ARCHITECT OF HUMAN DESTINY ?

Who Brings about Peace or Chaos ?

R.K. Kaushik

Publications

KALPAZ PUBLICATIONS

DELHI–110 052

ARCHITECT OF HUMAN DESTINY ?
(Philosophy, Religion)

Rs. 790

ISBN: 81-7835-179-X

Published in 2003 in India by
Kalpaz Publications
C–30, Satyawati Nagar
Delhi–110 052
E-mail: kalpaz@hotmail.com

Lasertypesetting by: Varsha Graphics, Delhi
Printed at: Mehra Offset Press, Delhi

Dedicated to

My Revered Father
and
Mother

Contents

Preface

A lot of water has already flowed, and more will ever be flowing under the bridge of human history. Undoubtedly, whether the water is natural in look, or red or black is not coming back. In this humble book of mine, I've tried my level best to see and understand as to which side it flows and why ? Why not to any other direction ? What's and who's there behind this whole current actually as a decisive force ? In a nutshell, my query is : What's the *Gangotri* or the fountain-head of the whole flow of water?

In fact, my poor mind has been weighed very heavily for long with this strong desire to know whether the web of this whole world of human history, whatever it's—good or bad—has ever been woven by the so-called 'thing' (matter) of Marx, or by the so-called 'thought' (idea) of Hegel, or by the so-called almighty God, or by the human spiders themselves with their own knitpins decisively as the architects of their own destinies? My mind was not at all in a mood to be content with this mere knowledge, but it wanted to know that if the same web was really ugly somewhere, who was to re-weave or mend it?

In this book my role is simply of an earnest and humble student, who wants to seek that truth. In this respect, what Swami Vivekanandji says has been a great morale-booster to me. He says, "Each work has to pass through these stages—ridicule, opposition and then acceptance. Each one who thinks ahead of his time is sure to be misunderstood. So opposition, and persecution are welcome." (on page 91, Vol. 5, *Swamiji's Works*).

So, I won't mind much, if a Lilliputian like me is at all ridiculed, or opposed, for what I humbly perceive as right and good for the whole humanity. Of course, there is nothing ahead of the time in it.

Moreover, let's remember what Swami Vivekanandji says in this context, "There are many who though immersed in ignorance, yet in their pride of their hearts, think they know everything . . . . This world is full of these; everyone wants to be a teacher, every beggar wants to make a gift of a million dollars." (on page 23 Vol. 4, Swamiji's Works) Simply by mugging up this or that scripture, some people think they are religious.

While religion is not in mugging up this or that, it's realisation of good in life. It's being. One, who transforms good into one's being, is truly religious.

In fact, I'm proud to be a seeker of truth only, no matter from which street or lane I get it. Frankly speaking, I know only this much that I know nothing, especially about our esteemed scriptures and some world fame books even. What I've written here is mainly based on the poor experience of my life and poor commonsense of a small man made of an ordinary clay like me. Actually it has been picked-up from different flowers like a honey-bee. My main motto of writing this all is to make myself a transparent goodman merely by changing my gear of thinking, feeling and doing, because I realise that I lack something very important in me, which has been causing me misery, and unless I change my whole mindset for good, I shall never be happier in my life. So, whatever all I'm doing in this book, it's all with the feeling of a patient, and not as a doctor. I am well aware that a sick person like me can hardly have any cure of any other sick mind.

For a seeker of truth there is no question of majority or minority. He's after truth only. No matter what one says and what one doesn't. In this context, it's again relevant to quote Swami Vivekanandji: "What you call majority is mainly composed of fools and men of common intellect. Men who have brains to think for themselves are few everywhere. These few men with brains are the real leaders in everything . . . . This majority is guided by them." (on page 333, Vol. 5, Swamiji's works). Can we forget Buddha in this context?

It's very relevant to quote here M. Northeote Parkinson, a well-known History and English Professor, who rightly holds: "It's not the business of the Botanist to eradicate the weeds. Enough for him, if he can tell us how fast they grow." So, all the great 'gurus' can show us what's right, and what's wrong. We're mistaken badly, if we think that they can eradicate our evils too. That is an individual's own business to do. At the most they can take us to the pool, but they cannot make us drink.

My purpose in this work is not at all to philosophy of any subject, or to explain any ideology or to start a new sect, or religion or ism for getting fame and the like, but only to know the truth, and at the same time putting all the great human 'gurus' and the scriptures in my highest esteem. I'm well-aware that mere knowledge of truth is not enough. It is more or less useless, unless I live upto it.

Some kind patrons of my book may resent my too much quoting of Swami Vivekanandji in it. To some extent, they may be right, but you see, if I have taken Swamiji's crutches here or there, my humble main object has not been to make at all a commentary on Swamiji's sayings, but I've quoted him, may be too frequently only in a proper context to make my humble point more clear, more weighty and more appealing, because I think Swamiji's approach to the subject has been master piece, no matter whether we agree or disagree with him. I feel understanding of one's point of view is more important. The question of agreeing or dissenting with him/her arises only afterwards.

I also believe that right of dissent is the keystone of the edifice of democracy and humanity. It was Voltaire, who rightly pleaded, "I disapprove of what you say, but I will defend to the death your right to say it." Of course, in a democracy there is no question of absolute rights or absolute freedom of anybody, no matter what one is. I hold we shall make our world a better one, if we've an honest dissent. Let's keep it into our minds that both democracy and humanity allow dissent, but not violence in any form. Talibanisation and democracy can never co-exist together. I've used the word Talibanisation, especially in the context of Afghanistan, where the so-called Talibans have done so many wrongs against humanity.

It was Samuel Butler, who rightly said, "Every man's work, whether it is literature or music, or picture or architecture or anything else, is always a portrait of himself."

I don't know whether this book is a portrait of mine or not, but I shall feel like a charged battery and feel that my humble efforts have not gone waste, if it helps us in bringing truth into light even a bit. I really feel I am only a humble pilgrim on the path of truth like so many, and hence I am sorry at present that I've got no answers of all the genuine or otherwise queries of my patrons. I hardly need to assure all of them that in this book I don't aim at turning anyone into an atheist or *'nastik'* or *'kafir'* in the usual sense of the term, but to sow simply the seeds of truth in the field; so that they may sprout, may be later on when I am no more here. But I am fully confident that they will grow and become such banyan trees one day that they are to provide respite to all the passers-by. I do agree that truth may be everywhere, but I do believe that it remains far away from us, so long we don't understand it, and try to follow it earnestly in life.

I recollect too what Francis Bacon said regarding books: "Some books are to be tasted, others to be swallowed, and some few to be chewed." I humbly aspire that whatever I write in this book must be aimed at seeking the truth only, no matter then it's either tasted, or chewed or swallowed or thrown away. I know beggars like me can never be choosers.

In his *Essays of Studies* Mr. Bacon says the following again :

"Reading maketh a full man,
conference a ready man,
and writing an exact man."

Definitely, who would not wish to be a full man, a ready man and an exact man of Mr. Bacon's concept? But I believe this wish shall ever remain only my dream-pipe, unless I earnestly aim at living according to the old principle : 'Live and let live,' which I think is the only patent cure against all our man-made miseries in this world.

Longfellow too uttered the truth when he said, "A simple conversation across the table with a wise man is better than ten years of study of books." I definitely wish very keenly to discuss these age old pertinent queries raised in this book with wise men just to be nearer to the truth, but you see in this world, whether this pious wish remains only my dream or it's materialised into a reality, scores in the womb of the future to tell.

Through this Preface I want to express that I really owe a lot to my both revered mother and father, who had been a constant source of inspiration and envy to me to believe in truth and no more in superstition or delusions. Further, I am very grateful to all my brothers, sisters, relatives and friends, who have always been helping me in my life even by going out of their means. I have now the privelege to say that most of them have also been associated with the growth of the manuscript of this humble book from typing to the reading of its proofs. What a fine persons all they are ! I envy them all indeed.

Through this Preface I want to express my heartfelt gratitude too to Sri Khushwant Singhji, who is known as the doyen of Indian media, and who inspite of being quite old had gone through almost twenty pages of this 'Architect of Human Destiny ?', and gave me his most precious boosting dose by expressing "your thesis is well argued and lucid", along with his valuable suggestions in his very kind letter dated 4th October 2000. Though I know that I've not written anything like a thesis, as it's not a master-piece attempt of the subject indeed. It is all in a rustic form. But I think the contents of a letter are more important than the envelop, if they are good.

Of course, I also owe a lot to Mrs. Prakashwati Kaushik, my wife, who has always been a great source of help to me at every time in my life and works. Here I recollect the advice tendered by the great Greek philosopher Socratese, whose marital difficulties have been well-known. He advised: "By all means marry. If you get a good wife, you will become very happy. If you get a bad one, you will become a philosopher and that is good for every man." Undoubtedly, I am happy. Hence, its credit must go to her. Though I am not a philosopher, I love philosophy, known as 'love of wisdom.'

But I don't know how far I shall be able to play the role of a good father-in-law with Dr. Nikhil Kulkarni, and a good father with Dr. Anshu Kulkarni and Ms. Arunima, both my daughters with these unusual views expressed in this book. Why ? Because I am directly responsible to them for all my commissions or omissions. Though I know they are with me in this mission.

I believe Preface is the right mirror of the mind of a writer to give the right reflection to one's patrons, as to what were the main reasons of writing a book. I don't know how far I have succeeded in this aim.

Last but not the least, Benjamin Franklin's advice too comes to my mind. He says, "If you don't want to be forgotten as soon as you are dead, either write things worth-reading, or do things worth-writing." What a fine advice he has given ! But I am aware how poor my pen is! What I have written, whether it's worth reading or not, it is for my patrons to decide. However, my earnest desire is to follow Buddha's sane advice, i.e., 'to do good to be good' only. It hardly matters to me whether I am remembered or forgotten, because the achievement of this ideal in my life has become now more important indeed for me to give a befitting see-off to my miseries from my life.

Now if we really want to achieve happiness in life, we have no short-cut and no alternative, except to do worth-doing, what we can, wherever we are. That's the only path to change ourselves and our world too in the capacity of the true architects of our own destinies.

R.K. Kaushik

Introduction

Every thoughtful person in this world experiences a sort of torrent of questions in one's own mind sooner or later just to see this world-scenario, what it is. Sometimes, he/she wonders to know what has happened, what's happening and what would happen and why?

You see there are two schools of thought, which give their respective explanations to solve this strange riddle.

People, who belong to first school, hold that there has been an eternal supernatural power, known as God behind all these happenings. He's the sole creator, the sustainer of this world and the killer of evils. While we go to work, He works. We are only his *'nimits'* or instruments. We can do nothing, except prostrating before Him, just to worship Him. The sole doer of each and everything in this world is He. And whatever he does, does good. Hence, we must be happy with His creation. Let's remember that without His blessings, we can't breathe even. 'Even a blade of grass can't grow without His mercy'. In a nutshell, we're all like 'His master's pet dogs on a long leash' only. Obviously, they paint a very gloomy picture.

People, who belong to second school, believe that if the so-called God created this world in six days, as referred in the Bible, and proclaimed at the end of that 'all was well', let Him read and re-read the bloody pages of human history too and then explain only what He meant by using 'all was well.'

They hold that we should no more behave like that stupid ostrich in sand dunes. We must remember that where there are wickedness and hypocracy, God can't live there. Moreover, there is no creation, but evolution only, as nothing can be created out of nothing. And there is nothing eternal, as everything is changing here. As such there is nothing beyond the Law of Cause and Effect.

So, according to this school God's nothing, but simply a projection or a caricature or a concoction of human minds only in our utter ignorance of the universe and this nature, just to infuse the necessary confidence in our ownselves to face boldly all the situations in our lives. It's our greatest misfortune that the dividend of this whole exercise has been more or less a zero. Because, in course of infusing blood of faith into Him, the actual architects of their own destinies—good or bad—have lost all the blood of faith in themselves, with the result they've become all more or less physically or mentally paralysed and perfect fatalists as well as escapists. They suffer from the psyche of 'weak and low.' Hence, Buddha the great human giant endeavoured to remove all the age long divine crutches from the armpits of all humans, and declared : 'God was one of the greatest superstitions.'

Let's realise that we may or may not have faith in Him, but faith in our ownselves as the true steersmen of the ship of our lives is like an anchor. So long as we don't realise that this world, whatever it is, has not been God ordained, but man-made, we won't make any sincere efforts to turn our hell into heaven indeed. Unless one exists, one cannot descend on earth with His rescue-crane to uplift the age old bogged down humanity from 'adharma'. Let's remember, fanaticism is more dangerous for us than even cancer and AIDS.

Of course, the denial of God does not mean at all that we can afford to be rash in our steering.

Now if we as architects of our own destinies really want to change the world-scenario to live in peace everywhere, no matter we are in a family, or in a *'mohalla'* or in a village, or city, or in a country, we have no alternative, but almost all of us will have to leave first the age long path of our ego. Because ego is nothing, but our excessive attachment with our ownselves even at the cost of others around.

So long we as human-spiders don't leave weaving the web of life out of our ownselves exclusively with our own knitpins to catch others in our nets, and do not think and care earnestly for others too at the same time, peace will ever remain a mirage, no matter whether there is God or no God, soul or no soul. So, the recipe of the world peace is our earnest following of the 'live and let live' principle or 'dharma'. The earlier we realise it, the better. Better late than never.

Of course, perfection in this world is only utopian.

1

Who is to Change it? 'Matter'? or 'Men'?

In one of his early works Karl Marx rightly wrote: "The philosophers have only interpreted the world in various ways; the point, however, is to change it." Obviously, being a great visionary Marx had a very high dream to materialise it, but the moot question before us is : Who is to change it? 'Matter'? or 'Men'? The important point to remember here is: Why did Marx have this great vision to change the material conditions of this world? Because he had a strong passion for it. It's creditable to Marx that others could not have such a vision even in the same material conditions. Again, the question is: Which is decisive—matter or men?

Undoubtedly, the changed modes of production or the changed economic conditions of Soviet Russia particularly after 1917 changed the Soviet mainly agricultural economy into a highly industrially advanced economic system during a period of about 50 years. In fact, it was an economic revolution in nature. We are badly mistaken, if we think Industrial and Human revolution are like Siamese-twins. It was only Marx's mirage to hold that as economic changes take place in the world, the minds of human beings, their thoughts, their ideologies, their outlook too would change automatically by an iron-necessity. Did they have these changes, especially in Soviet Russia, a country, which had the most advanced socialist modes of production? If not, how could they change the world?

I do admit that economic changes have been one of the most important factors to bring changes in the so-called entire super-structure, which is composed of the laws of the state, the religion, the very customs, traditions, the political social and ethical systems of the land concerned and its history etc. etc. But my humble submission here is that they have never been decisive or fundamental or basic factors in bringing changes revolutionary in character in the world. They themselves cannot revolutionise human minds essentially. Marx's talks are similar to putting the cart before the horse.

Lenin too said, "The world picture is a picture of how matter moves and how matter thinks." He added "the brain is the organ of thought." Again, the question is: whether the matter, what Lenin talks about, moves towards its right or left on its own? Do the contradictions or flaws, what he talks about arise on their own in the system? Are they not man-made? Don't they stop sprouting in the so-called last stage of the development of society, i.e., classless, casteless and stateless society? It means they are not essential parts of the development of the society.

Moreover, did not the society develop from the primitive communism to the slave-system without contradiction? It means the motion will ever be there in the matter, but not contradiction. Contradiction is not a wheel to move the matter. It's a foreign element, and not a part-and-parcel of matter. It can be debarred from the material conditions, if the men, who establish them, are farsighted enough. In this context, can we ever forget Sri Jamna Lalji Bajaj, a Gandhian capitalist and how he worked it? It's all due to passion for good, he did not allow any weeds to grow in his mind.

Let us ponder over it seriously and quite objectively, whether this 'matter' makes the picture of the world, or of the lives of the people, whatever it is—good or bad—on it's own? Let's keep it into our minds that every human possesses the same brain, made of the same matter, but the world picture or the picture of the life of each human has been quite different from each other. Were the pictures of the lives even of contemporaries like Ram-Ravana, Krishna-Duryodhana, and Gandhi-Hitler, just to submit some human species—not different from each other ? If the 'mind is the development of the matter in its highest state', does it mean that every mind thinks alike? No, obviously not. When pictures of each brain cannot be the same, that is a proof in itself that man is behind this picture of mind and he is responsibile for this picture, whether it is good or bad.

Of course, matter and motion are inseparable. But human minds cannot move or grow like hair on our heads on their own. Their direction of movement is determined by architects of human destinies themselves. Hence, socialism or communism, or any ism is not inevitable. Every ideology is to sprout only in a proper cultivated land by humans concerned.

Like Marx, Lenin and Stalin too had a dream to fulfill. Lenin holds: "People will become gradually accustomed to the observance of the elementary rules of the social life . . . without compulsion, without subordination, without the special apparatus for compulsion, which is called state". But the big question is how? How will this cooperative spirit sprout in people's minds automatically? After all, humans are not like robots, which work on dotted lines, as they have no personal whims, fancies, nature, interests, likes-dislikes, emotion-sentiments, weaknesses, thoughts etc. etc. So, do we treat all humans like snobs? When we have no required mindset, and, consequently, we fail to learn how to live on the planet earth, in spite of the state, how can we be accustomed to the observance of the elementary rules of social life, how can we live together in peace on a higher altitude of our mental state without the apparatus of state? Hence, I humbly hold that all their talks of withering away of state (a stateless society) too will ever remain mearly their dream-pipes. Actually, for all this change mere in material or economic conditions are not enough to bring the desired results. For this primarily we need to change our mindset, our outlook and attitude to our lives tremendously, which is possible only through men-making education. If we do it, all further lines will be almost clear for action.

Here I agree to disagree with Mr. Emile Burns, who says, "But the stage of communism implies much more than merely material sufficiency. From this time when the working class takes power and begins to change to socialism, a change also begins to take place in the outlook of the people." Let us no more live in a fool's paradise. Let's no more make castles in the air. Otherwise, let me know whether it had been possible even in the most advanced socialist economy? Mere material sufficiency or material change, intellectual fitness and perfect control over the state machine won't produce men of desired outlook automatically.

Of course, change is the law of nature. It will never stop. As the time changes, new discoveries alongwith our necessities and desires take place, all our economic, social, political, ethical and all other systems too change accordingly. Sometime our minds don't necessarily suit to our material conditions, we establish. Hence, we suffer. In a nutshell, if we change our minds, we can change our world as well. Otherwise, matter will change but men remain the same.

Does it not prove by itself that it is not 'matter', but men, who have been the real architects of their own destinies—good or bad? The obvious fact that there are as much pictures of the world as there are humans, clearly shows that matter has never been decisive in determining the very contours of our society and its history, but the humans themselves. Let Marx, Lenin and Stalin remember that everyone's brain, which is an organ of thought, is made of the same atom. But why does one think exclusively for one's own bread, interests, likes-dislikes etc., while another human thinks not only for his own bread, but for the bread of others around too in the same circumstances? Moreover, who makes the circumstances? Do they fall on our heads on their own? Of course, matter will ever be in a state of flux or change, even if we all humans are dead by chance. We cannot change the law of motion.

Don't we find people, who prefer to feed milk even to human cobras with their pious hands, which they even bite? So, earlier we realise the importance of the change of our mindset, the better. If we change ourselves first, all our 'thoughts' and 'things' are apt to change sooner or later automatically. But without changing our mindset first by our ownselves, no matter what material conditions we establish, the *'zulum'* on man by man in this or that form or flavour will ever continue.

So far we have been giving different flavours to our different conflicts. For instance, we say there is conflict among classes, or castes, or creeds, or colours, or races, or different sexes and different people of status etc. etc., forgetting that our minds are the real sources of conflict. This all does not mean I deny that if we see, hear, taste, touch, smell bad through our minds with the help of our senses, we don't do good too in the same way. But my point is that as long as we don't understand properly that we are living in a society and society is not made only of one person, but many, again as long as I don't understand that if I am to live here, so do others by peacefully resolving our mutual conflicts with proper understanding. Again so long we don't think that if a lizard has a right to live, a mosquito too has the similar right in this interdependent world, our conflicts in this or that form or flavour will ever stand flat opening their mouths to digest us ever alive, no matter, we are in a family, or 'mohalla', or country or at the world-stage. So, what is needed is, let me live according to my own *dharma,* i.e., the norms of my good behaviour, and you live according to your own. When we are all to live here without any doubt, why is there any ego of this or that, unnecessary conflict, tension and clash? Why don't we live here, by adjusting each other's mutual needs, without creating unnecessary conflict or trouble for any? The main *mantra* of our living is : why to worry for what none can help and why not to worry, which every one of us can avoid doing? After all we are only the 'manavas' or 'manush' who are to make our own world—good or bad.

This clearly proves that the world-picture, no matter what it is—good or bad—is not primarily the picture of how matter 'moves', and how 'matter' thinks, as Lenin thought about it, but the world picture has been primarily a picture of how the concerned humans—the true steersmen steer the ships of their lives either towards their right or left or towards forward or backward. Of course, they cannot do it without the help of steering, the petrol or the 'material conditions' or 'thoughts'. After all they don't steer it in a vaccum. Can our brains ever produce the picture either of heaven or hell on their own? A gramophone can never produce either sweet or shrill sound on its own. What it produces, all depends on the person, who plays records on it. Actually, whatever our life-picture, we humans paint, has been designed primarily by the values of life, we cherish. We do it consciously or unconsciously. A dogmatic mind only says that these values too have been pre-determined by matter? In this context, it is relevant to quote Prof. Promin, who says, "Genetics cannot determine values." That is why, it is rightly said that here nobody is a born saint or devil. Both saints and devils are made here by themselves. If both are the creatures, they too are the creators of their own circumstances. We can not forget that the circumstances in which they are born too are primarily made by some humans.

Lenin himself too once proposed: "Instead of debating on building heaven in their other world, let the faithful in religion and communists, who have no faith in religion, join hands to build a heaven on earth." Undoubtedly, I am a very small chap before him, but I am damn happy to know that a so-called materialist like Lenin too accepted the decisive role, what humans play in building either heaven or hell on earth ultimately. Of course, none can deny how important role both matter and idea play side by side in helping us in this respect.

Keeping in view these facts, obviously it was too much to expect from the Soviet people, who were not ready mentally to share their mutual bread with each other voluntarily, that they would be willingly ready to switch over themselves to follow the well-known Marxian economic principle, i.e., 'From each according to one's capacity, to each according to one's work/need' in the Marxian Utopian Eldorado, merely because of these economic changes. The unfortunate happenings in Soviet Russia in 1991 do tell their own tales themselves. In fact, the ground was not well tilled by them in advance. Hence, there was no question of sprouting those seeds.

In fact, we may or may not realise, but to act upon this lofty Marxian economic principle, the whole world needs men of different minds, different outlook, different attitude to life and nature. Can any economic or material changes bring these changes referred here primarily by themselves? No.

After 1991 it became quite evident that in the absence of men of desired outlook or mindset or mettle on the world stage, this Marxian high ideal would ever remain a mere dream-pipe or pious hope of Marx. Why? Because these economic changes, referred above or the so-called 'Proletariate-Dictatorship' too failed to bring the desired changes in the very consciousness, or outlook and nature of the Soviet-people. This was the foremost reason that the sandy edifice of Marx had collapsed even in its first tremor there. Consequently, these age old overlooked realities made the attainment of the last stage of socialism, known as communism, i.e., the classless, casteless and stateless society too as actually a mirage for the Soviet people.

Unfortunately, that is why, instead of withering away of the State in Soviet Russia, the country known as USSR had withered away even from the globe in 1991. Why it so happened there at that time, that is now a well-known history of that country?

But we can forget the main causes of its collapse only at our own peril. Those who forget the history, invite the same history to repeat.

It clearly proves that mere change in our economic or material conditions (as Marx, Lenin and Stalin thought) devoid of changes in human nature, their outlook, the attitude of humans primarily for the good of the people of the whole world, will be of as little value as the healthy body of a lunatic. To change the world, what Marx aimed at, we need to change our mindset first by our ownselves. Otherwise, our whole attempt will be futile.

I humbly feel it is not right to hold on the part of Marx that "men make their own history, but they do not make it under conditions by themselves." In fact, men are not like matter's pet dogs on a long leash to be free to move as far as leash of economic circumstances permit them. At least, the lives of great men all over the world nail this myth for all times to come. Let the communists realise that, at least, such great men, who make history, don't represent any class, but masses. They have vision and passion for people's service, no matter what tunnels of even adversed troubles or circumstances they have to pass through for the light. So, earlier we earnestly review our views regarding the world change, the better. Better late than never.

2

Can the 'Idea' of Hegel Change the World Decisively?

We all know India has been a very vast mine of thoughts, ideas and philosophies. Hence, it was known as the spiritual 'guru' of the world. But in spite of this fact in view, still the same history of sufferings and human miseries has been repeating here. In this context, it is most relevant to quote what once a Japanese asked Swami Vivekanandji and what he answered in return.

The Japanese asked: "When India possesses the philosophy of the *Gita,* the *Ramayana,* the Vedas, and the Upanishads, why then are her inhabitants dependent and poor ?"

Swamiji's marked reply was: 'If a marker does not know how to operate his gun, no matter how good the gun is, he can not get any credit.'

Let Marx and his guru Hegel realise that even good ideas conceived in particular circumstances of the society fail to sprout more or less, if they are not properly worked and nourished by a good farmer. Don't we still go on misbehaving with our fellow brothers and sisters as untouchables even in the 21st century? May I know who tilled those lands in which the seeds of untouchability in India and slavery in ancient Greece sprouted? Did they descend on earth on their own? Let us no more try to behave like that stupid ostrich in the sand-dunes.

Let us no more confuse spiritual knowledge with spiritual attainment. So long we don't have our rocky will and consciousness of attaining human excellence and good in life, our mere knowledge of truth, for instance, that we should not injure others, or that we shouldn't usurp other's property or territory, or that we should treat sisters of others as our's own, will be more or less useless as a load of sandalwood on the back of an ass. So mere spiritual-knowledge is not enough. It is like mere reaching or completing our half voyage. Spiritual attainment is most essential to complete it and to get happiness and peace of mind. Mere performance of this or that ritual or dogma in this respect won't help us, except adding to our ego further.

Here is the true reflecton of one's spiritual attainment in following stanza:

> *'Ghar se Maszid hai door, bahut door,*
> *Chaloo youn karleyn,*
> *kisi rote huve bachche ke aansoo ponch dalen.'*

Men-making religion is the demand of the present day world. The earlier we follow it, the better. Let us be confident that our life can be a *'yoga'* or a union, if we unite our good *'gyan'* with our good *'Karmas'*. And in case, we have a passion to unite them our life can become even *'Prayag'*.

It's O.K. that Hegel talks of the development of an idea in a dialectical method. Of course, like 'matters', ideas too are essential in life. But I humbly hold that if we think that merely by putting an idea before the people they'll change, we are only living in a fool's paradise. Let us remember this way ideas change, but men will remain.

To conclude I humbly hold that these sacred scriptures containing different thoughts are merely like our sacred cows. If we don't know how to milk them, they cannot provide us milk themselves. This shows how even the 'thoughts' of Hegel are ineffective to bring fundamental and decisive changes in the world. At the most they can take us to the pool, but they cannot make us drink. Both 'ideas' and 'matters' work as two charged batteries, only when they are put in the house of a good householder. Other people live and do all their works, but in complete darkness, in spite of their presence.

3

Will God Ever Descend on Earth and Change it?

The question has been very pertinent whether it is advisable for us then to wait for the day, when the so-called God will descend on earth with His rescue-crane to lift up the already age old bogged down humanity from the marshy land of 'adharma' to change the world?

We have just seen how if somewhere 'ideas' go forward, 'matters' too go ahead somewherelse to help humans to make their own history. Both cells are of equal importance for a charged battery. The idea how to remove one's hunger is there alongwith the condition of hunger. They can not live like poles apart or in a water-tight compartment. They always live together.

The idea of God too has been age old. He has been described as 'Trinity' i.e., three in-one. God is known as one, who creates the universe; one who protects all the living beings; and one who destroys the evils. But according to the Law of Cause and Effect, nothing can be created out of nothing, no matter how great the creator is. Secondly, we all daily witness with our own eyes, how the innocents are being butchered, or raped or exploited here in His so called kingdom day in and day out by their own fellow-beings. Thirdly, what to talk of destroying evils by God, the evil persons have their own kingdoms here. Don't they treat themselves as kings without crown? Otherwise, who is Osama bin Laden, or Veerappan, or Billa or Ranga, and the like?

Of course, most of us have the curiosity to know that if there has not been some creator, how then this universe came into being? They hold that there must be some power to manage the whole complicated universe or the world. But the fact is that it has all been our mere superstition that the universe must have been created by some Almighty. Science doesn't believe in creation, but only in its evolution. It is sheer ignorance that we believe it was created. Science says it has been evolved in centuries. Nature too has neither its beginning, nor its end like matter. It has always stood at all 'its' stages of evolution. It is not something standing or sitting out of the universe, but it has been working within as a part and parcel of it as a self-regulating tremendous force.

Science says that the real nature of matter is that it can neither be created, nor destructed by any, whatsoever. Of course, matter changes its form and it is always in a state of flux. It has been in a state of perpetual change by itself, because change is its fundamental nature.

We may or may not know the so-called God, but the greatest need of the hour is to know the nature and it's laws. The more we understand nature and its laws, the more we make the dark clouds of ignorance disappear from our minds. So, let us know first that the hole in the Ozone layer is being widened by us day by day. It is becoming a dangerous signal for the survival of beings.

Thus, objectively speaking the idea of some Supernatural Power seems to be simply our age old projection, or conjecture, or concotion, or conception of human mind in its utter ignorance of the universe and it's laws.

The God, who is supposed to be the most powerful navigator of the ship of this whole universe appears to be mere heretical, or a mere product of make-believe world, or a myth only. He is our greatest superstition only.

In the *Gita,* Krishna says: "I am the source of all creation, everything in the world moves because of Me; knowing this the wise, full of devotion worship Me." Lenin too held 'the world picture is a picture of how matter moves…' Krishna, perhaps, forgot that there is no creation and if there is good, there is evil too. How can He be the source of the creation of evils?

In fact, the believers in God have been pouring into our minds for ages that God is the doer of all things, whatever He does, he does right. It is He, who causes all the changes in the world. In case we fail to get justice in our present life, we are sure to get it in our other life to come. Believe in Him. It is said that our mind is like a parachute, which works when it is open. But the very talks of these believers, instead of opening our minds to think something worth, make them quite shut. That is why, all the believers in God propose here or there that God has been the doer of all things, we are only His *'nimits'* or instruments or tools in His hands. And we can do nothing, except worshipping Him. Thus, they make the whole human race inert or defunct or idlers, or escapists, or fatalists, or cowards and shirkers only. Undoubtedly, their mere assurances may get composed some of the people all the time, all the people some of the time, but they cannot get composed all the people all the time.

In brief, if milk is turned into curd by some useful bacteria, if two elements of Hydrogen and one element of oxygen are mixed together and make water (H_2O), why do we drag Him in these developments? If the seasons change, it is not because of the wish of some deity, but due to the revolution of earth round the sun. If days and night occur, it is not at all due to the will of some Lord, but because of rotation of earth on it's axis. If a child of a human cannot be a mule or horse or vice-versa, it is because of their different chromosomes respectively. All humans have the same organs of their bodies in normal circumstances, because of the development and growth of their different cells in the course of evolution in centuries, as nature has been the greatest genetical engineer.

Science says it is all heretical to believe: "That which cannot be perceived by the mind, the eyes, and organs of sense, but makes the mind, the eyes etc. speed to their work is Brahma. Brahma cannot be the object of perception or thought. Mind and speech turn back from it in dismay." (Swami Ram in *Woods of God Realisation*). May I have the privilege to ask this great saint that if Brahma cannot be perceived by our minds, the eyes, and organs of our senses, then how could he perceive or imagine that He makes our minds and eyes? If Brahma really makes our minds and eyes, then who was behind the minds, which crucified the great 'guru' like Christ?

If we do not believe in God, it all does not mean we can afford to keep our back towards science too. For instance, the science of magnetism says that opposite poles attract and similar poles repel. The head of the human body is considered North as all electrical currents originate in the brain. Hence, it is advised by science to sleep with our head towards South. When we sleep with our head towards North the repulsion in electromagnetic currents takes place, which can cause blood related disorders like B.P., Cholestral, or Insomnia. People are advised to sleep with their heads towards east preferably.

In fact, to see the whole world scenario, what it is without wearing any jaundiced-glasses, my remaining faith in His kingdom has further shaken very badly. And a natural question sprouts in my poor mind: whether the world is man-made or God-ordained at all? Had it been divine, there would not have been any wickedness in it.

Let me quote Swami Vivekanandji in this context: "You people of the West think you have God. What is it to have God? If you have Him, why is it that so much criminality exists... Hypocrisy cannot exist, where

God is". I think both are poles apart (Swamiji's works on page 416 Vol. 7).

So, I humbly feel that had God been at all a reality, He would have definitely got His wicked world changed through His so-called mere *'nimits'* or instruments, as He is called the sole doer of each and everything in the world. Or He would have taken, at least, *suo moto* action against all the evil-doers for the establishment of the kingdom of justice. In this context, I cannot help, but recollect an Urdu couplet as under:

'Bahut charcha sunte they pahlu mey dil ka,
dekha to katrae khun nahin nikla'

To find ourselves in a peculiar dilemma: what to accept, and what not then, the question comes to my mind: should we then behave like that foolish ostrich, who kept it's head under the sand dunes; so that it might not come to know the reality? No, not at all, as that would be like our Waterloo indeed. After all, we're all architects of our own destinies— good or bad. So, let's keep our minds in proper gear, just to follow the principle: 'Live and let live' to be good only. Let us examine it objectively as to why we have been suffering for ages? Because both 'things' and 'thoughts' have ever been changing, but Alas! men remain. Consequently, the same history of human sufferings goes on repeating again and again. And thus Marx's dream to change the world too remains merely his dream-pipe. Of course, humans change their 'things' and 'thoughts'. It is all irrelevant whether matter or idea comes first into being. We don't work in a vaccum. The most relevant is how men change themselves to change their world.

In this respect, my humble advice for all is: let us not to give undue weightage to what the most disgusted German philosopher Mr. Hermann Keyserling holds about human beings the world over in his *'Travel Diary'*: "If thou hearest that a mountain has been moved, believe it, if thou hearest that a man has changed his character, do not believe it." Why? Because it is merely a grave distortion of facts either to believe that 'man is essentially divine' or 'He is essentially a devil'. The fact is that man is neither essentially. He is what one makes oneself. Don't we know from history how Ratnakar had changed himself and his character one day, when he got 'gyan' and consequently, became a Balmiki, the great saint? Don't we know that if there had been Ravana, Duryodhana, Hitler and Mussolini, there had been Ram, Krishna, Mohammed, Christ and 'gurus' as well in the course of human history? There is nothing to be disgusted at all in this respect. Of course, to be good in this world is the hardest and the steepest climb. Lord Bernard Shaw mourned the death of Gandhiji in these words due to the same reason: 'How dangerous to be good in this world!' But let's remember we have no alternative, except either to be good or let's die *enbloc* then. We cannot accept Machiavelli or Hobbes as our guides, in this respect *in toto.*

Ghalib, the great poet too said:

> *"Bus ki duswar hai har kam ka assan hona,*
> *aadmi ko bhi mayasar nahin insan hona".*

This all proves that brutes too can be humans to change the world, provided they realise its' importance in life. Let's remember that if there's desired change in human nature or in our outlook, it would be a four-fold revolution—human as well as material, internal as well as external. Let us be sure that no God is descending on earth to right the wrongs. It is a human world, and we are to change it.

We can forget this at our own peril only that humans are no more to be treated like androids or robots, which start functioning on desired lines, the moment 'economic button' is pressed or switch of an 'idea' is on.

We shall never be able to attain Marx's very high ideal i.e., to each according to this work or need' mere by producing more in factories or fields, but by mere changing our mindset, so that we may automatically and voluntarily start following our principle i.e., 'live and let live' earnestly. There must be some incentive for private profit motive, keeping in view what the human nature is. Of course, even then no Welfare State can ever be a Laissezfaire State. The main lesson of Soviet economy to remember is that no good economy can go too far smoothly, riding on the back of populist subsidies.

Now time has come for us to realise that humanity doesn't make the leap from one system of production to another, except as the result of human action. Mr. Emile Burns in his famous book "What is Marxism"? endorses this view; "It was not enough to know that capitalism was only a passing phase and that it must be succeeded by Socialism. It was clear that this would not happen by itself, as a result of purely economic changes . . . there was no point at which capitalism would automatically turn into socialism as water turns into ice, when it's temperature falls to 32° Fahrenheit. Humanity does not make the leap from one system of production to another, except as the result of human action."

Human revolution first means in brief: 'One shot and all out. It is a sure shot'. It cannot be dropped down on earth by any divine crane. Moreover, both Buddha and Mahavir hold: 'God is the greatest superstition' only. Their view is very significant from this angle.

We shall never be able to [illegible] [illegible] [illegible] according to this [illegible] [illegible] [illegible] [illegible] [illegible] [illegible] [illegible], but by [illegible] changing our mindset so that [illegible] automatically and [illegible] follow [illegible] [illegible] [illegible] [illegible] [illegible] [illegible]. The [illegible] [illegible] [illegible] [illegible] in view what the human [illegible]. [illegible].

4

What Does the Replacement of Socialist Economy Only Mean?

Now after 1991 Russia had adopted the so-called market-economy in place of her socialist economy as a better alternative. In the spirit that 'A drowning country catches at a straw'. Undoubtedly, now it's economy is to be revived by and by. Both production and efficiency of the people are expected to go high again. But again it would be too much to expect to see a revolutionary change in the mindset of the people of Russia after sometime, because of these economic changes there again. The fact is that the desire of living exclusively for oneself is not according to the tune of the age and time. To change the world all of us without any exception the world over, have a dire need to change our mindset, which aims at both 'live and let live' at the same time as it's ideal. No economy including the so-called Socialist economy or market economy or even the so-called Gandhian economy can ever claim to produce such mindset automatically by itself. No economy can ever be insulated from evils.

Being architects of our own destinies it is the humans, who are to create the feeling of oneness for each other or the feeling of swim and sink together, feeling of purposefulness in life, feeling of fulfillment of some higher goal or mission in life earnestly, feeling of satisfaction of the creativity and the creative urge in our own minds ourselves.

In the words of Emile Burns "In capitalist society . . . the system makes "every man for himself, the main principle of life." I fail to comprehend how could the same principle of life change by itself merely because we established the socialist modes of production in Soviet Russia? How could our conscience change from individual to Social? This is also not possible again in the new system, what Russia has adopted in 1991.

Let them then decide, if they want to be exclusively materially giants, but spiritually pygmies. Let us remember Russia may or may not believe in a God, but the proper development of the spirit of the people of Russia too is a must. If they want to be happier, they too have no alternative, but to have their conscience pure and honest. Again, if they have no spiritual appetite, and their goal of life is only to be materially wanting, peace in their lives will ever remain only a mirage. They have to suffer in their lives. Their lives will be full of frustration with suicidal-tendencies allround. Why? Because man doesn't live by bread alone. Spiritual starvation is more dangerous than material starvation. Their goal of life 'every man for himself' is still not changed. The people of Russia still lack the high mission in their lives. They still live for themselves and not for others around too. I don't deny the fact that we cannot recite even Ram-Ram, if our bellies are empty. A good man doesn't live to eat, but eats to live.

The world is neither good, nor evil in itself. It is only a necessary means to an end. And the end of human life has for ever been peace and happinesss. Let us no more confuse pleasure with happiness. Let us remember if we lose peace and happiness in life, we lose everything in life. We must remember such parameters of good life, no matter whether we are in Russia, or America or in India.

Let the people of Russia now no more feel, as if they are on an unchartered sea. They must know in advance where they want to go? What is their destination of life? Whether they will ever be content with having some superfluous changes here or there in their economy now, or they want real inner changes in their lives to change the world, what Marx aimed at.

We must be well aware that if their new economy is according to the tune of their goal of life, it is well and good. Otherwise, there will always be all-round disturbances and turmoil in their lives.

Like others the people of Russia too are architects of their own destinies—good or bad. Hence, being mature people let them take the right decision now or never, as to what 'things' and 'thoughts' suit their goal of life. Nothing is inevitable by an iron-necessity. Nothing is pre-determined. Can we forget that the people of Soviet Russia were supposed to go ahead via socialism to communism? Didn't they move the needle of the development of their society and polity backward, i.e., again towards market economy as well as Western democracy? Of course, they are not carbon copies of anything.

It is certain that we can have peace from within and not without. If we fail to develop ourselves from within, we are apt to behave like sharks, tigers, scorpians, *'bagulas'*, wasps, cobras, leopards and the like only, no matter what economy we choose. This awareness is like our mariners-compass, which will indicate where peace lies. The important thing to remember is that our mere standard of living without standard of life can take us to a ditch only, no matter what economic changes we have.

Let the believers in God, wherever they are, reconsider and realise that our life is not what some hypothetical supernatural power makes it, but what we all humans make it either individually or collectively, no matter if it is good or bad. We have already seen that no economy and no ideology in itself is going to change the tigers from meat eaters to vegetarian. Let us remember human sharks have got no inclination even to change their world. They cannot do it.

It is told that some big cities in US and UK have now become number one or two cities in committing of sin in the world. As a result of it people cannot move out of their houses, especially in the dark. This all doesn't mean that any socialist or Gandhian economy has been immuned from such evils. Have the big cities in Russia or India not been infected with these crimes? Crime and sin are the products of a civilisation, which knows not, where it is supposed to go and where not. It knows only that everything is right. To achieve an end, every means is right. It knows that even by slitting my brother's throat in, if I can attain pleasure in life, I must go. Have not the people wearing even Gandhian Khadi been caught red-handed, while roasting even live people simply for their satisfaction of carnal desires? This all shows that no economy in the world and even our sacred Vedas or the Das capital or the Communist Manifesto, if they are kept in people's hands 24 hours in themselves are going to erect a Chinese-wall against evils, if the minds of the architects of human destinies are not lying in the right gear of thinking, feeling and doing. Lakhs of people daily read the *Gita,* the Quran, the Bible, the Granth Sahib as a routine. Have they made us better human beings necessarily? This all does not mean that we shouldn't read them. Rather we must. But my point is that we already know, what is right and good, but our mere knowledge cannot bear any good fruits, unless we transform our being into its light. Good or evil lies primarily in human minds. So, our minds need to be overhauled first.

So, no matter to which country we belong, we must ponder over seriously first as to which direction we have been going? Have we really been moving in the right direction? It is not right to believe that our matter or idea moves us primarily towards our right or left. On the other hand, it is the human beings, who move them or steer them. So, it is not without danger ahead, if we move on the road merely by aping either U.S. or U.K. or Russia or India or any other country. Let people of present day

Russia respond to their minds whether now they will be able to write a different history with these mere economic changes?

Mr. Emile Burns in his book *What is Marxism*? says, "Marx's whole account of Socialist Society shows that it will mean the end of wars. When production and distribution in each country are organised on a socialist basis, there will be no group . . . (which has) interest in conquering other countries . . . Socialist societies will not make war because there is nothing they . . . can gain from war . . ." Again, how lofty these socialist idea and matter are! But doesn't the commissions of Soviet Russia in Hungary, Czechoslovakia, Poland and Afghanistan after 1956 give a bitter taste in our mouth? The fundamental question now before all of us is can any economy or ideology in itself save the sinking ship of humanity? The answer is no.

Let us remind and refresh ourselves by knowing what Maxim Gorky once said: 'Science has brought so many comforts. There was a time, when we had to undergo so much trouble just to light a lamp, now we just switch the light on, and we have light. Now the journey of months can be completed within hours . . .' So many things Mr. Gorky said in praise of Science. By chance a villager got up and asked him: 'Sir, this is alright, but has science made men learn to be men? It is said that Mr. Gorky remained non-plussed for sometime. In fact, science might have stepped itself in an era of artificial life or cloning, but it must be clear to all of us that just like the Vedas, the Quran, the Bible, the Guru Granth Sahib, no economy in itself can save the unfortunate sinking ship of humanity. So it is beyond the science to make humans learn to be good men. No 'idea' and no 'matter' can come to our rescue. They too help those men, who help themselves; whose both inner and outer selves are reasonably strong. How to be good men actually is the domain or jurisdiction of men-making education and 'dharma'. Be sure no pills, or any rocket-launcher or missile can ever uproot the oasis of evils, actually built by humans in their minds, but only men themselves. Crime or sin knowns no border. Its true borders are good men only.

Science will definitely produce more bread for the starving people, more clothes for the naked, more milk-giving buffaloes and cows, more juicy fruits through cloning, but how can it force the have's to share their bread, even their spare clothes with the havenots? That is possible only when we build ourselves not only from without, but from within primarily.

Let's remember that once a favourite disciple of Buddha, Mr. Anand asked him if he believed in Supernatural miracles. Buddha replied: 'Is it not a wonderful thing mysterious and miraculous... that a man who commits wrong can become a saint by following the path of true enlightenment? (Printed in the column in "Meditations") in *Hindustan Times* on 7-5-2001.

The remedy of all remedies is that the mentality of 'I am to live, whether others may or may not live', which has entered everybody's attitudes today more or less the world-over, is to be replaced by the attitude of 'live and let live' at the earliest possible. In fact, the real salvation of each individual and each country lies in removing the exclusive 'self' from our minds. Because we grow, if we care not only for our own interests, our own bread, our own likes or dislikes etc., but for the interests, bread, likes or dislikes of others too around. If we do not do this, we arrest our natural growth automatically by our own commissions or omissions. In the same way, if we all individuals, and all countries follow this principle in our lives earnestly the world over, all of us will get both our material as well as spiritual development simultaneously. Then we shall feel happier, more cool, calm and peaceful. I humbly hold that if we think that merely by having changes in our this or that economy men or their world, their mindset or outlook too will change, we are badly mistaken. Men will remain. Matter will change, our being remains.

Let us remember Mr. Khrushcheva, an ex-late P.M. of Soviet Russia too once pathetically accepted the fact: "We still need the new type of character in men to live in the communist world." Can we change ourselves merely by holding *Das Capital* in our hands?

Can Marx ever dream to change the world without changing the character, the very nature and the very mindset of human beings? Can we do it merely by lying prostrate even before the hypothetical God? Oh, no. Never.

An eminent person from the West too accepted the same fact: "We in the West have failed to produce the type of man capable of living in the modern world".

It is note-worthy that Marx's inner desire was to establish a just social, political and economic order throughout the world, which has almost no chance for human exploitation and man-made inequality. He worked for it earnestly in London. All of us owe him a lot for all this. After 1991, it is inhuman to condemn the whole Marxism or the ideology of Communism after all what Marx had given to the world. It is also uncivilised to remove Marx's grave from some respectable place in Russia as well. Can we be humans by being inhumans?

But it is an undeniable fact that Marx's great dream 'to change the world' would for ever remain only his dream-boat with his mere 'thought' of Economic Interpretation of History' or Dialectical Materialism'. Human history does not move in a definite pre-determined pattern. Dialectical method, which too was adopted in old Greece to know the truth, is good. But they did not fail to protect even the Humpty-Dumpty Soviet economy and polity from their great fall in 1991? Of course, there were many causes for this unfortunate happening. But I humbly hold that no matter, what economy is now followed in Russia, people will not be able to fulfil Marx's great dream of changing their world without changing or overhauling their mindset indeed first.

5

Even the so-called Lord Brahma is Apt to Fail, if the Human Machinery is in a Mess

In this context, I want to express my firm views that hypothetically speaking if the so-called Lord Brahma, the creator too weaves the very web of the constitution of a country with His own divine knitpins, it won't work smoothly and efficiently, in case the human machinery is in a mess or in a rot. Dr. Ambedkar too expressed in the Constituent Assembly of India: "However, good a constitution may be, it is sure to turn out bad, if those who are called to work it, happen to be a bad lot." How correct he was is now more clear to us, when we look at the very pathetic conditions of our own Indian polity today!

In the same context, it is relevant to remind ourselves what Thomas Jefferson, a founder Father of the constitution and the 3rd President of USA said in the Independence-Hall in Philadelphia on March 4, 1789. The people, who gathered there asked him, "what have you given us?" Jefferson replied correctly: "A Republic, if you can keep it." In fact, if people are not worthy to maintain their Republic, it is apt to fall one day. This all proves how human factors have been superb either in writing, or making or changing human history.

In fact, it is not our constitution, but it is "we, the people of India" have failed our constitution. It is we, who make it stronger or weak and it is we who make it live or dead. The earlier we realise it, the better.

Swami Vivekanandji too uttered the truth, when he said: "But the basis of all systems, social or political rests upon the goodness of men. No nation is great or good because Parliament enacts this or that, but because it's men are great and good". (on page 192 Vol. 5 Swamiji's Works) What a fine judgement it is!

He adds further: "What guarantee have we that this or any civilisation will last, unless it is based on religion, on the goodness of men?" (on page 202 Vol. 5)

By religion he doesn't mean the conventional religion in vogue.

By religion he meant possibly men-making religion. Let is remember, unless we all the sailors of the ships of life make goodness our breathing—pipe, our breathing—pipe is apt to be chocked. Swamiji again uttered the truth: "Who is responsible for every action you do, every breath you take, and every thought you think? Isn't it you yourself? (on page 274 Vol. 7 *Swamiji's Works*)

Although Swamiji too says that 'we cannot breathe without His mercy'—something inconsistent with his previous statement. When we are responsible for every action we do, every breath we take, it is all meaningless to say that we cannot breathe without His mercy. It is all due to this inconsistency someone retorted and said: "So, when I am directed by His will, I am not at all responsible for my actions". (on page 274 Vol. 7 *Swamiji's Works*)

I do not appreciate the evasive reply of Swamiji, who said: "well, that can be said only in the highest state of realisation when the mind will be purified by work and you will see that it is He who is causing all to work . . . Otherwise, it is all but, a mere cant." (page 274 Vol. 7 *Swamiji's works*) It is a moot point when according to Swamiji' it is 'He who is causing all to work', how can the concerned poor person be responsible for the work, what God causes him to perform? The question of one's purification or impurification doesn't arise at all then. In both the cases, He must be responsible for all one's actions—good or bad. Otherwise, the best course for us to adopt is to leave dragging God in and out of human affairs for all times to come. Of course, dragging the God out of human affairs does not mean we can ever afford to be inhuman or uncivilised.

Let us remember that it was the people, who dropped atomic bombs on Hiroshima and Nagasaki in 1945, claiming that God was with them. Even Osama bin Laden, one of the greatest terrorists claims that God is with him and all his actions have been blessed by Him. That is why, he talks of *Jehad*, while actually *Jehad* aims at curbing one's selfish motives or exclusive self or one's evils. Is it not all befoolings or an attempt of camouflaging one's evil activities? And thus one's evil activities are apt to thrive under the garb of God's responsibilities.

This confusion can never be removed, unless we cease dragging God in human affairs. The so-called believers are bent upon to drag their beloved God in human affairs according to their sheer convenience. It is due to this that some friend of Swami*ji* questioned him again rightly: "But it is He who is giving me the wicked impulse?" (on page 275 Vol. 7 *Swamijis Works*) But like all other believers in God Swamiji too argued: "No, by no means. It would be blasphemy of the Lord to think in that way. He is not inciting you to evil action, it is all the creation of your desire for self-gratification" (On page 275 Vol. 7 *Swamiji's Works*) Let us accept the truth, when Swamiji rightly or wrongly believes: "you will see that it is He who is causing all to work', the question of our desire for self-gratification must not arise at all. Either we stop believing in that 'it is He who is causing all to work', we cannot breathe even without His mercy,' 'that the winds cannot blow without His blessings,' or accept the truth of that friend of Swamiji that 'when I am directed by His will, I am not responsible for my actions', and that 'it is He who is giving me the wicked impulse'. Why to try to win both the sides of the coin?

Although we know, if at all God exists, He cannot incite the human beings for any wicked impulse. In case we accept that 'I am directed by His will', and 'He causes all to work, we have no alternative, but to accept that He gives us wicked impulse too. In case, we accept that God causes us only good work, and we humans cause all our wicked impulses, then the difficulty is apt to arise. We will have to accept that there are then two creators of this world—One creates good, another evil—if at all we accept there's creation hypothetically even. Well, Swamiji must realise the very implications of his statement, when he says, "Rather say that He is causing the good work . . . while you are responsible for the evil action . . . that the Lord is causing the good actions, while he is doing the evil . . ." (on page 275 Vol. 7 *Swamiji's Works*). Let us then accept the truth of all truths that it is we all humans who are responsible for our both good or evil results, as we cause both the good as well as wicked impulses in our minds. When we talk of truth, why to have the crutches of untruth or lies at all? The most sensible view is: Being the steersmen of the ships of our lives, we are solely responsible for our destiny—good or bad. We hardly can digest the following Swamiji's view again: ". . . If one sincerely believes that the most wicked impulse is also prompted by the Lord, rest assured that one will not have to do those mean acts for long" (on page 276 Vol. 7 *Swamiji's Works*) The world knows that Osama bin Laden has been getting even innocent people killed the world over in the name of *Jehad*—a '*dharmayudha*'. Actually, in the actual film of our lives we human beings either play the role of a hero or heroin or a villain or a director or a producer or a lyricist or a photographer, and so on. If we assign any role to God to play in this film, it is apt to flop, because His very presence creates all round confusion only.

If we accept that human factors have been superb in determining our destiny—good and bad, whatever it is, it all does not mean we can ever undermine the importance either of economic conditions or ideas in our lives. We the steersmen can never steer the ships of our lives without the steerings and the petrol—is a fact indeed, but is it also not a fact that steering and petrol in the absence of steersmen are of no use? The fact is a fact that both of them can never determine the route of the voyage what the steersmen decide actually.

But the most neglected aspect of human world is good men—men, who think, feel and do good and no more evil, whatever they can, wherever they are to be good only. We never realise that it is only the good men who can change the world, what Marx had dreamt. We rightly care, and we must reform the species of our bulls, mules, dogs and even plants etc. etc., but do we ever care seriously about reforming our own minds, which are even more dangerous for the annihilation of our own species than these so called brutes? Earlier we realise that the key to world peace is not in God's hands, if at all He exists, but in men's, the better. Because they are the real architects of their own destinies—good or bad. We should not escape from our own responsibilities for our miseries. Of course, if there is any flaw in the constitution, it must be removed by experts.

In fact, there is no such crises of 'matter' or 'ideas'. They are quite in abundance with us here or there. If there is a crisis, it is the crisis of human spirit, not the crisis of the development of the so-called outer world, but of the inner-world i.e., the crisis of human will, human consciousness, human character, human nature and human values, and the like. In fact, the greatest need of the world is good men, because it is they alone who can maintain a constitution well.

6

Where to Get Good Men from ?

All of us wish to build the edifice of humanity, and all want and claim to change the world. But 'how', is the major question. Can we change the world without changing ourselves first? So, in every case we have no alternative, but to build our ownselves first, if we're earnest to build the world.

Again, the major question is: where to get such good, well-built, good natured human beings from? Undoubtedly, now the genetical science can change our physical and mental traits on desired lines through change of our genes. Science has gone ahead of it even. It can have several beings/persons of similar physical or mental traits through cloning. And now one more feather has been added to the crown of science, as on 25-11-2001 an American Biotech private firm has reported that it has cloned a human-embryo not to produce a human clone, but to evolve therapies for diseases such as diabities, cancer and AIDS. Again, on 18-12-2002 in *Hindustan Times* it is reported that a French scientist claims that a first human clone, a girl is born. The baby is an exact genetic copy of the cell donor, a 31 year old American woman.

Thus, let the creationists the world over beware that now science has almost reached the stage of snatching the age old monopoly of 'creation' (of course, there is no creation, but only evolution) from the hands of the hypothetical God. Science is capable of exploding the age old myth of divine right of creation. It is to produce life in the lab soon. Now the genetic science has climbed almost the peaks of The Everest in it's engineering (if at all the news of human cloning is correct.)

It is very relevant to know that the biologist Prof. Steven Rose of the Open University admits that genes play a role in our behaviour, but he clarifies that "America has a massively high murder rate . . . but that is not because they all have some 'rogue violent genes'. But it might have something to do with having 280 million hand-guns" or because of the mindset, what they've made of their own. In fact, there are 'no good or evil genes'. Thus, the message goes: let's no more think, feel and do exclusively 'to live', but also 'to let live', if at all we are earnest to remove our mutual sufferings and want to embrace peace and happiness in life. Let us remember in this atomic age we are either all 'to swim or all to sink together'.

A Professor of Physics at the university of Texas answered the most typical question: "Can science save us?", by stating flatly: "No". Let us remove our age old illusion to hear from science itself: "If somebody is thinking in terms of creating superman" through genetic-engineering, he is living only in a fool's paradise. So, let us know the biotechnical truths: Genetical science can, no-doubt, have several genetical copies of the cell-donors through cloning, but not several Gandhi's or Hitlers. why? Because both were the breeds of different education and religion. The historical instance of Ratnakar is before all of us. All of us know how he had changed and ultimately made himself a Balmiki, the great well-known saint later on, when he changed the very mindset of himself through '*gyan*' earnestly. Hence, good men should be produced. Of course, scientists don't deny that a clone may have a different IQ, personality and even looks, as genes are only one component of a person's identity. Environment is a big influence. Hence, clone may not be an exact copy of his/her cell-donor. Thus we should not worry that a Hitler clone can necessarily cause us a holocaust, just as we should not expect from the clones of an Einstein to turn out to be genious physicists, when they grow up.

But our fundamental question still remains to be answered: whether science can ever produce good men in a lab? It is obvious that the answer is: No, not at all. Because there are limitations of science too. It is beyond the domain of science to produce good men indeed. Good men can only be produced through men-making education, training and men-making religion only. When Rousseau said: 'Man was born free, but he is in chains', he meant that at the time of birth we are neither good, nor bad. It is only after our birth we chain ourselves with our own shakles of evils. But being the true architects of our own destinies we can free ourselves also from them, if we have the rocky will and earnestness to do so, because nothing is pre-determined. They're only man-made.

The very birth of epoch-making human giants like Ram, Krishna, Mohammad, Christ, Buddha, Mahavir, Gurus and the like causes a clear cut blow to the thesis of Mr. B.F. Skinner, who holds: We're not free at all to turn hell into heaven or vice-versa. He adds that we are 'predictable' and 'conditioned creatures' or "man is no different from laboratory animals," or man is not the master of his destiny, being 'merely a creature of his environment'. May I know how can we put these towering human personalities locked into the tiny hole of 'conditioned creatures' or 'laboratory animals'? Haven't they been the great masters of their own destinies? If they were creatures of their own respective circumstances, were they not the creators of them? Don't we bow before them out of our highest esteem for them, because they had their important hands in changing the values of the society, the very people, the very mindset and outlook of the common men of their respective ages and times? Their most important contribution to the entire world is that they had a great role in changing the world indeed. That is why, our heart felt respect for them is natural. Of course, we may or may not agree with them here or there for their commissions or omissions, but only senseless persons can say that 'they were not great'. It is not at all to deny that only very small persons act or react like cockroaches of gutters here in the world. I cannot accept that if they behave or misbehave with anyone, it is all, because their fate is pre-determined by some hypothetical power. Being a true architect of my own destiny— good or bad—I am fully responsible for my actions or reactions. I cannot escape from it morally or otherwise.

To think that man is the puppet in the hands of fate is nothing, but it is akin to challenge of man's true dignity. It is due to this Dr. Radhakrishnan rightly observed: "Man is not an aggregate chemical compound. He is not a slot machine with predictable responses to outer stimulation. He is not a puppet in the hands of fate, nor a pawn in the cosmic chess, moved by impersonal forces of nature, fate or destiny. He is the master of his fate, the captain of his soul". "Unless we accept the will of man is free, his dignity is a myth, his optimism is an illusion and history is fate." What is fate? Are all the humans of this world not the architects or makers or masters of their fate?

Science, no-doubt, can produce a totally self-operating bulldozer, but it can never produce a consciousness in men; so that they may not crush a crawling babe on the road. Of course, a most technically advanced computer helps a cardiac surgeon a lot in his works on the table from the beginning to an end to-day. But when we lack such desirable consciousness in us, and when we are fully conscious of this dangerous derailment on our parts too, it is because we have free will to misbehave or behave with our fellow-beings, being the true architects of our own destinies both good or evil. It is due to this fact that the same man can go even higher than the Everest in his goodness and excellence, and the same man, made of the same matter touches even the sea-depth, when he commits heinous crimes or sins, especially against humanity. Here man is the same, matter is the same, but his behaviour, his outlook and mindset and his consciousness are totally different in these two cases. Can we forget Ratnakar and how he became a Balmiki, the great saint later on? It is all the play or the magic of our consciousness, made by us. Escapism on our parts won't help us anymore in making ourselves, what we are—good or bad persons. Of course, we cannot deny that humans too have their own genuine or created limitations, which they fail to crossover sometime due to this or that reason, as perfection is utopian here.

Hence, it is not right for late Sh. Palkhivala, an Indian Constitutional lawyer to hold that "the basic pattern of an individual's and nation's life is pre-determined". I humbly feel with full esteem for the lawyer that it is a serious challenge to human dignity indeed. We should not mind such things much, when we have honest dissent with each other.

But the challenge is very serious with farreaching implications. Are we simply "laboratory animals", having no free-will of our own? Are we really the Peeping Toms at the keyhole of eternity? Are we like 'His Master's pet dogs on a long leash-dogs, which have freedom, but they can move about as far as the so-called Lords' leash permits and not beyond that, as Sri. Nani Palkhivala in his book *We the Nation* holds? I am not a lawyer, who can argue a case for sheer arguement. I am, undoubtedly, a very small fly, but with an humble urge to know the truth. May I know then if we have become greater dangers to our own species even to-day, does it not mean without doubt that it is we who have degraded ourselves as human beings, and, consequently, we are fully responsible for this, or does it mean that the same lord has loosened His leash consciously or unconsciously and thus we are not at all responsible for all these unfortunate things ? We can escape by saying: 'let the Piper pay for His music'. Let's remember if we fail to accept our parentage of the child (here it is our world or our respective lives), no matter the child is ugly or beautiful, we never shall be able to rear the said child in a proper way, with the result the child may remain a rickety child throughout with no scope for any change, whatsoever. Can we befool all the people all the time? The earlier we remove this cobweb, woven by us, the better. Otherwise, let us be ready to face more dangers ahead of all of us.

Here my humble query is: How can Mr. Palkhivala's 'Masters' pet dogs on a long leash' and Swami Vivekanandji's 'His chessmen' ever be the true architects of their own destinies—good or bad, as they are permanently disabled? Do we feel sorry or are we happy to know then the unfortunate classical misbehaviour of the priests of Somnath temple, when it was being looted by some cruel foreigners?

Here it's very essential for all of us to remember that men with the so-called divine (good) or devil (evil) nature are not born, but are made here by themselves. So, to think that in any highly industrially advanced material conditions the urge of exploitation of man by man is but natural, is nothing but our simple foolish over-simplification of this tendency, especially when we recollect the well-known name of Sri Jamnalalji Bajaj, "a spiritual son" of Gandhiji and well-known as "a Gandhian Capitalist". "Jamnalalji did earn his money, as all capitalists do, in the capitalistic way, but he held himself as a trustee of his wealth", because he had great spiritual urge, embraced simple-living and high thinking voluntarily and preferred to live in huts in place of bungalows, as Gandhiji did. Any one can argue that he was only one man, picked up from human history. But let us remember what one can make impossible, possible, everyone can do the same, provided one has the earnest urge and will for it. This living instance from Indian history has become all the more like a boosting dose to my belief that we are all the masters of our own destinies—both either good or bad, and not at all the slaves either of matter or an idea. Let us remember slaves are slaves and freemen are freemen, so long they make themselves so. It is merely our thinking that makes it so and thinking that makes it otherwise.

It is a scientific truth and not a scientific fiction even that Bio-technology is sure to produce 'men' one day in the lab, but it is beyond its limited power to produce good humans, who are the greatest need of the hour of our human world. Swami Vivekanandji too declared: "The older I grow, the more everything seems to lie in manliness". "This is my new gospel." Swamiji openly declared: "My mission is not Ramkrishna's, nor Vedanta's, but simply to bring manhood to my people." Can science ever deliver this good to humans? No, never, because of its limitations which are natural. Mr Palkhivala's His Master's pet dogs and Swamiji's own chess men can never bring this manhood to the people of this world, but only those, who really believe that they are actually the true architects of their own destinies—both good or evil.

Keeping all these facts in view now it is crystal clear that the 'manhood' what Swamijii's main mission of life was, cannot be achieved in a science lab either or in a factory or field, or by administering the pills to human beings, but simply by men-making education and training, and men-making 'dharma' only. It is not concerned with the field of science, and it is beyond science.

We have already seen how both Economic Determinism of Marx and Hegelian Determinism have been quite ineffective to bring changes in men first to change their world, what Marx aimd at. Now let us examine quite objectively again the case of this age old Divine-Determinism too in this respect in details.

7

Divine Determinism—The Most Hopeless and Dangerous Conjecture

It would be better to know Swami Vivekanandji's view before taking up their plea. Swamiji frankly asks: "What right has a man to say he has a soul, if he does not feel it, or that there is a God, if he does not see Him? If there is a God we must see Him, if there is a soul, we must perceive it; otherwise it is better not to believe. It is better to be an outspoken atheist than a hypocrite" (On page 127 Vol. 1) (*Swamiji's Works*). Even Gandhiji in his '*Experiments with Truth*' on page 206 accepts: "I have not seen Him, neither have I known Him".

In fact, the question of 'Divine-Determinism' arises only, when we know Him, have seen Him, felt Him, experienced Him anywhere, in any form or otherwise. What happens usually that most of us go on declaring from our tops that there is a God, and there is a soul. We have lofty talks about the so-called 'Atma'-'Pratama', 'lok'-'parlok', 'dharma'-'adharma' and the like only parrotwise. Our talks have been heretical only and not on the basis of our own experiences of our lives. When we ask them if there has been actually a God as the creator, the sustainer and the destroyer, where have then the bloody red pages of human history come from? They actually have no answer of it, and thus they remain non-plussed or they get bogged down in these or those unreasonable replies. When we ask them: have they themselves even seen or experienced or felt Him in their lives? They reply it only negatively. In fact, they have to prove their bonafides as the true 'bhakats' of 'Bhagwan', and as such they have no alternative, except to drag Him in, and drag Him out of human affairs simply according to their conveniences.

Kingslay Martinn approvingly quotes Rashdalls' view that the explanation of the world's evils is that God is not omnipotent, and perhaps, due to this reason "A struggling and defeated Deity" was Rashdall's phrase. Perhaps, Nietzsche had said that "God is dead" in the same context. Facts are facts. We are not looking at Him through negative glasses.

In fact, we have been living in a make-believe world only. It is we who have made our God as the greatest mystery. The so-called religious Pandits boast and declare that because He is beyond the cause and effect, He cannot be known or felt or experienced by us. They hold that though He is almighty and everywhere, He is formless. Hence, the knower cannot be known by us. In fact, they are more interested to keep this mystery quite intact or beyond the poor access of the common men. The question is—have they made the common men more religious in the right sense of the term or more humane by their modus-operandi at all? I would like to be apologised for these frank views. How long would they go on concealing Him behind the bushes of time, cause and space?

I cannot endorse Swami Vivekanandji's view that mere belief in the Lord can ever make us good humans by an iron necessity. I humbly feel to be good or to be humane depends more on what mindset we have formed; how conscientous persons we are. Belief in God is not essential to be humane. Do we not know that even robbers, criminals visit the temple and pray Him, lest they should be nabbed red-handed? Don't we know that even Napoleon, Hitler and Mussolini believed in God?

So, I do not think the following view of Swami Vivekanandji is based on facts. He holds: "If men believe in a God, they may become good, and moral, and so make good citizens." It is a fact that we have both good and evil impulses or ripples or waves for action in our minds. How can then we accept Swamiji's contention "that every impulse for action comes from Him . . ." In fact this view conceives in one's mind, when one believes that we humans are only His '*nimits*', and the Lord is the doer of all things. And whatever He does, does right. Is it not a bogus plea of creationists?

Once, Sri J.K. Krishnamurti was asked: 'Well, belief in God has been a powerful incentive to better living. Why do you then deny God? He replied: "I am not denying God. It would be foolish to do so . . . First of all, why do we believe. You believe because it gives you satisfaction, consolation, hope . . . Actually, your belief has very little significance, because you believe and exploit, you believe and kill, you believe in God and murder. The rich man also believes in God, he exploits ruthelessly, accumulates money and then builds a temple or becomes a philanthropist . . ." Is it not all actually happening under His nose the world over? Are not crimes and sins thriving under the garb of divine belief? This all does not mean that all believers in God are criminals or sinners. But when the question of belief in Him comes up, let us realise the reality and what does this belief mean generally? What believers have been doing generally at home and in the country?

Actually, there is now no question of belief or no belief in Him. We may or may not have any faith in God, but if we have faith in our manliness, in our own good doings, what we can, wherever we are only to be good, if we earnestly not only believe, but actually follow the principle 'live and let live' in our lives, we are apt to change ourselves and our world too simultaneously for good. Otherwise, on the one hand, we shall go on believing in Him, worshipping Him as usual, but we are apt to find our ship of life without a good mast or it is unnavigable on the other. why? Obviously, because of our hypocritic character.

So, our belief in God becomes meaningless in itself. It's no use to believe in a God and cheat or exploit or rape or ill-treat or butcher the living gods and goddesses at the same time. So, first of all such window-dressing of our belief or religious-shopping or camouflaging of our real skin or colour must be stopped altogether.

Those, who have actually the very good of these living gods and goddesses at their hearts or in their minds, their belief or no belief in Him makes no difference. They live and actually can die as well for them. Of course, there must not be inherent clash between the hypothetical God and these living gods and goddesses, but in actual life we see that we remember our God, but forget these living gods and goddesses. Let us remember God was not at all an end in Himself, but only a means to an end. And the real end was the welfare of these living gods and goddesses. That is why, I humbly hold that no religion, whatsoever is an end in itself, but only a means to an end. If a religion fulfils this end, it is worth accepting. Otherwise, it is worth-rejecting totally. So, our belief or faith in Him is all meaningless, if we donot believe and have no faith in our own manliness, and good-doings, and in these living gods and goddesses. Being the true steersmen of the ships of our lives, we may or may not have faith in Him, but if we lack belief or faith in the welfare of these common living gods and goddesses, we are sure to see our moving ship is stopped then and there. We may or may not faithfully worship our God, but if we ill-treat our elders especially at home, this faith or belief in Him is all meaningless or purposeless. What a hypocrisy we are doing! To whom are we befooling or dodging? If we do not love those, who are known to us, and quite visible to our eyes, can we ever love and worship Him, who has ever been quite unknown to us?

Sri J.K. Krishnamurti says: ". . . The men who dropped the atomic bomb on Hiroshima said that God was with them. Belief . . . divides people . . . To know . . . mind must be free from . . . all ideas about God. All that you know about God are words, the experiences of others . . . we can see him eye to eye by serving the humanity . . . There is hope in men . . . organised religions . . . offer only a false solution to the basic problem. When you quote the Bhagwad Gita, or the Bible . . . surely you are merely repeating. Are you not?" What we actually and often do is that we pass on to others the belief or other's faiths—right or wrong, not based on facts without any valid questioning. It is no use to quote anything from anybody, unless it is based on facts, reasoning and commonsense and the like. So, let us not run anymore in this meaningless rat-race.

For instance, we talk of Karma Theory. Of course, we must. As a general rule in our life it's O.K. 'As you sow, so shall you reap'—as a general principle is to be accepted by all reasonable persons. For instance, if I put my hand on fire, it is apt to be burnt, but people in general have been in the habit of dragging their hypothetical Lord even in such affairs and they put their unnecessary if's and but's here or there by telling very confidently that my hand would never be burnt, if the Lord does not will it, as if their Lord has been a magician, and being so He can stop my hand from being burnt, because He has some Alladin magic to play with me. What a funny plea they have got! Hence, they are ridiculed.

Let is accept that only good people can make a good society. According to Karma Theory as propagated usually nothing bad should happen, at least, to good people, but you see here in this world, what it is even worst things too have happened to good people, not because they must have done some wrong in their past lives essentially, as believers in Karma theory put it so confidently, as if they have got some solid evidence of it with them. First of all, it is still disputable whether there is the so-called rebirth. Who knows about it authentically? Is it not all a guess-work? Then the question is: Why is it happening with the good people? Karma theory has no valid explanation of it. There is a sense in it that this world is human and not God-ordained at all. It is not a one-man show even, but a show, staged by crorers of people, no matter the show is good or evil. That is why, Rabbi Kushner had admitted frankly and asked: "why bad things happen to good people?" He too holds that if we go on linking our fortunes or misfortunes with the will of God, we are sure to distort facts. So, let us no more behave like blinds. He too retorts by asking us: 'Do the mosquitoes bite us due to our past or present bad karmas? In fact, let us accept the fact in question. The fact is that all of us have been the successors of apes. We might have become humans in appearance, as a result of evolution but brute in our nature still works very powerfully without any brake here or there and without any clutch and thus as a result of it even good people have not been left by us without making them the very targets of our claws. In fact, the she-mosquitoes need protein from human blood and she bites. This shows that the web of human life has been woven by human spiders themselves exclusively with their own knitpins, no matter the web is good or bad. And it is only these human spiders who can re-weave the same web, if at all it is not worth-accepting somewhere. So, it is rather dangerous to drag Him in and drag Him out of human affairs, as we usually do it simply according to our convenience. I repeat here again that denial of God does not mean at all that we human beings can afford to be inhuman or uncivilised in any way. The most important thing to remember is that we may or may not have any faith in God, but in case we do not have any faith in our own manliness or manhood, we are sure to behave like those unfortunate priests of Somnath temple, which was being looted by some inhumans. Let us believe that our life is, what we make it—good or bad. Escapism from one's responsibility makes one experience living death.

Let us know that Mr. Edmund Burke, who had no belief in God, was not very much inclined to hear the lecture of one of his close friends in a church. On the great insistence of his friend one day, Burke went to the church to listen to him. Edmund Burke asked his friend, when he ended his lecture: "I have a question. You said in your speech that a man, who is good, virtuous, a believer in God, goes to heaven. And a man, who is not good, not virtuous does not believe in God, goes into hell . . . My question is", Burke said, . . . "I want to know: if a man is good and virtuous and does not believe in God, where does he go? A man who is bad . . . but is a believer in God . . . where does he go?" In fact, the whole talks of Burke's friend were from the make believe world. They were all heretical. The truth is: heaven or hell is nowherelse, but is here on earth. It is all due to the fanaticism of the believers in God, we found great people like Galelio and Totostoy in a hell. Had God been there, He would not have allowed, at least, such great architects of their own destinies in a hell. Hence, I humbly believe that belief or no belief in such a God is all irrelevant.

So earlier we realise that both our happiness or sufferings or miseries in our lives have not been any of God's making, but ours own, the better. Actually, our own experience of life says that our life, whatever it is—good or bad—has not been the result of any God's mindsport or God's '*leela*', but it has been the actual result of the mindset of all of us either individually or collectively. So, earlier we stop hijacking Him in human affairs, the better. It's all our sheer escapism to say that whatever has happened, or is happening, or would happen, it is all because of God and thus it is good. It's nothing but our *fate-accompli* pre-determined by the

Lord. Such senseless approaches are meaningless. They invite dangerous escapism on our parts. Let us no more behave like that stupid ostrich in 'sand' dunes.

To say that 'whatever He does with us, is right' is a dangerous dose to kill the men. It is nothing, but the most dangerous' poison.

Had god been the sole doer of all things in this world, He would have definitely taken, at least, a *suo motu* action to change the two belligerent minds in the *Mahabharata*, and side by side, would have changed or removed the very causes of that big fight, instead of seeing, the blood-bath later on like a passive-spectator of the melodrama, staged by humans.

When Gandhari saw all her sons dead in the battle field, she too reminded Krishna pathetically, but out of the same age old 'illusion'. What she said was: "You could have stopped the war", and thereafter cursed Him too. I humbly believe her illusion was that it is the Lord, who ignites the fire and it is He only who douses it. Firstly, keeping in view the world, what it has been—good or bad, it is very very difficult to believe—whether He exists, and, secondly, He does anything at all. Thirdly, those who hold that the war was inevitable as their *fate-accompli* predetermined, they must remember that the concept of inevitability of happening must have been quiet foreign to the very concept of God. So, earlier we stop hijacking God in and out of human affairs, the better. Again, earlier we realise, that God may or may not exist, but it is we humans, who wage war, and it is we, who can establish peace in the world, and not any divine hypothetical force, the better. Merely our lying prostrate before Him in the belief that He is the sole-doer of all things in the world, would not help us at all. Better follow earnestly the age old principle. 'Live and let live'. If at all He exists anywhere He cannot be pleased to see us being passive 'Karmayogi'. In fact, the very philosophy of 'God's sole doer of all things in our lives' is so deadly a poison that it is apt to make us all '*Akarmanya*', in place of '*Karmanya*' in our lives. So earlier we leave it, the better. Mere worshipping our respective God as a routine, creates illusion. Will it make us better human beings essentially? Has it made us less egoists?

So, earlier we realise that the world, whatever it has been, it has not been divine, but man-made, the better. The priests of Somnath temple too were suffering from the same deadly poison, when the temple was being looted. It made them perfect escapists, cowards, fatalists and shirkers only. Our history of follies, sufferings and miseries has failed utterly to wake up the nation which has been fast asleep in deep slumber. Consequently, the same history has been repeating non stop again and again, because of the same doses of illusions, what we have been taking for ages.

Frankly speaking, even the saints like Swami Vivekanandji too was not an exception of this self-imposed illusion. I humbly hold that it was sheer blind faith in Him, Swamiji pleaded: "Who would live a second, who would breathe a second in the universe, if that blessed one were not filling it?" (on page 133 Vol. 2 *Swamiji's Works*) When one cannot live even a second, and breathe a second even without the Lord's blessings, who would like to do anything else, except prostrating before Him just to worship Him and to please Him ultimately? You go to any of the so-called religious places particularly, and you can witness it with your own eyes an army of the so-called masked *sadhus,* who are more or less idlers. Most of them have nothing to do with getting 'gyan' or spiritual-attainment. A very good percentage of them lives to eat and is found actually indulged in this or that evil. Although they keep the name of 'Om', or Ram or Krishna or Mohammed or Allaha, or Christ or God or '*wahe guru*' simply on their lips and not in their minds just to pose before the people around that they are religious people. I do admit that there have been some of them, who are really exceptions, and they are not living the lives of slaves or parasites, and their lives are assets for the world indeed. But their number is only on the tips. Here I remember an old saying which rightly denotes that a person, whose life goes on and on smoothly without doing anything, would never like to do anythingworth-doing in one's life. Such is the case with this army of self-declaring *Sadhus*. Undoubtedly, I have been a small person, but let us ascertain whether this mass of the so-called 'sadhus' has been living the life of a *Karmanya* or perfect *Akarmanya*, a person who never sets an example before the society for one's worth-thinking, feelings and doings? Let us remember this is the net result or the right output of this dismal philosophy, we have been advocating for long.

What a deadly poison we have been sipping for ages and that too in the name of God! What they treat it as a nectar, has been actually a poison. If here an innocent is butchered, or raped or exploited by his/her fellow-beings, these theists at once drag their Lord in just to console the concerned victims by patting their backs that they should not mind it much, as it was only their *fate-accompli*, predetermined by the Lord on the basis of their own past or present Karmas; as if they know surely everybody's past or present record of one's commissions or omissions. It definitely gets innocent mass of the people composed for a considerable time. But does it not all mean that crimes and sins have been thriving and multiplying in these lanes of blind faith and innocence under the garb of God's responsibilities? Actually, how long would we like to behave like that stupid ostrich? And what is the utility of such beliefs to the individuals or the society as a whole? Has it all made us better human beings and less egoists?

Can such poisoned minds ever even think of changing themselves and their world too? Of course, they can play the role of a leopard or a good chameleon only. Let us remember that for changing ourselves and our world, we shall have to change our psyche first altogether.

When according to Swami Vivekanandji 'we can neither live, nor even breathe without His mercy, the same faith demands that we must hold this view too that the Lord must be standing somewhere and must be pumping our blood circulation even. But in this case Swamiji denies this plea. How inconsistent it is! Swamiji holds: "Not that He is standing somewhere and making my blood circulate." (on page 133 Vol. 2 *Swamiji's Works*). Of course, I am damn happy that, at least, Swamiji accepts the truth.

But his statement becomes quite meaningless, because swamiji makes his Lord the very cause of both our rise or fall, or the source of our breathing or choking. I humbly hold that excessive attachment even with the Lord blurs our vision and, consequently, we fail to see truth as truth. In this world, what it is made by all of us, unfortunately, the innocents or the common men may or may not be able to live or breathe even a second freely, but can Swamiji deny that the hard core criminals and sinners have their own rules to follow, and thus they are seen breathing freely most of the time?

Hence, I humbly believe that the determinists—whether they are materialists, who propagate that the 'things' or the material or the economic conditions have been the decisive forces in human history, as they change, they change the world as well, or the Hegalion Determinists, who hold that the 'thought' or the 'Idea' has been the decisive force in human history, as 'thoughts' change, they change the world too, or the Divine Determinists, who say from their tops that all hopes, religion, the whole universe and everything in it have come out of Brahma—the God—all have been trying their level best to carve the roads for us through so dangerous their tunnels, that we fail to come out of them and there we see there is no hope of light, but complete darkness in them. Hence, in their kingdoms we humans would neither be able to change ourselves, nor the world. When we claim that all human beings have been the sole architects of their own destinies—good or bad—themselves, it clearly means that humans have not been dictated to make their destinies either by the 'things' or 'thoughts' or by the so-called Brahma, but they themselves determine their own history, their own destinies, their own lives and their own world too, no matter they are good or bad. They are like human spiders who weave the very web of their lives—good or bad—with their own knitpins, and in case they are quite earnest, they can re-weave the same web, if at all it is not in the welfare of the entire world.

Human beings are not cogs in a machine. Here no-doubt, those people may be full of pleasures, whose circumstances suit their tempers, but only those people can ever be happier, who can suit their temper to any circumstance-either good or bad. Of course, this ideal is very lofty and difficult to follow, but to attain happiness, humans have no other alternative to it. It is undeniable that the circumstances too sting to those, who fail to make themselves their masters and not servants. It is right that poverty breeds crime and sin to some extent, but we witness with our own eyes that people's affluence too breeds crime, if they fail to control their minds as masters and themselves become their slaves. If we fail to make our minds work properly on desired channels, or we have our sick or filthy and vulgar minds or we fail to strengthen our conscience; it would not be well-equipped to determine: what to do, and what not in a given circumstances, no matter we are poor or rich then. Our minds are apt to spit fire and erupt 'lava'. In fact, crime and sins know no barriers of class or caste or creed or place, and the like. They know no such frontiers or borders. Their only barriers are our well built minds only on desired lines by our ownselves. Earlier we understand this thing as architects of our own destinies, the better. Better late than never. Let us no more try to seek any motive of 'ego' in this truth. The need of the hour is to know ourselves what we are, and what we ought to be to make our world a heaven.

In the same context, it is again relevant to quote Swami Vivekanandji, who says, "I am a materialist in a certain sense, because I believe that there is only one . . . Only he calls it matter and I call it God. The materialists admit that out of this matter all hope and religion and everything have come. I say all these have come out of Brahman. But the materialism that prevailed before Buddha was that crude sort of materialism which taught "eat, drink, and be merry"; there is no God, soul or heaven. Religion is a concotion of wicked priests". (On page 138-139 Vol. 2 *Swamiji's Works*). He adds further: "It taught the morality that so long as you live, you must try to live happily; eat though you have to borrow money for the food, and never mind about repaying" (On page 138-139, Vol. 2 *Swamiji's Works*).

But you see, unlike the materialists or the Hegalianists, or the Divine-determinists, we believe that there has not been one, but crorers of people, who have actually been the real architects of their own destinies—good or bad. We believe by our own experience of life that all the 'thoughts' and 'things', all the hopes or religions have been the brain children of the human spiders, who have actually been weaving their webs of life—good or bad with their own knitpins, and it is only they who can remove the red-blood patches on the webs, if there are any. If we believe that humans are the real steersmen of the ships of their lives, it all does not mean, they are free to steer it, as they like it whimsically.

After all liberty is not the absence of restraints. It is only the replacement of the undesirable restraints by desirable ones. So, in a civilised polity there is no question of absolute freedom and unlimited rights for anyone, whatsoever. Actually, the denial of the existence of a hypothetical God does not mean the denial of the observance of the rules of the land concerned, or it does not mean human steersmen can steer their ships rashly or whimisically, press the clutch or accelerator and apply the brakes like eccentric fellows, because rashness means that there's all possibility of a fatal accident. Let us beware of it all in time.

Hence, there is no question to follow the '*charvak*' philosophy, i.e., 'eat, drink and be merry', no matter there is God or no God, soul or no soul, as it too is apt to drag us further towards our hell only.

Let us remember that science observes both our unquestioned acceptance and un-explored rejection unscientific. So, what we need is not to accept anything, which is not based on reason and which is not meant for the welfare of the general masses. When we find this divine—determinism merely a hopeless and dangerous conjecture of human mind, there is no question of it's acceptance by us.

8

For Pandit Nehru—"Human Character of the Nation" was More Important

Pandit Nehru had sounded us even from the rampart of the Red fort on Aug. 15, 1950: "We have to progress in many directions . . . All this is necessary and has to be done. But behind it all lies the human character of the nation, and if this goes wrong, then all else is of little worth. I have sensed a process of . . . little mindedness . . . affecting all our national activities . . ." (Pandit Nehru)

Undoubtedly, for Panditji material progress of India was very dear, but actually dearer for him was the "human character of the nation". He was well aware that Marxism would not have succeeded in achieving its ideals i.e., from each according to one's capacity, to each according to one's work/need', and a 'stateless society', because it failed to build the human mind or the desired human-psyche for the same. What we actually need not the removal of 'I' or me, or my or mine, but the dissolution of the myopic spirit or little-mindedness, what Panditji had referred above, which has been associated with these 'I' or 'my' or mine by our filthy minds, into the wider ocean of humanity by all of us. This is the only meaning, when I say that material investment is O.K., and it is a must, but investment in men is more important. So, it is not the 'I' which is to be removed, but only the 'I's mind is to be overhauled. When we earnestly follow the principle: 'live and let live' in our own lives, it is only then we can say that our investment in men is proper, and now we are sure to get it's good dividend. No solution is final. A seeker of truth remains on the voyage of the exploration of truth constantly. His 'Sadhana' goes on life-long.

How human factors have been important and basic to change the world, Pandit Nehru wrote on the objectives of planned development in a Third Plan document: "Although planning involves material investment, even more important is the investment in man". On the theme of India Today And Tomorrow in the inaugral Azad Memorial lecture Panditji made the same point amply clear. He said: "What I am concerned with is not merely our material progress, but the quality and depth of our people. Gaining power through industrial process, will they lose themselves in the quest of individual wealth and soft-living? That would be a tragedy, for that would be a negation of what India has stood for in the past." In a nutshell, to throw away our own little-mindedness to the garbage or to the dustbin of history is the greatest religion of all the people of the world. Unless all of us do it intently and earnestly, let's make it a point to remember' that our minds will remain more dangerous than even a volcano, about which nobody knows, when it can erupt it's 'lava', more dangerous than atom bombs, AIDS and the so-called cancer. We talk of Ram, Allaha, God and 'Wahe guru', but we fight with each other even on these names of our esteemed 'gurus! why? Because, these names remain only on our lips and the very messages of these 'gurus' do not reach the very depth of our minds—the real wombs, where the germs of both peace and war conceive, and where ripples or waves of both love and hatred for each other rise, and if they subside, they leave their marks behind to come up again and thus they make our *sanskars*. So let us be careful which ripple or wave conceives in our minds and which does not actually. Being the true architects of our own destinies, let us then be very much careful, while weaving the very web of our lives or the world as human spiders with our own knitpins, to ensure that no more such web should be woven by us, which makes us love exclusively either Ram or Allaha or God or 'Wahe guru', and not all the living gods and goddesses of the world without any bias of any sort. In fact, if we love either of them exclusively, we are not truly religious, but only posing to be religious.

Undoubtedly, all of us want peace and happiness, but like Osama bin Laden some of us hope to get the same even by piercing others' bodies and minds with their needles, while persons like Gandhi moved openly in Noakhali without getting any protection just to put actual balm on the wounded bodies and minds of both the Hindus and Muslims; because the cardinal principle of Gandhiji's life was 'means justify the end,' and not 'end justifies the means'.

I recollect when someone reminded Pandit Nehru that China had made 'tremendous progress'. He replied: "But at what cost?"

Pandit Nehru made this point amply clear in some other context by saying, "I have felt more and more that basic lesson that Gandhiji taught was right and that was that means should never be subordinate to ends'. In context of Gandhiji's philosophy of 'means justify the end', it is most relevant to quote him from *Hind Swaraj*. Gandhiji viewed: "Do you not tremble to think of freeing India by assassination? What we need today is to kill ourselves. It is a cowardly thought, that of killing others. Those who will rise to power by murders will certainly not make the nation happy". What Buddha thought for elimination of human misery, one will have to eliminate his own exclusive self, Gandhi meant the same thing by killing ourselves later on.

Today the whole world is sitting on the mouth of a volcano and it can emit it's lava at any time, because most of us, wherever we are either in a family or in a country or in any part of the world—least bother for the means to attain our end. People defame even Marx by accusing him to think of bringing revolution only through violent means by turning haves into have' nots. But to think like that we're mistaken. Marx nowhere propagated his violent means, at least, in the so-called democracy like UK, where for him revolution was possible through constitutional means too. No doubt, Marx was a Jew by birth, but not a Shylock of the Merchant of Venice. We all know Shylock was after a pound of flesh of Antonio for his own end. In fact, Marx was one of the greatest human beings, because he did each and everything for establishing a just order in the world, no matter his theories in the *Das Capital* or Communist Manifesto were right or wrong.

In this context, Swami Vivekanandji's advice too is very noteworthy. He says, "Let us perfect the means, the end will take care of itself. For the world can be good and pure, only if our lives are good and pure . . . Therefore, let us purify ourselves, let us make ourselves perfect." (on page 9 Vol. 2 *Swamiji's Works*)

Hence, it is more relevant to remind ourselves that instead of confining ourselves simply to beautifying our idols of God with costly costumes, instead of decking our abode of God with flowers and buntings, etc., let's pay our sincere attention first to making ourselves from within more pure; so that all the living gods and goddesses of the world may be loved by all. Consequently, when we are changed, we may also be in a position to change the world too.

This clearly implies that change in the world is possible not through the corridors of change in the modes of production, consisting of both the instruments of production and relation of production, but only when our mindset is changed and made pure by us. Thus, the starting point of real revolution is neither the 'thing' of Marx, nor the 'idea' of Hegel, but humans themselves. If humans are changed, their minds, their very 'things' as well as 'thoughts' too would change themselves automatically sooner or later. Thus, the main carriers of revolution are humans themselves.

If we really want to change the world, we shall have to change our very psyche, or the very gear of our thoughts, feelings and doings for the good of all the people first. We boast that unlike other animals we're thinking animals, because we are privileged to have minds. But is it not a fact that we switch this privileged apparatus 'off', when it is needed the most? Instead of reacting against hatred, anger, jealousy and vengeance, do we ever remember how to respond to them with love? If we really do not, how can we boast to be the thoughtful animals? In fact, we stop thinking properly, when we need it the most merely due to our own anger, and consequently we become more dangerous animals than even sharks, tigers, cobras, scorpions, '*bagulas*' and the like. It is these human sharks, human-tigers, human-cobras, human-scorpions and human-*bagulas* who have been making the whole ocean of humanity dirtier, filthier and more vulgar. So, the greatest need of the hour for us is to cease to behave like scorpions or sharks or tigers or cobras and bagulas for all times to come. Being humans, we are all subject to errors. Let us repent earnestly, if we have done any avoidable commissions or omissions for the welfare of the entire humanity. After all we are all humans—neither divine, nor devil essentially by our nature. Let us behave then like humans only for the good of our fellow sisters and brothers from now onwards, at least. Let the dead past, burry its dead. Let us leave the past, think of the present to make it better just to hope for a brighter future too.

It all does not mean I would ever like to be befooled again and again by those, who are adament to behave like human-cobras, or human bagulas and the like deliberately. Not that at all. Such unfortunate situations do come very often particularly in the lives of all right-thinking humans. But all good men of foresight always give proper thought to them; so that they may be in a position to respond to them in the most befitting manners, keeping in view the welfare of all the people of the world. Even in adversed circumstances good people are happy, because they choose the work, what they do, of their own choice, free-will and hope, and the people around in their immediate contact too are of their own choice, whom they love the most. I feel we shall be able to know Pt. Nehru better, if we know the relevant views of others too beforehand as under.

We may or may not have faith or belief in God, but if we have no faith or belief in our ownselves, we have no future. Being the steersmen of the ship of our lives we would not be able to steer our ships even an inch further then. In this context, it is relevant to quote Swami Vivekanandji: "What a mass of superstition this is! . . . why was reason given us, if we have to believe? . . . I am sure God will pardon a man who will use his reason and cannot believe, rather than a man, who believes blindly instead of using the faculties He has given him." (on page 11, 12 Vol. 6 *Swamiji's Works*). Self-imposed religious people are seen telling: "We are very religious people." "What religion they have, no one knows, because they have swallowed some grandmother's story, and priests have asked them to believe these things . . ." (on page 13-14 Swami *Vivekanandji's Works*, Vol. 6). So, reason is a must along with faith in oneself.

In fact, religion has nothing to do with what they do usually. They live under illusions only. In fact, these people believe in all those things, which are not worth-believing by any angle of reason. Sri Narasimhaiah says, "Ancient astrology had its origin in Astronomy. But Astronomy is a science . . . How such planets which are huge lumps of matter situated millions of miles away can be intruders in the affairs of man . . . Besides, it is ridiculous to attribute all kinds of human qualities to planets . . . It is not difficult to prove that no day is inauspicious and everyday is innocuous . . . Horoscope also has astrology as its basis . . ." (On page 189, 191 in his book *Science, Non-science and Paranormal*).

Even Sri S. Chandrasekhar in the same book *Science Non-Science and Paranormal* says, "Those who wish to believe in astrology should realise that there is no scientific foundation for its tenets."

Professor David Hilbert, one of the greatest mathematicians of the last century holds: "When you collect the ten wisest men of the world and ask them to find the most stupid thing in existence, they will not be able to find anything stupider than astrology."

Of course, "...the role of the moon as the principle raiser of tides on the earth has been known for many hundreds of years and was first explained in terms of gravitational theory by Isace Newton in the seventeenth century."

Sri H. Narasimhaiah, the V.C. of Bangalore University opines in the same book. "...There is no evidence of the working of any Supernatural force... (on page 163-164 science, *Non-science Paranormal*)

Sri. H. Narasimhaiah Condemns in his book: "The problem before us is whether matter can be created from nothing . . . Such . . . is a paranormal phenomenon defying all known laws of science . . ." He further chides: ". . . A scientist or a student of science is quite rational in his approach to problems inside the laboratory. But it is shocking to find the same 'rational' man being hopelessly irrational in trying to solve the problems of life. It is not uncommon for a professor to teach Darwin's Theory of Evolution in the class and to accept an entirely unscientific theory in the church." (On page 191-193 science, *Non-Science, Paranormal*).

Dr. Narasimhaiah laughs on those teachers, who actually lack scientific vision and approach: . . . "A physics teacher emphatically tells his students that matter cannot be created or destroyed but outside the class he believes—that a watch can be created from nothing . . . It seems as though their thinking faculty has taken a holiday . . . Does not science have its limitations? . . .It is also argued that science may make bulldozers, but cannot train the emotions of the driver not to allow the the bulldozer to roll over a crawling child . . . It is futile to discuss anything with a person, who has a close mind. Thomas Paine says, "To argue with a man, who has renounced the use of authority of reason is like administering medicine to the dead" (On page 308-309 science, *Non-science, Paranormal*).

Dr. Narasimhaiah confirms: "Life in its simplest form as a sub-microscopic entity came into existence on the planet nearly two billion years ago. In the enormus interval, life has slowly, but steadily passed through various stages . . . Any aeroplane is not science anymore than a temple is religion. (*Science, Non-science, Paranormal.*)

He further adds interesting truth in his book: "There seems to be more truth in the statement of Voltaire that man created God than in the belief that God created men . . . There is no creation. Everything is evolution . . ." (*Science, Non-science, Paranormal*)

People, who argue had God not been a creator of this universe, there would not have been His temples or churches or books, which talk of God only, Swami Vivekanandji says, "Temples, or Churches, books or forms, are simply the kindergarten of religion, to make the spiritual child strong enough to take higher steps . . . We hear so many talking about God and the soul, and all the mysteries of the universe, but if you take them one by one, and ask them, "Have you realised God? Have you seen your soul?"—how many can say they have?" (On page 43 Vol. 2 *Swamiji's Works*).

Dr. H. Narasimhaiah too clearly confirms and assures us further in his book that "Man is the master of his destiny, the architect of his future. He makes his own hell and heaven, and he makes it here and now . . . Humanism is opposed to all theories of determinism, predestination and fatalism. Humanism examines everything . . . in the light of reason . . . Humanists do not believe in making petitions to God through prayers or rituals." (on page 312, 314 *Science, Non-science, Paranormal*).

Hence, I humbly believe that it is exclusively the domain of science to decide about the existence of universe and life too on the basis of scientific facts, but when I see religion starts declaring about the universe and life too, I feel it trespasses it's domain, which is very dangerous.

Dr. Radhakrishnan too endorses this view that man is the master of his destiny—good or bad. He says, "If anyone asks why we suffer, we need not point to the stars above, or say that God has punished us. We have to put it down to our iniquities, our disloyalties and our deviations from the ideals, which we profess. We have the best ideals inscribed and embodied in our constitution, but how many of us are carrying them out properly".

Another scientist and rationalist Dr. Asimov says, "I am afraid that I do not know of a single scrap of scientific evidence that supports the notion of transmigration of souls". (in *Science, Non-science, Paranormal*).

Keeping all these scientific facts in view let us examine Pt. Nehru's views further. He says, "Whether there is such a thing as a soul, or whether there is a survival after death or not, I do not know and important as these questions are: they do not trouble me in the least." What a right approach he had! Because goodness of men was dearer to him.

During his vist to Ceylon in 1939, when his Indian host suggested that they should go to the temple. "Temple", he stormed, "what temple, why?" while inaugrating the power dam in the Damodar valley Pt. Nehru said, "These are our temples." He boldly proclaimed his scientific belief: "I find myself incapable of thinking of a deity or of any unknown supreme power in anthropomorphic terms and the fact that many people think so is continually a source of surprise to me".

Wasting time as idlers do either looking towards idols or deities or to the stars for hoping any good from them, or doing penance was nothing but "damn nonsense", according to Pt. Nehru. He said in these words: "I am not a religious man" to Stanley Jones, an evangelist. He said, "So many things are done in the name of God and religion with which I cannot agree, that I have dismissed them both from my life." He added: "I am trying to serve my country. If service to my country is religion, I am religious. If it is not, I am not". (Pt. Nehru) He clarifies: "No orthodox religion attracts me", "But if I have to choose it would certainly be Buddhism". A man's way of life must concern itself more with the good of the society, rather than the salvation of one's self after death, according to Pt. Nehru.

"No, one may not lose faith in man: God, we may deny, but what hope is left for us, if we deny man and thus reduce everything to futility" (Pt. Nehru) Actually Nehru's ambition was that "India . . . looses her religiousity and turns to science . . ." How rational and scientific mind Pt. Nehru had! How relevant he is today!

During the Individual Satyagraha campaign in 1940, Pt. Nehru came to see Mahatma Gandhi at Sevagram. After the meeting, when he got up to bid farewell, Kasturba Gandhi, the wife of Mahatma blessed him saying: "God will look after you." But being a perfect rationalist Pt. Nehru turning to her asked her: "Where is God, Ba? If he exists, he must be fast asleep." What a logical conclusion he derived! Logic to him was in inheritance.

Sri Motilal Nehru too was not an orthodox person. Hence he too said: "I do not believe in his (Gandhiji's) spirituality and will never and I have told him that I shall never believe in God, atleast, in this life".

Once, Nayantara, Nehru's neice asked Pt. Nehru: "Do you believe in God, Mamu?" Jawaharlal replied: "Now that is a very difficult question to answer" Because "it all depends on what you mean by God." Pt. ji's Western education had taught him to see everything through three lenses of what, why and how? That is why, Pt. Nehru advised all of us: "worship is good, but doing penance and counting beads out of a phantom fear is demoralising". Once, he went to the extent of saying that he "looked upon a cow as on a horse".

If Pt. ji went to a temple, he admired the idols only as works of art and sculpture. He preferred other things more important than to go on decking the idols there. He said: "When there is so much to learn and so much to do so".

Religion as practised in the world generally repelled Pt. Nehru, because "it seemed to be associated with superstition and dogmatic beliefs". Pt. Motilal too holds: "I have heard of saints and supermen, but have never had the the pleasure of meeting them, and must confess too a feeling of scepticism about their real existence. I believe in men and things manly." "Religion" wrote Jawaharlal Nehru in his *Discovery of India*, "as I saw it practised, and accepted even by thinking minds, whether it was Hinduism or Islam or Buddhism or Christinity did not attract me." According to him religious theories were only assumptions or speculations about an Unknown and the world. He saw in religion an element of uncritical credulousness, a reliance on Supernatural. Panditji believed in picking up good things, no matter whether they come from the west or the East.

Panditji said: "I want nothing to do with any religion concerned which keeps the masses satisfied to live in hunger, filth and ignorance. I want nothing to do with any order, religious or otherwise, which does not teach people that they are capable of becoming happier and more civilised on this earth, capable of becoming true men, masters of their fate and captains of their souls. To retain this I would put priests to work also and turn the temples into schools." We have made temples more as abodes of God. We have failed to turn them into the refineries of humans unfortunately.

"The cultural mind . . . should have its doors and windows open. It should have the capacity to understand the others' viewpoint fully even though it cannot always agree with it. The question of agreement or disagreement arises only when you understand a thing. (Pt. Nehru).

Panditji did not accept anything which is not based on scientific facts, no matter where it comes from. Even he did not agree with his mentor 'Bapu' on many points. On Jan 15, 1934 there was a serious earthquake in Bihar. Gandhiji sought divine will in it, and said, "a divine chastisement sent by God for our sins . . . for me there is a vital connection between the Bihar earth-calamity and the untouchability campaign." Obviously, Gandhiji was bitterly criticised by many including Tagore and Pt. Nehru particularly. Tagore retorted: " . . . what is truly tragic about it is the fact the kind of arguement that Mahatma Gandhi used by exploiting an event of cosmic disturbance for better-soothers". Having heard it, the great Mahatma responded: " . . . with me the connection between cosmic phenomenon and human behaviour is a living faith that draws me nearer to God, humbles me and makes me readier for facing Him." In fact, blind faith in God was allergic to Pt. Nehru. He preferred human character, human excellence and strong human will to do good to be good to blind 'bhakti'.

Nehru wrote in his Autobiography: "I read with great shock Gandhiji's statement to the effect that the earthquake has been a punishment for the sin of untouchability. That was a staggering remark and I welcomed and wholly agreed with Rabindranath Tagore's answer to it." Actually, had Gandhiji's view been even a bit correct scientifically, the human world would have been full of earthquakes, floods, storms and such natural calamities, because of our tigerish behaviour. So, let us inculcate our scientific vision and outlook to see and know this universe in scientific light. Let us no more waste our valuable time in seeking God here or there. Let us think, feel and do good to be good and men of character, what Pt. Nehru wanted.

Therefore, if we really want to change ourselves and our world, we shall have to change our psyche, our outlook and behaviour for the good of the people of the whole world first. We must remember our character is determined by our behaviour. This takes us to the pertinent question: what is a good human behaviour? Because a nation is measured as good by the good people it has, and not by the consideration of how many 'things' and 'thoughts' it's people have.

9

What is a Good Human Behaviour ?

Our old 'dharma' has been bogged down in rituals and dogmas. It might have made us either Hindus, or Muslims, or Christians, or Sikhs and the like, but it has failed to make us either good Hindus, or good Muslims, or good Christians and good Sikhs etc. At least, it has failed bitterly to make us good humans—the greatest need of the world. Of course, exceptions are there. But do we ever look towards this world and it's living gods and goddesses as mere humans? Has it not fractured human minds and hearts? Instead of uniting two minds together, has it not disunited two-brothers and sisters and made them quite apart from each other? It shows how futile the conventional religions have become now! Of course, it is we who have divided humanity into fragments, and this is the cause of all troubles.

We humans the world over need a new dharma, which revolves round the central theme: "Do to others, as you wish to be done by", but we're not supposed to do anything, which overlooks the very well-being of the people at large. We can call it as men-making religion or by any other name, we like. If we really boast to be humans, this new *dharma* is the least-expectation from us. It nowhere calls us to leave either our family or our world to worship an Unknown, but only to behave and behave properly with all the living gods and goddesses merely as architects of their own destinies. Dr. Radhakrishnan says, "The essence of all dharma is not doing to others, what you do not wish to be done to yourself." If most of us live accordingly, then change in the world is an automatic certainty. Being mere humans do we ever follow in our lives the very essence or the spirit of *dharma*? Are not we supposed to make the following i.e., to do good to all, what we can, wherever we are only to be good, and avoid doing any evil or any harm to anyone, whatsoever, what we can avoid certainly—the two main columns of the very edifice of our lives—individual's or otherwise? Of course, we have to keep the welfare of the people at large in the very core of our minds. Good human behaviour mainly depends on these columns.

The world is not in an imminent danger from commet, but we are sitting on the mouth of a huge volcano, if we fail to think, feel and do good. In fact, the real religion does not live either in our books or scriptures and lectures, or discourses or religious places or rituals or dogmas or in the caves or on the peaks of The Himalayas and the like, but in our realisation. Religion is realisation of good in life. It is not essentially worshipping, but being. Hence, I cannot digest a French philosopher Voltaire's, view that 'all religions are absurd and contrary to reason.' I humbly feel without men-making religion this planet earth is apt to be reduced merely to a forest of brutes.

In fact, had we followed the men-making religion in our lives in it's true spirit, the hell would have been turned into heaven automatically long-long ago, because it must have flushed the filth from our minds. So, 'to do good to be good' is the very essence of the real religion.

The very concepts of good and evil change according to the time, place, circumstances, persons etc. This all does not mean everything is good and nothing is evil in this world. Everything may be O.K. in love and war, but in actual human life, and day-to-day living this cannot be applied. No religion is an end in itself, but it is only a means to an end. And the end is human welfare at large. In case it serves this purpose, well and good, otherwise, it is an antithesis of religion. It is in this context, a thing, which is nectar for me, may be poison for another. A religion of a father or mother, or a brother or sister or teacher or doctor varies from each other. We must keep it into our minds the very motive of our works, before deciding what is *dharma* and what is *adharma*.

Swami Vivekanandji rightly views: "Nor is it right that I should be judged by your standard or you by mine.". This is the only recipe of world peace. Hence, let us realise that here nothing maketh '*pap*' (evil) or '*punya*' (good), but our motive and repurcussions of our doings. So, let our thinking, feelings and doings no more create fissures anywhere. Let them act as only a balm.

What we need the most is not merely a proper harmony in our three aspects of personalities i.e., knowing, feeling and willing, but a very good rapport among our good thoughts, good feelings and good doings as well. We know a successful criminal too has a proper harmony among his three aspects referred over here, and, consequently, he succeeds to dupe us without leaving even a minor trace behind his/her crimes for the investigating agencies to probe.

What the human world lacks today is the proper rapport in it's good thoughts, feelings and doings. When we lack this, we remember our immediate end and forget the means. Let us realise that Hitler's Germany was not lacking intellectually in any way. Hitler's thought was to conquer the entire world. Was the feeling for what Hitler considered to be the right end lacking there? Hitler believed: 'War was a necessary instrument to keep the nations alive and not dead.' Were Hitler's efforts or his doings to attain his aim lacking in any respect? No, not at all.

So, what was actually lacking in Hitler's views from the point of view of the welfare of the people of the whole world, was a proper rapport in his good thinking, good feelings, and good doings. Actually, for him everything was good, which served his exclusive 'self' or the 'self of his country'. He remembered 'to live' only, and erased 'to let live' from his mind. It's results must have been the most horrible indeed. So, to change the world we need not any men, but good men in the true sense of the term. Because good men only think, feel, behave and do good, wherever they are only to be good.

In fact, our trouble is not that we do not know the truth. We all know it. Even the most-criminal minded persons know it. Who does not know that we should not injure others, that we should not cast an evil eye against the sisters of others and the like? But how many of us follow them in our lives? So, merely knowing of truth is not enough. We must feel it, and act accordingly. This human world is in a crisis, because we are the most hypocrite persons. We wear only masked personalities. We say one thing, and do another. There is a very dangerous type of duplicacy in our character. We lack the requisite strength to act according to our good knowledge and feelings. That is why, Dr. Radhakrishnan rightly says, "Why is it that we are doing, what our inner most conscience tells us is something, which is wrong? That is because in human nature itself there is a polarity, there is dichotomy. In other words, we know what is right, but we have not devoted the strength, the will-power, the capacity to get rid of our weakness . . ." So, let us have the will to remove it. Unless we all the architects of our own destinies make our minds perceive rightly as to what's a good or evil behaviour of ours, and unless we get them convinced for it strongly, the dark clouds from the firmament can not be removed by themselves. Let us make our values of life right and strong too, because it is our values that determine our behaviour.

Actually, we know a lot, and we know not only evil, but good too. But we have no will-power to raise our lives on what we know good for ourselves and for others too. We have a paralysed conscience to live according to the Satya, we know. Moreover, whenever we find ourselves standing on the wrong ground, we have the tendency to escape from our own responsibility for it, thinking that the Lord must have upset our *buddhi,* because He is the doer of all things. This illusion is the main cause of our every derailment. Moreover, our eyes are very keen to see the faults of others. We have often no guts to peep into our ownselves.

To overpower this weakness we all immediately need the *yoga,* the very union among our three good aspects of personalities. *Yoga* is the science to know how to maintain a true harmony among our body, mind and spirit or consciousness together. I humbly feel that the actual yoga may or may not be the science of union of ours with a hypothetical divine entity, but it is definitely a union among our three good aspects of personalities. When we reach this stage of true union, a Ratnakar turns himself into a Balmiki, the saint. When we have this true union, it brings harmony, peace, happiness, more powerful human bonds together. It is all due to the magic of *yoga.* By flushing the toxins of his mind, a *yogi* gets all the toxins of his body flushed by and by. So, let us no more confine our yoga to our physical exercises only. The true yoga can be had only when we extend it's domain upto our minds and consciousness as well.

Today most of us take it for granted that our main cause of unrest in life is Mr. A or Mr. B or anybody like that, because he/she has not changed himself/herself. Everyone accuses another that he/she has not changed his/her mindset. Almost, all of us never think that the main cause of trouble in our life is 'we ourselves'. In other words, we want to see change in others, but ourselves maintain the status quo. Practically speaking, it is no doubt the hardest and the steepest climb, not to react anger for anger, jealousy for jealousy, hatred for hatred, but in case we are earnest to calm down our mind we have no alternative, except to respond to somebody's negative gesture i.e., anger with our utmost love, affection. If we really respond to others hatred with our sincere love, we shall find ourselves really a changed, happier and more peaceful person from within particularly—a person quite at bay from the ceaseless fire of hatred, jealousy and anger, that burns both our body and mind. The main 'mantra' to remember is that we can change ourselves, but we cannot change others. Of course, there is limit of patience in our individual, national and international life. If suppose, Pakistan or India is bent upon creating trouble or our neighbour or our own brother is bent upon disturbing our mental peace on this or that pretext due to little mindedness, we cannot allow others to make our bodies or minds a delicious soup for others to sip after a limit. We shall have to be very careful to avoid such situation in life. We cannot escape from our duties.

Dr. Radhakrishnan clarifies in this respect further: "The trouble about human nature is that it knows what the results of a particular line of conduct will be, knows them to be disastrous and yet it has not the power to take itself out of the rut, face problems with courage and compassion and avert the catastrophe, which we know is inevitable today. Again we know these nuclear armaments . . . and nuclear tests are also going on and it is possible that by a mistake the world may go up in fragments . . . we all want peace, but we have not the courage, we have not the strength to retrace our steps and say that our problem after a war is going to be exactly the same as it is today." So, lets develop our courage to be good.

Good education does not necessarily aim at exclusively making us to know, what we do not know already, but it aims at bridging the unfortunate gulf among these three good aspects of our personalities referred just now. For a good human behaviour it is a must.

Dr. Sahib further points out to us what to do to overcome this crisis. He suggests rightly: "Our task today is to deal with the souls of men, it is there that the changes have to be brought about." Dr. Radhakrishnan points out: "Before outer organisations are established, inward changes have to take place. An outer crisis is a reflection of an inward chaos, and if the chaos inside the minds and heart of men . . . If that is not removed we cannot bring about a more satisfactory world order." What we need the most is to set our mindset right first by our ownselves, and to have a true harmony or union or *yoga* among three good aspects of our persoanlities Without a healthy mind, our position is akin to the healthy body of a lunatic.

For a more peaceful, calm, cool and happy life, everyone of us should drop one's own feelings of anger, hate, jealousy, etc., from one's own mind. It is his real inner bath.

Had men been essentially angels or divine and no devils, we would have needed neither police, nor military, nor any lock, nor any courts, nor any law, nor any provision for punishment, nor jail, and the like. So long brute in our nature is also there, the Marxian dream of a Stateless Society is not possible. Unless our nature is changed by all of us, our unnecessary problems, anxieties, botherations, troubles, misfortunes, miseries and the like here or there in this or that form will ever remain standing on their flat-feet. So, what we need the most is not to change our garbs or robes or outer appearances or masks, but our whole mindset and our inner-conscience. Without it, the genuine peace in the world will ever remain a mirage or a flop-show only.

Wild animals are no more a challenge to our survival, as we are to to our own species. Dr. Radhakrishnan rightly warns us: "The greatest challenge man faces today is from man himself. The Chinese philosopher

Las Tzu said: "All is clear. I alone am clouded". When our knowledge is increased, our behaviour has to become worthy of our knowledge". He clarifies: "There is not inevitability in human history. The very fact that we are human beings means that we have the power not to be mere servants of nature, but shapers of our world . . .". In other words we cannot think or say that we cannot change our fate or we cannot do this or that to change the world. Being the true architects of our own destinies, the history won't excuse us for our bad commission or omissions on this or that pretext.

One may pluck out my eyes, one may chop off my nose, ears and amputate my arms and even legs, but all these would not kill me. But the moment you blast my belief that human nature cannot be changed and it is all futile to think for the re-making of human nature, you shall see me completely dead within no time. Can we ever forget how Ratnakar became a Balmiki, a great saint one day ? Can we ever forget how Ashok turned himself from a warrior into a man of peace ? Is it not the magic of one's change of mindset ?

According to Ruskin: "Education does not mean teaching people to know, what they do not know; it means teaching them to behave as they do not behave". Thus, real education aims at bringing out the best in men. Education is an instrument to throw away the garbage from the minds. A torrent of water submerges the whole village or city and devastates the whole standing crops, disturbs violently our whole life and sweeps even humans in its torrent-current. In the same way, men, whose innate tendencies or instincts are not properly sublimated, can only make people around difficult to breathe. So, let us learn how to live and behave in this world.

There is no such divine force, which can save the sinking ship of humanity from any catastrophe or disaster, except the magic of good human nature. So, let us no more make our life like a masked ball. Why this duplicity, hypocrisy and superstitous dealing? Be sure that the key to heaven on earth is with all the architects of destinies. They are none else, but humans themselves. But the key cannot open the doors to heaven by itself. For all this humans will have to change their nature, outlook and behaviour first. Let us rememeber that most of us weep to see others before them, but we laugh at them, when they are not before us.

Most of the problems we have been facing in our lives, are our own creations or products. They are mostly concerned with human nature. I do agree that there are certain inborn inequalities concerning our genes or heredity, which I do not think that any dose of education could have made Ramsay Macdonald into Hack Hobbs or vice-versa. But these natural inequalities can never be road blocks in making ourselves men of good nature. Our world grows rickety, and mouldy today, because of our bad nature. The most dangerous trend apparently visible now is that the burning desire to be good is now receding by and by everywhere because we seldom realise what revolutionary changes we can bring in our lives by behaving good.

Due to this we are falling in our own esteem. It is in this very context Edward Markin once said, "I would prefer to loose a leg or two, a hand or two, even both rather than fall in my own esteem". Because falling in one's own esteem is akin to one's living death.

What we all need the most is a shake up in our nature. Why? Because in Dr. Radhakrishnan's words "it is human nature that has brought about all the great changes that have taken place in this world." If it is bad, it causes us the great unrest and disturbances, if it is good it causes us our mental peace and happiness too. Thus, the choice is ours, whichever we prefer.

The dream of Marx to change the world is not going to be materialised merely by changing the economic or material condition of the world, but by having changes in human nature first by humans themselves. So, let us enlarge our vision and understandings to have this shake up first. If we have this shake up in our nature, we are sure to be good humans as well. Only good humans can behave well. They live in peace themselves and let others too live in peace at the same time through their good behaviour.

10

Our Age Old Stereotyped Talks are no Real Solutions for Peace

From the times of Socratese, Plato and Aristotle, and even before them philosophers of the world have been hankering after peace. In other words, the attainment of peace in life has been the greatest motto of the lives of human beings everywhere for long. But, unfortunately, we have been seeking peace in worldly things like money, fame, name, worldly comforts and worldly pleasures etc. Undoubtedly, bread is important in life. We cannot imagine even to live without it, but man does not live on bread alone. Our simple hysterical talks and our stereotyped solutions for peace, no matter from where they come, would not help us at all to attain peace of mind and happiness in life or to lift up the ship of our life, which has been bogged down upto the sea level of the marshy land of confusion for ages.

Swami Chidanandji Saraswati too spoke about peace in New York (published in *Hindustan Times* on 11-9-2000). He holds: "You do not have to look for peace, find peace or create peace. All you have to do is remove the 'I' and remove the want . . . 'I' is one of the greatest obstacles to peace. I is our ego. I is our sense of ownership, doership and pride . . . the truth is that we only go to work, God works. We can do nothing without His grace . . . As soon as we realise this, then we can take our little 'I' and merge it in this big 'I', the universal I, the divine I. Then we surrender our lives and our every action to Him. Then we say, God, let my tiny drop of water merge with your great ocean. Let me be a tool for your will and your work."

Swami Chidanandji Saraswati adds further: "The more we have the more we want. People always think that if they attain something more, whether it is more money, a better job, a degree, a good husband, then they will be happy . . . These external things never bring any lasting happiness. We must give more and want less. Then we will know true joy and peace". "Peace comes through prayer . . . Just pray. Then you will see the magic."

Even before Swami Chidanandji Saraswati, Swami Vivekanandji had diagonised the same disease in his own way. He found the same symptoms, causing the disease and said (on page 100 Vol. 1 in his own works): "This 'I' and 'mine' causes the whole misery." "Me and mine is a superstition". (On page 7 Vol. 8 Swamiji's works).

Swami Vivekanandji goes further in this respect: "Misery comes through attachment, not through work. As soon as we identify ourselves with the work we do, we feel miserable; but if we do not identify ourselves with it, we do not feel that misery . . . Each wave in the Chitta that says "I and mine" immediately puts a chain round us and makes us slaves; and the more we say "I and mine" the more slavery grows, the more misery increases. Therefore, Karma Yoga tells us to enjoy the beauty of all the pictures in the world, but not to identify ourselves with any of them. Never say "mine". Whenever we say a thing is "mine", misery will immediately come. Do not even say, "my child" in your mind. Possess the child, but do not say "mine" . . . Do not say "my house", do not say "my body" . . . Instead of the sacrifice of pouring oblations into the fire, perform this one great sacrifice day and night—the sacrifice of your little self." (On page 100-102 Vol. 1 *Swamiji's Works*) Swami Vivekanandji elucidates his plca further: "Who can live a moment, breathe a moment, if the all-powerful one does not will it?" "We can only worship Him. Give up all fruits of work; do good for its own sake . . ." (On page 107 Vol. 1*Swamiji's Works*). But Swamiji himself warns us: "If a man worships Jesus Christ and thinks he will be saved by that, he is mistaken entirely. (On page 47 Vol. 4).

As a humble seeker of truth my humble suggestion for peace and happiness is that we neither need to surrender this 'I' or merge it in the so-called hypothetical bigger divine 'I', just to work merely as a tool or '*nimit*' of His will, nor we need to surrender our lives, our every action to Him, nor we need to remove all our wants or desires, as suggested by Swami Saraswatiji. We cannot do such things in this life, what it is. Let us remember the fact in question that each wave or ripple in the chitta that says "I and mine" does not shacklc us or does not make us slaves necessarily by itself. It is nothing, but the conjectures of these great Swamiji's. Of course, ordinarily such waves put a chain round us and reduce rather the 'masters' to the level of 'slaves'. The fact is such things happen with such persons who act as slaves only. In a nutshell, every wave of 'I and mine' does not enslave us. You stop every such wave in your mind, you will see to it that the work at hand too stops; no matter what the motive of work is—good or bad.

The more serious question to ponder over here is: Can we ever even

doings, but not arrogant. Arrogance enters in, when some self works behind the scene and thus it changes a good motive into a bad one.

Let us remember here the soldier's 'I' or 'my' remains quite intact as such, but the difference is that his 'I' here works on a very higher altitude of spirituality only.

The soldier in question knows well both the art of attachment and detachment at the same time in his life. He knows well how to give the right ordering of his loyalities in life at a time. He too knows that for peace and happiness, he is not to indulge himself either in his excessive attachments, or in excessive detachments in life. He realises well that if his country dies, he cannot live, and if his country lives, he cannot die.

In a nutshell, the moment we change our attitude in our lives for good, the same 'I' or 'me' or 'my' or 'mine', which have been great headache for the welfare of the bigger ocean of the people, becomes a balm or calmpose or tranquilizer for all. They make everybody's life happier and more peaceful.

It is not the magic of our lying prostrate and praying to God ritualistically or dogmatically, but what we actually do in this world under age old illusions, but the magic of the dissolution or the merging of little 'I' in the vast ocean of humanity only. In a nutshell, our objective of peace can be achieved, if every 'I', instead of removing it from one's mindset, raises its working on a higher plane and, instead of removing his or her all desires, every 'I' aims at attaining higher mission in life. That is the desire not only to live, but at the same time to let others too live around earnestly.

In India the so-called Joint Family System was in vogue. It helped our society to go ahead smoothly and peacefully. How? Because it was a system in which every member of the family used to dissolve one's own spirit of selfishness attached with one's 'I' voluntarily into the wider unit of the family. True love and mutual sacrifice were the true archs upon which the huge edifice of Joint Family System stood. Thus, the eldest one in the family acted like a banyan tree. Everyone's interests and safety were well-ensured there automatically by each member of the family, because everyone acted with the spirit of 'swim and sink together'. In fact, there was no such issue like 'bread for me' or 'for my child' or 'for my wife' exclusively, but everyone's life was based on the principle, i.e., 'from each according to one's capacity, to each according to his need'. That was the very foundation on which the most ancient pious Indian commune in the form of Joint Family System worked. Of course, it was not like the Plato's commune in which there was no individual family and property. It was, in fact, a commune of some close elder as well as younger members of the same family, living together in all respects, and sharing all properties as well as responsibilities together alike. There was no question of development of one at the cost of others. It was a real commune, because everyone had to work according to one's capacity and everyone used to get according to one's need. It's strong walls remained quite intact, so long as all the members of the family went on voluntarily dissolving their own self-centered spirits attached with their 'I', 'me', 'my' or mine' into the bigger unit of the joint family, but they started tumbling down, when the same members, instead of dissolving their little mindedness attached with their 'I's, started keeping it before their self-centered minds. So, the cracks in the walls of Joint Family System were quite natural. It so happened only, when, instead of acting like a hero, 'I' started acting like a villain in the whole show. And the whole show was bound to be flop in such an unfortunate condition. Who changed the very material conditions of this Joint Family System? Obviously, it's short-sighted members did.

Our simple spiritual knowledge without the spiritual attainment is apt to spit the lava of egoism, selfishness, anger, jealousy, etc. which always grind humanity by their turn. So, what we need the most is not to mitigate the existence of these I or me, or my or mine, but the very self-centered spirit attached with them. Let us change our mindset or attitude of life only. Let us bury our 'frog in the well' attitude. If 'I' sucks some human's blood somewhere, the same 'I' can donate his/her blood for the survival of the same human, provided I's mindset is changed by I's. So, what we need the most is not to treat the patient like a quack only. Let us understand that these age old suffocating minds only need spiritual oxygen to stand and work properly. In short, what we all almost need is to transform our being or our nature. When we realise its importance, it is only then we can live a religious life, because religion is realisation, as to what we should do, and what not.

Everybody knows that if I cast an evil-eye against anyone, it is not my eyes which are at fault, and it is not my eyes which are to be removed, but only my evil outlook or evil angle of vision.

Of course, no job is so tough, as steering one's own mind for the steersman. One, who knows this art, is happier and more peaceful in life.

So, the best solution is: let this I's exclusive 'self' be dissolved by I's ownself into wider ocean of humanity at family level, national and international level too. There is no need to remove this 'I', or 'me', or 'my', or mine at any level at all. And there is no need to remove the so-called State's—sovereignty, but let every 'I' and State and its people work with the true spirit of 'Basudheva Kutumbkam', and let it no more be used/misused to harm others in any way. Thus, 'I' is not to be uprooted from the ground as such, but it is only to be trimmed or pruned by all of us concerned, wherever we are in the right spirit; so that the vine of 'I' spreads here or there in a controlled way and let everyone feel happier to see it blooming and giving to all it's pleasant fragrence and fruits. Therefore, there is no other way out but to change ourselves and our world too. Otherwise, peace will be a mirage for us.

Let us keep it into our minds that our whole work in the world will be at a standstill, if we remove the necessary hinge or attachment from our minds, as our all attachments are not evils. Instead of the contraction of the 'self', we only need it's expansion. And 'Basudheva kutumbakam' is nothing, but expansion of the circle of self only.

Today, the whole world seems to suffer from the spiritual decadence on the one hand, and on the other, self-proclaimed philosophers go on repeating parrotwise their solutions of miseries, what they have simply borrowed from somewhere. In fact, the original, but purposeful thinking has been stifled for centuries and our minds have been stuffed with only irrational beliefs, and being choked, our minds have stopped working properly.

Even then for instance there are Smaritan auto-pullers, who return the very purse or the articles left by commuters by mistake in their autos, to their owners, while bad cops snatch the very purse, the jewellery of a lone lady, who is by chance injured in an accident on the road. Instead of taking her first to the nearest hospital, just to save her precious life, these inhuman cops, what else they do with that unfortunate victim, is now beyond my poor imagination even to describe it further. This world sometimes looks like a den of criminals and sometimes looks like a banyan tree too under which passers by take rest freely. It is all due to the magic of the attitude of human beings to life only.

It requires not that we should leave the world or our family. Let us live in the world, let the world of our evils no more build their oasis in our minds. Let all the members of a family, or a nation follow the old principle 'live and let live' at the same time only for peace everywhere.

Hansie Cronje, who was sacked as South African's cricket captain after he admitted taking money from a book-maker recently, had blamed his errant behaviour on some satan for, forgetting both devil and divine (evil and good) live in one's mind only. He said: "In a moment of stupidity and weakness I allowed 'satan' and the world to dictate terms to me. The moment I took my eyes off Jesus, my whole world turned dark". We live in the world of escaping from our own responsibilties. Here is nothing good or evil in the world, but men maketh.

There's a good saying here:

'Mujh ko ati hai hansi is hazrate insan per,
Fale bad to khud kera lanat kare shaitan par

Flattery of God too is not a sure visa to heaven. Both hell or heaven are man made here. Hence, Anatole France, preferred to go to hell, rather heaven, because hell contained here even such interesting people like Galelio and Tolostoy.

Let's not to try to snatch the very birth right of a 'mom' to say 'my child'. Let us no more snatch the birth-right of a child to say 'my mom' too. The moment you do it, the very foundation of the family is to be terribly shaken. We are not like these Swamis. We are all worldly people. Let us remember a mother may or may not pardon the thief of her necklace by chance, but not the person, who snatches this right of her. You remove this 'I', 'me', 'my', 'mine', you shall see to it that every member of the family goes uncared for at the same moment. No house is to be looked after well then, and the ladies are apt to forget their purses even, wherever they are. This is the magic of the removal of 'I' or 'my'. The moment you remove the poor 'I' from the scene you remove the necessary hinge, which unites people and things, and thus everybody and everything becomes terribly apart. Then everybody is turned into nobody then and there. We should no more talk like philosophers, and act like fools.

Undoubtedly, when this 'I' thinks: 'I am on the steering wheel, and I am to kill every passers by, the little 'I' becomes a menace to world peace. Thus, good or evil does not lie essentially in each 'I' in itself, but actually in how 'I' thinks, feels and does or how 'I' steers the ship of one's life in this world. So, it is not the 'I' which is to be removed or buried underground, but the immediate need of the hour is to bury the very little mindedness of 'I's only, which causes all sufferings. Let us then merge our little 'I' in the bigger ocean of crores of 'I' only.

If the mother's milk gives physical health to the baby, the calls like 'my mom', 'my child' give psychological doses to these respective persons. Both are necessary for their welfare. After all, how can we reduce a mother and her child to the level of a robot, which has no feeling and no sentiments. They are true architects of their destinies—good or bad.

Practically speaking, if 'I' withers away from the world as Swami Chidanandji Saraswati wants, everybody in every house and every other elder or younger member of the family is apt to forego from one's essential care and affection, what one gets in a family. This disappearance of 'I' will be like the stoppage of the electricity current from the power house, and, consequently, there is all blackout there. In fact, this 'I' provides us the very sense of duty, the sense of ownership and the sense of possessiveness. If this 'I' goes the sense of duty, where we are either in the family or country, the sense of ownership and pride and the sense of possessiveness too go along with it's absence. In fact, the same 'I' becomes like a naked electricity wire, when it becomes a symbol of our ego, or when it carries the *germs of* selfishness with its wings and flutters like a dirty bee. Such things happen only when 'I' becomes not a humble servant of ours, but a cruel master and thinks that 'I am only to live and let others may or may not live, but 'my' life, 'my' honour, 'my' interests, 'my' likes-dislikes, etc., are supermost. Then only 'I' becomes a menace or a hurdle' on the path of the universal peace and brotherhood. Only this 'I' must go from one's mind.

The important point to remember is that every 'I' has not been a problem. When Swami Vivekanandji advises: "Have faith in yourself first . . . say I can do everything . . ." (Page 74 Vol. 6 *Swamiji's Works*). Do we ever question Swamiji's 'I' here in this context? No, because his 'I' works here with a good motive. Here again, we all like Krishna's I, because it works for the welfare of all beings of the world. Krishna says, "Look at me, Arjuna. If I stop from work for one moment, the whole universe will die . . . but why do 'I' work? Because I love the world." Here Krishna's 'I' does not keep hate with it's wings, when it flutters, but it does it so only with love for all. Hence, we are happy with His 'I'. This 'I' of Krishna is good, not evil. If you remove this Krishna's 'I', how would Krishna then be able to love the world? So, it is to be kept intact. It is our dogmatic approach of self-proclaimed religious persons has eaten us like white-ants. Let us beware of them.

It is my considered view that it is these 'I', 'me', 'my' and 'mine' that bring the whole human machinery in a full momentum. If 'I' is not there, who is to steer the ship of one's life in the absence of the sense of duty? Of course, if I steers rash, this 'I' is to be brought to the book. Suppose, if 'I' is erased from the municipal register, who is to own and look after the private and public properties? We can only imagine that the moment you remove this 'I' from this mind of a driver or pilot, what will happen to a moving car or train and a flying aeroplane in the sky then and there. Are we ready to face these grave consequences? What we are all to check is only the rashness of the 'I', if there is any, which is usually attached with the same 'I', when 'I' is on the steering wheel and 'I' threatens. 'I' can kill anybody, I like'. Hence, why to board a wrong carriage, which is going to cause our undesirable waterloo? Imagine, if 'I' is not there on the stage, who is to run the factory, the fields, the schools, the hospitals, the offices, the labs; and who is to fight with pride at the border of the country? When 'I' is absent from the stage, the necessary attachment or hinge with the people and things too becomes absent and the whole show becomes flop. Thus, with the removal of this poor 'I', the first casualty will be of one's duty. Then no one is there to play either as a hero or a villain, etc. In a nutshell, if you remove this I's family from it's employment, you'll see the minds of all I's going too on their permanent holidays. Do we achieve peace mere by chanting 'Om Shanti, Om Shanti' parrotwise, unless we change our mindset for good? Who would accept that God is to play the multiple roles in our film of life? And we 're supposed to play only His *'nimit'* or as an instrument?

Mr. Parthasarthy in his good book *Vedanta Treatise* suggests: "The ego which claims "I am doing this", "I am doing that", "This is mine", "I am the sufferer" . . . such thoughts must be done away with. Your thoughts of possessiveness, "my wife, my child, my body, my mind", etc., have to be renounced. A man of renunciation is one who gets rid of this . . . spirit of 'me' and 'mine'." Had these pious suggestions been desirable, natural and practical, they would have been the integral parts of the lives of most of the people long-long ago. Mr. Parthasarthy too takes every rope as a snake. If 'I' is to leave the feeling of a doer, should he leave his family and adopt *sanyasa*? How can I accept that He works, I only goes to work? Who would believe that 'I' is only His instrument and it is He who is to give every 'I' a package of food, clothes, and shelter? Does He ever do that? Who is to believe this age old white-lie? Even after shedding one's sweat throughout the day, a poor 'I' goes to his bed half-fed, half clad and shelterless in the night! This shows either that He's nowhere or He keeps His eyes, ears, mouth and other senses quite shut. Should Mr. Parthasarthy snatch this poor I's right to feel his mental and physical agony and suffering too, even when if 'I' works, but does not get his due and, consequently, faces ail troubles? How can we transfer this responsibility from his present 'karmas' to his past ones without wearing the mask of the escapism? I don't deny that all I's never work according to their capacities, but hanker after their full fruits. Let such I's must suffer. But what about others, who work and still suffer? Can we overlook these painful realities of our lives? Let us remember that the attachment of a mother with her would be babe only induces her to bear all the pangs of birth and inconveniences both before or after the birth of her child. Now Mr. Parthasarthy wants to cut off this necessary hinge between a 'mom' and her 'babe'! Can we ever dare to do it? I humbly hold that so long this hinge does not become a hurdle in the proper growth of other babies around in a family or elsewhere, we should not even touch it all. So long as 'my child', 'my mom' don't become a source of unnecessary tension, they must be well-protected. Otherwise, the very foundation of a family or country is going to be shaken. Everybody's property is nobody's—is a well-known phrase. We are to remove only bad hinges or bad motives of work. Otherwise, there will be lawlessness and chaos everywhere.

Mr. Parthasrarthy, honestly speaking, I am not challenging anybody in this humble book. I am only a small seeker of truth like you. Let us imagine how happy a mom is!, how happy a child is!, and how happy a devotee is in one's mind, when one calls 'my child', 'my mom', 'my God' respectively! Certainly, if a mom is so much blind in her '*moha*' (excessive attachment) with her child that she being like a slave goes even to administer poison to other babies around out of jealousy, or if a 'bhakat' out of sheer fanaticism becomes so blind that he is ready to apply a dynamite to destroy the idols or statues or religious places of other's faith, the concerned 'I' must be severely punished under the law. Otherwise, to apply the dynamite of renunciation on all others alike will be Mr. Parthasarthy's and other's most dangerous prescription. A good doctor never ignores human psychology.

Some arm-chaired philosophers occasionally suggest: 'Do your work for duty sake; but surrender the desire of fruit to the almighty God!, just to bury one's ego. O.K. One's ego must be buried quite deep underground. But they want to remove 'I' along with the motive of work. May I know who works without any good or bad motive in this world? When He is nowhere, to whom should we surrender our desire of fruit? Let a doctor not prescribe a medicine, which kills the patient even like a quack does. So, what is to be removed is only our bad motive, and not all motives. Otherwise, their prescription will be worse than the disease. No navigator navigates without a mast. Let is no more live in the world of fancies.

Further Mr. Parthasarthy holds: "renunciation is the secret of success". But do not we see here that even Krishna is attached with Arjuna, His friend and devotee? Hence, Krishna could go to any extent to protect Arjuna. Could Krishna ever be ready to renounce saying 'Arjuna, my bhakat and my' *sakha*' (friend)? This shows neither all attachments, nor all detachments are good. We must be proficient in the art of both attachment and detachment. Krishna was the most proficient knower of this art. He succeeded in His mission. Nobody counts how many 'I's you have removed, but how much little-mindedness we remove from our lives.

On page 202 in his book Mr. Parthasarthy says "Do not claim anything as yours, you gain everything." Actually claiming what is ours or our due is not evil, but to claim all as ours, what's not ours is evil. Otherwise, each child, each house, each country, each God is going uncared for. We spoil public buses, but do we ever spoil our own car? Of course, we should not enslave ourselves like Hitler, who cared not whether one lived or died. Let our approach not give stink of any thoughtlessness.

Apparently, it looks very attractive and charming the said proposal of Swami Chidanandji and Swami Vivekanandji that 'all you have to do is to remove the 'I' and remove the want . . . 'I' is one of the greatest obstacles to peace. I is our ego. I is our sense of ownership, doership and pride . . . The truth is that we only go to work, God works. We can do nothing without His grace . . . We can take our little 'I' and merge it in this big 'I', the universal I, the divine I . . .' But let is keep it into our minds that our mind is like a parachute, which works only when it is open. The proposal has been accepted by the devotees without questioning its suitability or appropriatness and without minding it's dire consequences.

Before accepting the very existence of God, let us accept the fact we know nothing about God. We have neither seen Him, nor felt His existence, nor experienced Him, taking His rescue-crane, besides the poorest, the most downtrodden, the most innocent and the most uncared for people of the world particularly, just to help them in time of their grave need. Of course, we know and witness with our own eyes Samaritan humans, donating even their precious blood to the needy, and taking injured on the road to the hospital to provide the necessary medical aid to the needy on time. Even such people go beyond their personal reach. But may I know, whether we ever experience such a Samaritan god, coming to the help of the needy? Had it not been a fact, there would not have been the loud cries of the innocent victims of butchery, rape and exploitation and the like in this world under His nose? You cannot befool the people anymore by attributing even these human Samaritans, who might not be believing in Him, as His simple *nimits*. Had God ever been coming forward in this respect anywhere in this world, the great Samaritan Marx would not have talked of revolution, just to provide true 'liberty', 'equality' and 'justice', and everybody's due to everybody without any bias? Has God ever taken any *suo moto* action against the evil-doers in this world? I do not think so. Well, no serious person can blow-off the issue in question, simply by throwing his missile (of the most powerful kind) of 'atheism' towards a small chap like me anymore. Hypothetically speaking, how can then we surrender or dissolve our 'I' into the divine 'I', when He has been unknown to us?

In fact, how would one believe in this Swami Chidanandji's unbelievable illusion that 'the truth is that we only go to work. God works? Does God do bad even? Who does not know that we have crorers of good and evil waves or ripples or impulses daily in our *chitta* or minds? If it is a fact that 'we can do nothing without His grace', then whose grace was working behind, what Ravana or Duryodhana or Hitler or Mussolini, or Osama bin Laden or Veerappan, or Billa-Ranga did or is doing, and especially the people, who crucified our great guru Christ, and ex-communicated Galelio and Tolstoy from their religions, because they stood for some great truth in their lives? Let us remember the dust can never be settled well, unless it is settled right. You cannot befool all the people all the time. Now enough is enough. I, myself, do not believe in generating unnecessary heat, but only necessary light. One can kill me, but who can kill the truth? I am a small chap. Any parrot of scriptures, can make me fall flat on the ground, undoubtedly. Here the question is not of 'me', but of truth only. How can then we merge this little 'I' in the so-called big 'I', the universal 'I', the divine 'I'? How can then we ever be simple tools of the divine 'I'? By making us his simple tools, does Swami Chidanandji Saraswati want from us really to be escaped from the true responsibilities for what we have already done-good or bad both in our past, or doing in the present, or would do in the future?

I do know that no wise men can ever behave like parrots, but it is a fact, that I know nothing about our esteemed scriputres. I have only my poor common sense with me and the common experience of lives of others too side by side. All the devotees believe that God is the sole doer of all things in life, and whatever He does, He does right. We can do nothing, except lying prostrate before the Lord to pray and worship Him.

The mechanisation of this world too has come to their rescue. What do these devotees do at the most is that while busying themselves in their more important works, they get their preferred cassettes displayed to give a religious tinge to the whole situation.

Now one thing must be clear to all that mere giving a religious tingue to the issue will not be enough. Heaven won't fall on our heads if we keep the issue of God's worshipping pending, but the edifice of humanity is to be shaken, if in craze of removing 'I', we fail to remove the filth of I's mind indeed. So, let us remove only the filth of I's mind at our earliest possible.

For a daily bread-earner, who daily digs his well and quenches his thirst. if at all it is possible in this world, what it is, bread is his the great

God. He is busy in his own life to attain pleasure. Hardly he has got time for these unnecessary gossips. Moreover, he lacks the requisite understanding for all these matters too. On the other, what these the so-called affluent people do? Because they know that the doer of all things is the Lord, hence they have a play or the replay of their cassettes, containing either the *Ramayana* or the *Mahabharata*, or the *guruvani* or the devotional songs at the most in their drawing or sleeping rooms or in their cars just to pose to the world that they are religious people unlike so many. For them religion and rituals are synonyms.

In fact, keeping all these facts in view, God is nothing, but like a ghost. A ghost is nothing, except the projection or the caricature of human minds. He too is the projection or conjecture or the concotion or the conception of priests' minds in their utter ignorance of the universe or nature.

My humble submission is: Let all the believers be free to have immense faith in their God. But in case, they have no faith in their own steering of the ships of their lives or in their thinking, feeling and doing, good to turn the hell into heaven, the sinking human ship cannot be saved from being sunk deeper then. Hence, I do not agree with Swami Vivekanandji, who advises all mothers: "to look upon your children as a nurse does" (on page 88 Vol. 1 *Swamiji Works*). Do not say, 'my child'. Let's know how the same nurse, a simple cog—behaves too like a mother, and not a nurse at her home. We may be doing this or that thing in our 24 hours, but the question is what do we do to shake up our nature? Has it been changed for good by us? Let us no more be hysterical in our approach.

God seems to be the greater superstition than 'me' and 'mine' of Swami Vivekanandji. They cause us misery only when they are attached with our little-mindedness. How can it be practical for a mother not to say 'my child' in her mind, and at the same time go on possessing the same child, suggested by Swami Vivekanandji? How can it be possible not to say, 'my house', and at the same time go on possessing the same house? We accept that Arjuna was a *nimit* of Krishna in the *Mahabharata* but may I know, whose '*nimit*' Duryodhana was in the same war, whose '*nimits*' Hitler and Mussolini were in the Ist and IInd World Wars, and now whose '*nimits*' people like Osama bin Laden and Veerappan are? If He works and we only go to work, then how many roles does Swami ji's Lord play? In case being escapists, we hold that there is nothing like good and evil in the world, but our thinking makes it so only, then the question is how long shall we go on behaving like that stupid ostrich?

Let us remember the truth in Swami Vivekanandji's own words:

peaceful in life, simply by performing our duties as architects of our own destinies—good or bad? Rather let us feel obliged to the person, who has given us such an opportunity to mend ourselves.

Regarding desires Swami Vivekanandji removes the age old confusion very rightly (on page 148 Vol. 2 *Swamiji Works*): "We all understand that desires are wrong, but what is meant by giving up desires? How could life go on? It would be the same suicidal advice, killing the desire and man too. The solution is this. Not that you should not have property, not that you should not have things which are necessary and things which are even luxuries. Have all that, you want . . . Only know the truth and realise it. Have no idea of proprietorship . . . All belongs to the Lord. He is in the desire that rises in your mind. If you put God in your every moment, in your conversation . . . in everything, the whole scene changes, and the world instead of appearing as one of woe and misery will become a heaven."

Here Swamiji's solution that 'all belongs to the Lord' is not worth-accepting indeed in the light of what happened in Soviet Russia in 1991, and what really forced her to change it from it's socialist economy to market-economy, and what really caused it's unfortunate disintegration. Of course, in Soviet Russia nothing belonged to the so-called Lord, but to the State, except consumers-goods, because Soviet Russia did not believe in the existence of a Supernatural power. Let us read and re-read human psychology before jumping on to a solution.

Let us remember we cannot ignore, what actual human nature is before deciding this matter. Actually, a little feeling of individual ownership and individual profit-motive—both are necessary to keep and maintain a vibrant economy. In fact, the introduction of these two things act like a soothing-balm or like propellers in the ship of human life. It was felt that everybody's property was nobody's. When this feeling becomes strong, it becomes a road block on the path of individual initiative and efficiency. The increasing lack of individual initiative and individual-inefficiency in their works led the Soviet-economy to collapse to a great extent.

So, in case if we follow Swami Vivekanandji in this respect and make everything belong to Lord, instead of state, even then the same problems are to be faced by us. In India we have even gone ahead of it. We have assigned the work of individual-upliftment to our hypothetical God, and consequently we have started thinking that 'we can only worship Him'. The net result of this dismal philosophy is before all of us. That we have become like complete defunct, escapists, fatalists and even shirkers from our duties and responsibilities to a great extent. These are the practical unfortunate gains of the said philosophy indeed. Do not we recite daily in our prayer or worship: *'Vishaya Vikar mitao pap haro deva, Swami pap haro deva'*. . ., as if the said Lord has got a contract and thus He is supposed' to descend on earth with His rescue-crane one day to uplift the already age old bogged down humanity? Let us remember that mere prostrating before God won't help us in eradicating our evils. If we follow earnestly this principle: 'live and let live', that will be an automatic eradication of our evils from our minds. Do we not recite daily in our prayers: *'Tera tujhko arpana kya lage mera, swami kya lage mera'*. . . hypocritically? Does it not happen that the moment we cease to pray like this, we try to seek every opportunity to snatch even other's due? Of course, exceptions are there. Has it made us less egoists?

So, this hypocrisy has failed to provide us any dividened. It has failed to remove our miseries indeed, because we have not learnt that we are not only to live, but we have to follow 'let live' earnestly in life.

Thus, in my humble opinion the right solution of our problems does not lie in making the Lord, the Master of each and everything and every property and in delegating the right of our own upliftment even to the said Lord, but in having every faith in our ownselves by understanding that being the true architects of our own destinies—both good and evil, we can now turn hell into heaven, as we have already turned heaven into hell before, provided we change our attitude in our lives and cease to attach the little-mindedness with our own. 'I' or me' and 'my or mine' anymore. This is the recipe of world peace indeed. Well, we cannot accept, Swamiji's contention here that He is in the desire that rises in your mind,' because we have both good and evil desires in our minds.

Here in the world the hypocrites put God in their every moment, in their conversation, and even when they sneeze and yawn, but most of them remain where they were before. Of course, exception of it are there. Well, Jesus too says, "the kingdom of heaven is within you". If it is a fact, it is also a fact undeniable that the kingdom of devil too is there in our minds and not in this world, which has been dubbed as '*mithya*' or illusion. So, it is not a fact as Swamiji believes that 'if you put God in your every moment, in your conversation . . . in everything, the whole scene changes, and the world . . . will become a heaven'. My humble view is that we may or may not talk of God, but if we believe in 'live and let live' principle earnestly, we are sure to change ourselves and our world too. Let us remember the old saying: 'A camel may pass through the hole of a needle, but human-cobras and human-sharks can never enter the heaven on earth.

Some people hold that when Jesus said, 'whoever is not with 'me' is against 'me'. He didn't mean by 'me' as 'I', but 'Truth'. But let us not overlook the living truth that this 'Truth' may have It's eyes, but not feet to walk, or wings to flutter of 'Its' own. Hence, so long humans, being architects of their own destinies suffer from their little mindedness, this 'Truth' remains buried deep in the books. If the very few work like Swami Vivekanandji or Buddha, it is because they insulate their I's or my's family from the little mindedness and ego.

The words like 'I', 'me', 'my' or 'mine' are not evils in themselves. They are only the carriers of our feelings—good or bad. What is needed is not to uproot them, but only to change the myopic view, what we attach with them, unfortunately. Swami Vivekanand too himself used these words, because he did not attach any malafide-intention with them. He said: " . . . that 'my' love for my country, and especially for my countrymen will be the same whether they receive 'me' . . . or spurn me from the country."

(On page, 156 Vol. 3 Swamiji's works) This shows how great mind Swami ji had!. Do we question his 'my' and 'me'?

Mr. Nilanshu Ranjan in his article 'Look for happiness in the present' in the column 'Meditations' in *Hindustan Times* on 14-5-2002 writes, "Pythagoras says that people who go on seeking and searching bliss and happiness are unfortunate . . ." But in this world all seem to be seeking bliss, happiness and peace. Are we then all unfortunate? Of course, it is a different question: that one seeks peace, but gets pleasure. But according to Pythagoras we should not have even our mind or desire for peace. Let us imagine, what will happen to us, if we follow him in this respect. Of course, how foolish we have been that we seek bliss and happiness in capturing more powers, in having a better position or status of ours, or in having more fame or name or money by hook or by crook, or simply in changing even our life-partners, or our car, or our architectural beauty of our house etc. etc! We are badly mistaken, if we think that these changes in this outer world of ours will definitely give us peace and make us happier. Even Sri Chidanandji sought peace through prayer. Didn't he ?

In fact, peace can be had from within and not without. Of course, from outward-changes we may or may not have pleasure, but not peace. Have we ever been so particular to change or build ourselves from within as we have been keen to have outward changes? It all does not mean we can deny outward changes to ourselves, so long we live here. It only means that this world is only a necessary means to an end. And the end is bliss, happiness and peace. If our world helps us in achieving this end, our world is good. Otherwise, it is evil. Of course, if we behave well, we can have peace automatically. But we behave for peace. Don't we've our minds for it?

When we accept the fact that world is only a necessary means to an end, it means we cannot give up all our desires. Without desire we cannot pull on our lives even. Do we ever imagine as to what is meant by giving up all our desires in life? In fact, those who advise to give up all our desires, they give us only a suicidal advice to kill the desire and man too. When we seek peace we cannot have it, unless we desire for a higher plane in our lives. In other words, first we must have a mind or desire for peace, it is only then that we can have it. Of course, it is also a fact, that civilisation does not mean multiplication of our wants, but their voluntary reduction. Being creative and, to have a meaningful life, if we have a mind or desire for higher values of life, what is unethical in it? Let us remember, to have a mind or desire to achieve higher mission in life means strengthening the very foundation on which the very edifice of humanity is erected.

My humble submission is that to think that all our desires make our lives miserable, has been a blunder, we have been committing for ages. In fact, our miseries in life sprout not from all our desires, but from our excessive desires for satisfying our exclusive self, no matter by what means. Miseries are apt to be there in our lives, when we have a mindset that we are only to live, and when we least care whether others around us are too live at the same time. In short, our life will always be full of troubles or botherations, when we do not follow earnestly the principle: 'live and let live' side by side. Can we ever even imagine not to have desire to eat to live, desire to drink water, desire to breathe and desire to live like masters of our world and not its slaves at all? The moot question is: Can we ever live in a state of no mind and desire at all?

The fact is that we cannot live in a state, when we have no mind or desire for peace and happiness in life. Hypothetically speaking, the moment we have no mind and even no desire for happiness and peace even, it will be like our living death. The very mind, the very desire for peace transfuses life even in the dead bones. If we have no goal-oriented mindset of ours for peace, our life will be akin to the dismal life of cockroaches of the gutters, because unlike humans, they know not, why do they live, and why do they die? The lives of cockroaches begin and end with the fulfilment of their goal i.e., eating, drinking and resting etc. only.

Of course, when we suffer, we run towards our temples, mosques, churches, gurdwaras nearby to gain peace. It is a different question whether our sufferings come to an end or not. But do we not go there with a mind or desire for peace? Being humans we cannot keep our minds locked up, and we cannot keep the mouths of all our desires shut. Of course, being foolish we instead of fulfilling our higher desires, we fulfill only our lower desires in life.

Being humans we can never live in a state of no mind, or when we have no desire or goal either for higher or lower life. Mr. Nilanshu Ranjan quotes Pythagoras, who advises us: "Do not be goal-oriented. Goal-orientation is the way of mind. Mind exists in ambition, in future. So drop the mind that is, to live in the stage of no mind." Is it possible when we have no goal-oriented life, or when we have no mind, no desire for our present or future? It is wrong to attribute people as unfortunate, who live in the mind, who live in the tomorrow, and who live with a goal or desire to fulfill higher mission in life. This view of Pythagoras is akin to switch the light off in life, and consequently, there is no hope for light. There is only darkness everywhere. After all, we're all the architects of our own destinies. If we live, we live with some mind or desire to make or unmake our own destinies—good or bad.

It is equally wrong to say as Mr. Nilanshu Ranjan does that an enlightened person lives in no mind and no mind is the state of enlightenment. Again, it is wrong to say "the Enlightened one cannot be goal-oriented for he has no future, for him all is present."

Buddha renounced his family life, because his life was highly goal oriented. His goal or highest desire in his mind was how to get all the people emancipated from their miseries. Hence, he asked the people to give up their exclusive self for it. So, Enlightened like Buddha can never even imagine to live in the state of no mind or no goal, or no desire for higher life. An Enlightened's life is always goal-oriented both for present and future. For him all is not present. He lives in future too. His mind, or desire for future acts like an oxygen to him. Only cockroaches of the gutters can live in the state of complete mindlessness, because they live for present and for themselves only. When we have meditation, we do not live in a state of no mind, having no desire. It is a state when we focus our minds for a certain time for higher life. When Buddha renouned his family, was he in a state of his no mind? Did he not have a higher goal in renunciation? Did he not have a desire for the people's emancipation from their miseries? He did it with an empty mind, with objectivity and without any prejudices.

Swamiji too had a mind and goal when he expressed:, " 'I' have a seed planted here and wish to grow" (page 343 Vol. 8 *Swamiji Works*). Thus, it is no use to make scapegoat these words for our own evils. They become evils, when they are allowed to take the germs of 'little-mindedness' with their wings by us, as the flies do and flutter here and there and leave their rubbish, wherever they go. We can never be without having a mind or goal in life, no matter when our mind and goal are for higher values in life, we get peace and happiness certainly.

Let us remember we may live like a lotus in the pond, as Swami Vivekanandji suggests us, but we must remember the main difference here in the position of a lotus in a pond and the humans in the world. The difference is that the water in the pond may or may not be dirty, but the whole world can never be dirty. Our world or life is, what we make them either individually or collectively. So it is never justified to dub the world as illusion or a dream. Whether it is good or evil—the baby is ours. Let us own it—whatever it is, if we have even a small sense of morality. We are to detach ourselves not with the whole world, but with the evils, we have attached with ourselves.

In fact, for peace and happiness in life we have to avoid our extreme desires only. Swami Vivekanandji too says, ". . . He who wants to love God must get rid of extreme desires; desire nothing except God. This world is good so far as it helps one to go to the higher world. The object of senses are good so far as they help us to attain higher objects. We always forget that this world is a means to an end, and not an end in itself . . . and as soon as it has ceased to be so, it is evil. So wife, husband, children, money and learning, are good so long as they help us forward . . . if the wife helps us to attain God, she is a good wife; so with a husband or a child. If money helps a man to do good to others, it is of some value . . . The mind should always go towards God . . ." (on page 7-8 Vol. 4 *Swamiji Works*).

In fact, a husband, or a wife, or a father, or a mother, or a child becomes like a slave only in extreme attachments or when they have extreme desires. So, let's remain the masters of all our trades and avoid all our extremes, because they cause us miseries and make us like bonded labourers.

It is praise-worthy of Swamiji's contention here that he was in favour of avoiding our only extreme desires and not all desires. And as such it has no usual stink of escapism. Of course, he advocated that we should desire nothing, except God. Let us take God as desire for good and excellence in life, instead of God, which has been unknown to us since His conception. It is good that Swamiji believes that this world and our objects of senses are good, so far as they help us to attain higher mission in life. Swamiji rightly said that the world is only a means to an end, and not an end in itself. Thus, he rightly said that wife, husband, children, money, learing are good, so long they help us in going-forward.

Swami Vivekanandji made it further clear: "This world is neither good, nor evil. Life is good or evil according to the state of mind in which we look at it, it is neither by itself. Fire, by itself, is neither good, nor evil . . ." (On page 75-76 Vol. 1, *Swamiji Works*)

So, it is through our right and positive mindset we can change our hell into heaven on earth. If we come down in a plane, and demolish the W.T.C. building in New York or anywhere else and get thousands of people—our own brethren-dead, this mindset with which we have been doing such dismal acts to create panic or terror in this world, it is not made by any deity, but it is made either by you or me. It knows how to kill our own sisters and brothers; it knows how to snatch other's bread, other's properties, other's freedom, but, unfortunately, we the architects of our own destinies have failed to make it well-equipped; so that it may know how to save other's lives; it may know how to love others; it may know how to share our own, whatever we have, with others alike; so that being creative and having an earnest desire to live a meaningful and purposeful life, all of us may be in a position to live peacefully and happily in this world. One thing very important to remember is: that with a weak and low mindset we fall, and with a high and powerful mindset, having an earnest desire to reach the highest altitude of 'manhood', we can rise and we can be one day a Ram, or Krishna, or Buddha, or Mahavir, or Mohammad, or Chris't or a 'guru'. Of course, for our physical or material and mental development, we need proper education, but for our spiritual development or to be a good human first, we need men-making education and dharma, which increases our '*buddhi*' or *vivek* or power of discrimination, as to what is to be done by us, being humans, and what is not to be done in this world.

Our world in itself can never be '*satya*' or false. Of course, our evil-desires or little-mindedness, with which we think that we can build huge edifice of humanity, are definitely false, or myths or illusory in character.

So, let us remember good or evil does not lie with every 'I' necessarily, but with 'I's mind. Hence, instead of dreaming to remove the poor 'I', why should we not remove the filth of 'I's' mind? Why should not we ask earnestly our every 'I' to resist, whenever evil impulses or waves or ripples want to conceive in our minds with a proper thought; so that they may not be a cancerous growth later on? Why should we not ask our every 'I' to allow only good impulses to come to our minds, which are meant to do good of the people at large? Let us remember that if 'I's' mind creates fissures somewhere, it can act as a soothing-balm too somewhere else, provided our mindset is good. We can never rise merely by either wearing a particular ring in our hand, or by looking at stars, or by looking towards even deity to descend on earth with its rescue-operation, but by our good karmas only, as we fall only by our bad karmas.

Here's, what Sidhanshuji Maharaj, another of today's great Swami plays the same tune, what Swami Chidanand ji Maharaj did in New York. His views have been printed in Meditations in *Hindustan Times* on 22-10-2001, but I humbly feel again that they too are in the same stereotyped flavour. He views: "No matter how much we wish to know His ways or get a glimse of Him, our senses fail to gratify us. The Lord is invisible. The sense cannot catch Him. The nose cannot smell His fragrance, the mind cannot comprehend Him, the tongue cannot taste Him. He is beyond the reach of all our senses, and even imagination." He further adds: "Thus, it proves that the power of the Lord is supreme. His glories are infinite. He is Brahma: the all knowing and eternal". "That is the supreme power. His rule prevails throughout the world; our body is actually His property. Whatever resources that we have are His endowments. He has the supreme power of transformation when it is the right time . . . We have made our entry into this world on His discretion and we shall leave it when He wishes to. All the worldly possessions that we require during our life time can be wished away by Him in an instant. Before His supreme will, you cannot do anything . . .". "The only thing that a human being can do is to prostrate before the Almighty."

What a strange caricature of God Swami Sidhanshuji Maharaj too has drawn actually! It is an old wine in a new bottle. How? Because, it has already been told to us: that without His will a blade of grass cannot grow even, that even we cannot breathe without His blessings. Everything is old, but in new garbs only. Undoubtedly, I am a small chap before these great Swamis. Hence, I apologise to them for my frank views.

When we see the innocents are butchered, raped and exploited and what not in the kingdom of his Lord, I have really the humble feelings that perhaps, Sri Sidhanshuji's Lord may reign here, but does not rule at all. He does not govern indeed. In other words there may be God's government here in this world, but no God's administration at all. These are our mere illusions that—'we have made our entry into the world on His discretion and we shall leave it when He wishes us to. That all the worldly possessions that we acquire during our life time can be wished away by

Him in an instant. Before His supreme will you cannot do anything' and so on and so forth. This is apt to help the criminals to thrive under the garb of their God's responsibility. Unconsciously, out of His Lords bhakti, Swamiji is putting a premium on our vices by holding such views. How hopeless it is to hear that 'The Lord is invisible—He is beyond the reach of all our senses, and even imagination . . . The mind cannot comprehend Him . . . He is Brahma, the all knowing and eternal . . . He is the supreme power. His rule prevails throughout the world . . .!' When He is all-knowing, why does He tolerate the innocent's butchery, rape and exploitation of all like that in His own kingdom? Is He all powerful or completely powerless? When everything is in a state of perpetual change here, how can he be eternal and beyond the Law of Cause and Effect? Well, Science believes that everything in the world changes. Does Swamiji challenge the science.?

By saying simply the same thing that a human being can do in this world is to prostrate before the Almighty only and nothing more, Sidhanshuji Maharaj too makes us complete defuncts, escapists, truants and all that like his predecessors, because the only work, what he too has assigned us to do before God is nothing, but an easiest route to escape from all our responsibilities, wherever we are. Actually we do not need such a hopeless God at all. Strange! He claims 'God cannot be known and is beyond even our imagination, and our mind cannot comprehend Him', still, he claims to know and imagine what His God is! If still any devotee claims to know Him only through his Atma, Science does not accept its' existence.

The main problem is: if God's *bhaktas* cannot know Him, how can they worship Him without knowing Him Will they do it as robots simply? The approach of all theists towards their God is as if they want to win both the obverse and reverse sides of the same coin. Because, on the one hand they claim 'how can you know man without knowing God', and on the other, their plea is: 'He cannot be known'. We are in a dilemma: which is '*satya*' and which is '*mithya*'. Is it not all the magic of our own glorification of God only?

To conclude let me submit my humble opinion then. I earnestly believe that now when today science knows much about the universe nature and its laws (certainly, our knowledge, especially about the universe and nature will never be complete), we can afford, perhaps, not to try to know the God (who's declared—cannot be known) anymore, but we can never afford not to know the men, who being the true architects of their own destinies—good or bad—can certainly attain good and excellence in their lives, provided they are earnest, sincere and well-guided in their approaches. It is only then that they can have self-realisation. It is now no use to repeat again and again like parrots that God is the almighty creator of the world. Now Swami Vivekanandji too accepts the truth regarding creation in the following stanza. He says, "we have seen first of all that this cannot be proved, this idea of a Personal God creating the world; is there any child that can believe this to-day? Because a 'Kumbhakara' creates a 'Ghata', therefore a God created the world! If this is so, then your Kumbhakara is God also, and if any one tells you that He acts without head and hands, you may take him to a lunatic asylum. Has ever your Personal God, the creator of the world to whom you cry all your life, helped you . . . is the next challenge from modern science . . . (on page 413 Vol. 3 *Swamiji's Works*).

If a ball is thrown up in the sky, and it dashes to the ground within no time, how does the God come into this picture? It's causes must be sought not outside, but within the phenomenon itself. Law of Gravitation of Newton clearly explains as to why does the ball come back to the ground, no matter theologians may not accept this gravitational pull behind it. So, let us no more try to hijack the Lord in and out of human affairs according to our convenience. That is why, perhaps, being stunned Albert Einstein once said: "I want to know how God created the universe . . ."

It's good Swami Chidanandji Saraswati talks of peace in his lecture in New York, but I humbly feel that the way he suggests for peace is the way to lull only, and not peace at all. It will really be a stage, when whole human machinery comes to a halt. That will be worse than the disease itself.

Why? Because peace can be had only by building the men or by changing our mindset for good by ourselves, and not by building necessarily the so-called abodes of God or by installing idols there, or merely by lying prostrate before the God or by glorifying the God, as we have been doing so far. Let us no more be fanatic about it.

When we say that peace can be had from within and not without, it means that only our myopic vision or little-mindedness, which has been the greatest barrier in attaining peace, must be replaced by us by our old vision of '*Vasudheva Kutumbkam*'; so that we may not only believe to live, but at the same time believe earnestly to let others too live' in this world. This ideal only can be had by us, when every 'I' works on the higher altitude of human excellence. To say 'we go to work. He works only' is nothing, but the main product of the so-called dismal, low, weak and escapist mentality only. Being architects of our own destinies, we are to discard it, keeping in view that we are supposed to do good only.

When we say that God was conceived in human minds in their utter ignorance about the universe and nature, we clearly mean that His conception mainly was meant to build the men to prevent them not to be brutes. But, somehow, due to some illusions, we have remained confined more or less exclusively to building His abodes here or there after one another or to His glorification unfortunately, and have forgotten to build ourselves, i.e., our mindset on somewhat higher altitude so far. Have we not made mere '*Hari-darshan*', God's *Ibadat* or '*puja*', His chanting of name or 'Gurubani', or performance of this or that ritual or dogma—the be-all and end-all of our religious life so far? Of course, I do not, and I cannot deny that there have been if great 'gurus' of ours like Ram, Krishna, Mohammad, Christ, Buddha, Mahavir, 'Gurus', there have been insane persons too in this world. But are not these great men on our tips ? In a nutshell, have we not been repeating so far that "peace comes through prayer" or "we can only worship Him" or "the only thing that a human being can do is to prostrate before the Almighty"? Let us honestly introspect ourselves: How far we have attained our main goal ? I humbly believe men are neither essentially divine, nor devil in their nature. They are, what they make themselves. Of course, there has never been any clash in between building the God's abode and building the men. But our problems crop up, because while building the God's abode we forget our main goal, i.e., the building of men. This deliberate or otherwise negligence on our parts has again left us on the same road-crossing, from where we started our voyage of life indeed. No-doubt we' have built ourselves from without. But can we navigate our ship smoothly without building ourselves from within? So, building the men from within prioritywise is most urgent.

It is only in this context, all of us will have to meditate on what Edwin Markham once gave his very kind, timely guidance to us to follow. He said :

"We are all blind until we see nothing is worth the making, if it does not make the man. Why build these cities glorious ? If man unbuilt goes. In vain we build the work, unless the builder also grows."—Edwin Markham.

The point to remember is that if man is well-built, not only from outside but from within, everything will be automatically well-built sooner or later. And if man remains, everything remains. Consequently, the same human history of miseries is apt to repeat again and again. Why? Obviously, because men are the true architects of their own destinies-good or bad.

'It was the best of time, it was the worst of time', said Charles Dickens in his famous 'A *Tale of two Cities*'. It is not the events or circumstances that cause elation or depression in life. It is our attitude, our mindset or approach towards our life that is the fountain head of our happiness or sufferings indeed. Positive attitude gives oxygen, negative attitude chokes our mind, our breathing pipe even. Our positive attitude makes our every single minute, our every place, our every day as auspicious as it can ever be. What matters more is our attitude to life. Undoubtedly, we can live beyond our death with our positive attitude of mind, which knows not our 'little-mindedness' almost.

Obviously, who am I to build anybody? Everyone is to build oneself. Let everyone have his own blueprint regarding it. Let the men-making persons, psychiatrists and psychologists come forward the world over to suggest the ways, how to keep the human bricks and human slabs together jointly as intact as it is possible; so that the human edifice may be everlasting, and, consequently, a small chap like me may ever be happier to see the natural sunshine as well as sunset on it, no matter personally I may or may not be here in the world. So, merely our talks of peace are futile, unless we remove the real causes of a war, i.e., our 'little-mindedness,' or 'myopic view of the world' attached to this poor 'I' by us. Instead of removing this poor 'I' then, earlier we remove this poor 'I's filth of mind, the better. Better late than never.

There is no more any question of any illusion, or doing anything in disgust. After all, we are all the true architects of our own destinies—good or bad. We can move even mountains, provided we have the good-will and we are earnest to attain good and excellence in our lives. Peace is apt to kiss everybody's feet, if everybody removes one's filth or rubbishness or little-mindedness or exclusive self from one's own mind oneself earnestly and sincerely. This is the recipe of real peace. Mere age old God's hypnotism won't help us in this respect. We have no alternative, except to elevate every 'I' to work on a higher altitude of life, if we want to establish peace genuinely in our own world. Peace lies not in removing the poor 'I', but in removing its' filth, unfortunately, attached usually with 'I's mind only. Removal of 'I' from the scene will mean only killing the 'I' and getting both 'I's mind and body completely paralysed. Are we ready for it?

Now this chapter can't be ended by me whimsically without particularly knowing this poor 'I', what it is, which has been a bone of contention for ages. Naturally, my kind patrons too are apt to ask me, who is this 'I', I have been talking about in this whole chapter? In order to solve this age old riddle for all times to come I humbly dislike to talk about it from any heretical world, but I would prefer to express how I feel or experience about it.

I believe. That it is 'I', who thinks, feels, or does either good or bad in life. Obviously, this 'I' is not our mind, but it is the same architect of one's own destiny or a human spider, and nothing else, as our mind, which is the highest stage of the development of matter, doesn't move either to its right or left on its own. If I thinks, feels and does good, it's all, because 'I' elevates to himself or herself to a higher altitude of thoughts, feelings and doings and on the other, if 'I' thinks, feels or does any evil anywhere, it's all because the same 'I' degrades himself/herself to that level. Why? Because, 'I' fails to perceive one's own mind, as to what is to be done, and what is not to be done in a situation with the power of '*buddhi*' or '*vivek*' or discrimination of one's own mind. This power varies from man to man. I know nothing, about the soul, when people treat the same 'I' as an immortal soul inside our bodies.

I firmly believe that the same 'I' hears both good or bad by means of one's ears, speaks both good or evil through one's mouth, and sees good or bad with one's eyes. Actually, this human body is a composite living machine or like an assembly of different instruments or organs or senses, by means of which this same 'I' speaks, hears, sees, works, and moves about, but this 'I' is quite different from them. This 'I' works as the good or bad master, and the body, mind and all other organs are one's poor servants only. In other words, this 'I' is neither our mind, nor our body, nor eyes, nor ears.

But when this body goes or the very life from the body goes like the light, this 'I' too goes from this world, because in their absence the same 'I' has no separate *locus-standi*. Hence this 'I' is not eternal, as there is nothing eternal in this world. Everything is in a state of flux or change.

In this context let us remember that no I's mind ever works on its own. It moves towards its right or left at the command or the dictates of the same 'I'. Here I don't deny that, undoubtedly, different systems in one's body work naturally and independently of the 'I's command. For instance, the question of I's likes or dislikes doesn't arise in so many works, what everybody's brain does. Again, for instance, my heart never circulates or pumps blood or throbs at any 'I's command.

But do I ever experience that my mind or my eyes, or ears, etc., work on their own without the I's command? Obviously, it is underiable that when I's command is somewhat weak, I's mind, I's eyes, ears, mouth all go astray in their respective works, but when I's command is strong enough, all the bodily instruments too work according to I's good or bad wishes more or less.

In this context, here one may allege that because I'm the so-called non-believer in God, I can't experience or see God or soul with my mind and eyes respectively. Well, I am an humble seeker of truth and I have got no other means to know it all, except through my mind, what nature has given to me as a wonderful gift.

Thus, this 'I' is the doer of all things—good or bad in life. This 'I' is living or sentient. It's conscient. It is the 'I' that experiences both pleasure or pain. This 'I' is responsible for the good or bad fabric of life. Nothing is God-ordained or pre-determined here.

Let us remember nature helps those, who help themselves in strengthening their values, will-power, consciousness, their 'Buddhi' (intellect), 'Vivek' and power of discrimination. It is understood that when somewhere 'I' goes for good behaviour, obviously it means 'I' works in complete harmony among one's consciousness, one's intellect and one's power of reasoning. And when 'I' goes for some evil action somewherelse, it means this harmony is disturbed. Does not an 'I' look at a virgin as his own sister with a pure mind and eyes? Doesn't the same 'I' look at the same virgin with an angle of the satisfaction of one's carnal desires with the help of the same mind and eyes, made of the same matter? Thus, I's working depends upon, what mindset I makes.

Let us remember the truth that if we earnestly make our respective minds perceive rightly, what is good and what is evil, with our respective intellect or '*buddhi*', or if we make our minds capable to perceive pleasure or pain, happiness or sorrow wisely in advance, our respective minds will be in a position to treat the temptation or impulse of thinking, feeling and doing evil as really a pain and not as pleasure, and the impulse of doing good as really a matter of happiness, and not as pain at all.

The main cause of our miseries in the world is that we fail to make our minds perceive rightly and wisely in situations, which everyone faces in one's life. When we, the architects of our own destinies, fail to do this, we smoke, we steal, we rape, we exploit, we misbehave, we kill innocent people around, but when we succeed, we stop smoking , stealing, raping, exploiting, mis-behaving and killing innocent people then and there. The very design of our working of our minds, eyes, ears, nose, hands, feet all changes accordingly. So, the greatest need of the hour is to train our minds to treat pleasure as pleasure and pain as pain rightly and wisely and even not to treat pleasure as happiness at all. Here I don't see and experience any role for the thing like the so-called soul to play in these whole exercises, what 'I' does with the assistance of I's mind and different senses. I's values of life and conscience too determine the very colour of I's behaviour, as I chooses them.

Mind is the organ of thought, which the same 'I' applies either rightly or wrongly. This clearly shows as to how 'I' is decisive in determining the course of human history itself. Undoubtedly, here what works, I does, are done through I's mind only.

Mind works like the main control-room or the most technical natural computer for all its activities—both good or bad. 'Sanskars' mean the good or bad effects, produced on 'I's mind by 'I's good or bad repeated actions. Thus, 'I' is one's own best friend, as well as worst foe too, because primarily it is 'I', who is the maker of one's own 'sanskars and nature.' One's parents, or one's 'gurus' and one's society only help the person concerned in this respect.

Thus, if 'I' is Mr. 'X', this 'I' is an architect of one's own destiny—either good or bad. In other words, this 'I' is the human-spider, who weaves one's web of life, whatever it is with one's own knitpins. This 'I' is the overall master or the captain of the ship of human body. This body serves as a carriage to each architect of one's own destiny. Again, this 'I' employs one's own mind or different organs or the senses of the body-mechanism and thus makes the carriage run or stop.

The mind, which is a part of our brain, is a natural machine, fitted by nature in one's body, by means of which the 'I' thinks, remembers, receives messages from or gives directions to different sense-organs. The brain is a meeting place of all the nerves, which carry sensations from all parts of one's body to the brain. When the brain dies, all the systems' of 'I's body too stop working. But this brain is separate from this 'I'.

Again, the million dollar question is: who is this 'I'? Is it not either he, or you or me as an architect of one's own destiny good or bad? In fact, this 'I' is the dynamic sum total of 'I's consciousness, I's values of life, 'I's will-power, 'I's 'Sanskars', and 'I's power of intellect (*buddhi*), '*vivek*' and power of discrimination of I's mind. Hence, we should no more be dishonest to make our minds or bodies, or eyes, or ears, or mouth, or hands and feet scapegoats for actually ours good or bad thoughts feelings and doings. Obviously. This 'I' plays as a hero or a villain in the whole good or bad show. It is the sum total of an 'I' which determines the whole behaviour—pattern of each and every 'I', no matter what type of this sum total is, but 'I' chooses, selects and makes them, what they are. In short, once an 'I' which determines all these constituents parts of this sum total either consciously or unconsciously, the sum total too determines the whole 'I's behaviour in its turn in a situation from behind the scene afterwards.

The question is, how can then we renounce this 'I'—the very navigator of the ship? Undoubtedly, if 'I', being an architect of one's own destiny, does not renounce one's ego, one's little-mindedness, what 'I' often attaches with the 'I's mind, then 'I' has no future. 'I' is apt to be doomed then soon. So, let every 'I' be most careful, while steering one's ship of life to reach the Eldorado of peace and happiness indeed.

In this context, let me make it humbly clear that our mere prostrating before a hypothetical deity, as most of us do, won't help us much in this respect. For me this exercise of ours is more a safer escaping route from our respective responsibilities. It won't make us necessarily good humans indeed. Will 'I' ever beware of it to reach I's destination of peace and happiness with certainty?

Let every 'I' mind it that it is the stuff of 'I's mind, that matters much more than anything else in I's life. If this 'I' is crucified or nailed, who is to shut out the junk material out of 'I's mind in that state of affairs, and who is to convince I's mind to perceive good as good and evil as evil with the help of one's power of 'buddhi' (intellect) 'vivek' and power of discrimination consciously? Has 'He' ever come to any 'I's rescue in this respect? If yes, why have 'I's miseries been multiplying? Let us beware of it before it' is too late for 'I's.

After all, if at all He exists anywhere, let us understand the fact that 'He' has neither made any 'I' dirtier from within, nor from without. When every 'I' himelf/herself is responsible for either being pure or impure, hence, unless every 'I' earnestly takes one's inner and outer bath by oneself, no 'I' can ever be cleaned. Good persons and good scriptures can only take every 'I' to the pool, but they cannot make any 'I' drink. If each 'I' makes oneself conscious of this truth, it is not at all a question of the ego of any 'I', but the question of I's responsibility only. Earlier, every 'I' realises it, the better. Better late than never.

11

Our Life is, What We Make it—Good or Bad

Our life or world, whatever it is—good or bad—is not predetermined by any deity, but is made either by you or me or by all of us concerned. When it contains evil too, there is no sense to hijack God in it's making. Hence, logic demands from us to accept this truth that our life or world, whatever it is—good or evil—can never have been God-ordained, but it has been man-made. Being the true architects of our own destinies, let us then have necessary moral guts to own the baby—beautiful or ugly, and it's parentage, if we are really earnest to reform it. Those, who hold that there is neither good, nor evil in the world, but only thinking makes it so, they are humbly advised not to behave like that stupid Ostrich, which kept its head under the sand dunes. Earlier they stop behaving like fanatics, the better. Better late than never.

So, it is no use to go on dubbing this world as '*mithya*' or '*maya*' (dream), or illusion and it has no sense to get ourselves indulged anymore in having a hate-campaign against the world—Our own baby. Our moral sense demands to accept it with a positive mindset.

Let us then listen to the sane advice of Swami Vivekanandji; the great saint, who clarifies: "This world is neither good, nor evil . . . life is good or evil according to the state of mind in which we look at it, it is neither by itself. Fire, by itself is neither good, nor evil. When it keeps us warm we say, 'How beautiful is fire!' "When it burns our finger, we blame it. Still, in itself it is neither good, nor bad . . . so also is the world. It is perfect . . . " (On page 75-76 *Swamiji's Works*)

In fact, the real womb of both good and evil is our mind. Of course, our mind too never moves towards its right or left or forward or backward on its own. Which side it moves, depends upon its beholder. So, let us no more even imagine to run away from our families or the world like escapists. Let us live in the world, make it a better place to live in by following our old principle 'live and let live' in its true spirit, or by our good thinking, feeling and doing, what we can, wherever we are to be good only. In fact, we won't need then to go to the shore of the Ganges if we make our lives as pure as the Ganges itself and we won't need to visit any temple then, if we make our lives better than any temple of the world. Of course, I have no allergy against them.

Do we ever realise how difficult it is to live a purposeful life or a life of high missions—one after another in series than to run away from our responsibilities, no matter we are in a family or in a country? Do we ever realise that living in caves means at the most worshipping one God, but living among our sisters and brothers in this world means we must live a purposeful life, and, consequently, it will mean thinking, feeling and doing good for crores of living gods and goddess here? That is the real heaven on earth.

It is very relevant to quote Swami Vivekanandji in this respect. He says, "It is useless to say that the man who lives out of the world is a greater man than he who lives in the world, it is much more difficult to live in the world and worship God than to give it up and live a free and easy life. (On page 42, Vol. 1, *Swamiji's Works*).

The question is how can these escapists change their world, no matter whether they live here, or in some hypothetical '*Lok*', viz., '*Vaikunth*', the heaven without changing their minds first for good? Can they dare to deny the fact that whatever our world is—good or bad—is our own brain child? What a contrast ! That while the positive thinking of Marx talks for changing the world, the negative thinking of these hate-campaigners against this world only knows how to dub the world as '*mithya*' or like that, and run away from here. Of course, we should not be slaves of our worldly desires, and we should not be bewildered or hypnotised by the glittering of the world. Otherwise, instead of its' masters, it is apt to make us its slaves.

If there is human-hypocrisy, human-wickedness and criminality in the world, it clearly proves that the claims of believers that God exists, is quite hollow and it has got no substance in it. If Swami Vivekanand ji holds "hypocrisy cannot exist, where God is", how can He reside in the minds of hypocrites? How does Swamiji hold then that "God is ordering our lives" or 'He is the Governor or maintainer of this world?' His claim then that "it is He (God) that works. We are only His instruments," seems to be quite hollow.

Let us remember our only good doings can make us great, no matter whether we are householders or sanyasins. Swami Vivekanandji endorses this view. He says, "Each is great in his own place." (On page 47 Vol. 1, *Swamiji Works*). He further adds, ". . . that to be an ideal householder is a much more difficult task than to be an ideal sanyasin." (On p. 62, Vol. 1, *Swamiji Works*).

So, let us no more keep our minds clouded with age old illusions, because they have been great barriers in our ways to change ourselves and our world too. If the entire world is in a state of perpetual change, it is according to the Law of Motion of nature. What is unnatural or '*mithya*' in it ? This change is its nature. It is inevitable. One, who is born today, is apt to die another day. One, who is young, beautiful and strong today, is apt to be old, may not remain so beautiful, and strong tomorrow or day after. It is a scientific fact. What is false or dreamy in it ? Rather it is the greatest '*satya*'. And if there are more cases of treachery, betrayal, hatred, jealousy, vengeance, cunningness, selfishness, and the like in the world than pure love, affection, sympathy etc. etc., are not they all the products of our own filthy minds? Why do we not realise that it is we, who have turned this human world into a hell, and it is only we who can turn the same hell into a heaven simply by removing our exclusive 'self' from our minds? So, why to make the world a scapegoat of our own evils? Swami-Vivekanandji too accepts the truth: "People think that this world is bad and imagine that heaven is somewhere else. This world is not bad." (On page 129, Vol. 8, *Swamiji's Works*) I humbly feel our mere negativism in our thinking is our greatest barrier to see the world in its right perspective. Let us no more behave like jaundiced beings.

These theists or the so-called believers in God forget that when 'His Master's pet dogs', who have spoiled this world, how can they be expected to keep the so-called hypothetical 'Vaikunth', the heaven, a better place to live in?

Let us remember our hand is holier that helps, than two hands, which simply pray. Let us not forget that our prayer too as a boosting dose of our morale, is a blessing, but as an escaping route from our own responsibilities, is a mere curse.

If natural calamities come time to time in life, it all does not mean nature is decisive to change the world history. Nature is an automatic force inside all the things of the world. It is responsible for all the changes in the world of nature only. Nature has nothing to do with the usual changes in human world. There is no chaos in the world of nature. If there is a chaos, it is all due to humans in the world. Do we not know, what moves or changes in nature, that is all, as if well-caused, planned and well-settled by nature itself? Nature is never whimsical in its behaviour. It acts and reacts due to certain causes, no matter then who suffers and who does not. But it has nothing to do with man-made miseries.

In short, is it not truer to say that nature evolved all the beings, including humans in the course of centuries, and these humans in their own turn, being the true architects of their own destinies, have made their own world, no matter whether it is good or bad? Even these humans, unlike other animals, have made even their gods and goddesses in their utter ignorance of the universe and the nature. How strange it is that we may be knowing about God a lot, but our knowledge about our ownselves is equal to nil still ! We are not aware of the fact that we can be better human beings only when we know our ownselves. Merely knowing about Him is not enough.

Most of us go to temples, mosques, churches and 'gurudwaras' to worship God to perform all sorts of rituals and dogmas, to mutter many 'mantras', to chant from scriptures in the hope to see God eye to eye there. Why to go there and seek Him, when the living gods and goddesses have been everywhere? But we can do this only, when we transform maximum good into our beings, remake our mindset, get rid ourselves of our own selfish nature and little-mindedness. Even if Truth is God, it's victory or defeat depends on the persons, who possess it, as truth has eyes, but no feet to walk and no wings to fly or flutter on its own. It is only due to this flaw here in this world, what it is, every Christ is apt to be nailed, every Lincoln and Gandhi are apt to be shot at, every Galelio is apt to be ex-communicated from his own religion and every Dayanand Saraswati and Socratese are apt to sip the cup of poison again and again, and consequently, the same history of human miseries too is apt to repeat again and again, so long brutes do not change themselves and become humans. The truth will ever remain buried under the debris, so long we go on feeding our tigerish nature.

Swami Vivekanandji rightly holds, "The Karmayogi need not believe even in doctrine . . . He may not believe even in God. He has got his own special aim of realising selfishness. . . ." Because he has strong faith that it is he, who makes his own life or world, what it is good or bad.

Simply by going on a pilgrimage like Badrinath or Dwarka, or Mecca-Madina, or Veitcan city or Nanak Sahib, or simply by having an '*akhand-kirtan*' (non-stop chanting of the Lord) or '*waheguru*', or by simply having a 'roza' in Ramzan days, or simply by going to church on a Sunday and lighting a candle there will never help us in either changing our mindset, or our world. Indeed we do all these rituals and dogmas just to please our God primarily. It is all due to this reason men remain !

In fact, to change myself I shall have to assess myself honestly, what actually I am. Am I not simply the one among the crorers of architects of our own destinies—good or bad—to live side by side with others in this world? Why then I feel like a football bladder, fattened just to hear my praise and like a deflated tyre to hear my due or undue censure ? Why to behave like other's slave ? The less I am dependent on others for my happiness or sorrow, the better. Can I overlook the fact that all, who either praise or censure me, do not do this always with a mind of my true welfare?

Hence, to make or mar my present or future lies with me. Otherwise, my slavery will persist. Of course, if anyone is bent upon creating some nuisance, we shall have to keep a distance with such a person.

To live a purposeful and meaningful life we all need a different mind indeed. How foolish we have been that we believe that we need such a mind only, when we reach the last stage of our lives and by that time we must enjoy life with whatever mind we have got! Don't we realise that our good mind has always been our real precious asset? Again, don't we realise that it is we only as architects of our own destinies, who can make our lives either a heaven of hell with our own good or bad mindset?

But to live a purposeful life, and to keep our little mindedness at bay from ours, we all need 'meditation'. In fact, now meditation as the surer road to our mental peace and happiness is being accepted by the people the world over. Even in jails meditation is now being used as a necessary instrument of reforms of the criminals. The seeds of change in our individual, national and international life are apt to be seen quite apparently, if we know what meditation is, as an instrument of change of our mindset.

12

Meditation—both Science and An Art of Our Conscious, Good and Natural Living Only

If we really want to change ourselves, and our world around, we shall have to equip ourselves with a different mindset and work with a different psyche. For attaining such state of our minds and mindset, we all need meditation as our daily routine. In fact, the life of a true 'Sadhak' (seeker of truth) remains quite immersed in continuous meditation. For him it is not at all a one time, but the whole time or 'whole life affair'.

The question is what is meditation ? In fact, meditation has been an age old science and an art to keep our minds composed, because it controls the very flow of our thinking, feeling and doing altogether. So, today it's importance has been realised in a more noisy and stressful world, which is akin to a boisterous sea. Today within no time we have fits of anger, hatred and jealousy. Meditation keeps our minds calm and more balenced even in adversed circumstances. Through meditation we can have better control over our minds, no matter there is happiness or sorrow. It does not believe in escapism to see the problems, tension, anxieties and botherations. In a nutshell, it makes us like a good captain, whose merit is not tested, when the sea is calm, but when it is like an errant or violent child. As a navigator reaches the destined sea-shore through mariner compass, a good man reaches his/her destined goal through meditation.

Yoga is a more comprehensive term. It is the name of the state of the union or the perfect harmony among our body, mind and spirit or consciousness. It is possible only when there is a perfect harmony among our three aspects of personalities, i.e., when we work with a perfect union among our good thinking, good feeling and good willing. It may or may not be our union with the so called God. In fact, 'yoga' means union. Union of what ? Can union of evil forces be called a yoga? No. 'Yoga' is possible, when there is a union of good forces only. One, who unites things and people is a 'Yogi'. And one, who unites only our evil forces, he brings not unity and construction, but disunity and disintegration everywhere. Hence, one, who does so like Osama bin Laden, is called a criminal or a sinner, and not a 'yogi'. In a nutshell one, who unites or one who brings harmony among people or things or in the society is a 'yogi'. And one who brings disintegration or destruction is anti-thesis of 'Yoga'. Let us remember harmony is life and disharmony is death. Harmony comes, when body, mind and spirit work as one for good.

I humbly hold that while the so-called 'Pranayama' (inhaling and exhaling of our breathing) represents more the physical side, the meditation represents more the mental side of the same 'yoga'. Both of them are like the branches of the tree of 'yoga'. Both are part and parcels of the same tree.

Now the obvious question is: Is meditation concentration only ? According to Swami Chitanaya Keerti: 'Meditation is not concentration; concentration is a mind exercise to focus on a particular subject'. *(Hindustan Times* in Meditations on 4-6-2001). For instance, a writer, or an actor or a student or a scientist, or a painter, or a singer. goes on even sometime losing oneself in one's own respective activity or work, and, consequently, may know nothing about what is actually happening around oneself. It is akin to the state of our forgetfulness voluntarily. Why does it so happen ? Because of this intensive exercise of concentration on the part of a person concerned. Let us remember that a 'thug' (criminal) too succeeds to achieve his perfect aim, leaving no trace at all behind his crime for the investigating cop to probe, because of the same concentration of his mind. But meditation is different.

According to *Oxford Dictionary* to meditate means 'to look about, or to give oneself up to serious thought' (esp. religion). It further states: to meditate means to "focus one's mind for a period of time for spiritual purposes" or it is "a method of relaxation".

The most important thing to remember here is that for meditation our mind must be inwardly, and not outwardly. Or we must have our inward vision. In other words, it means meditation is not at all meant to seek peace and happiness in outwardly things, as we often do, but only in inwardly spiritual attainments. We have to look in and not out for real peace and happiness. Of course, we can have pleasures simply by looking out. To meditate one has to turn one's gaze within. So, we have to adopt the policy of pick and choose, as to what is to be meditated upon and what is not. It all does not mean at all that we can overlook outwardly things in life. It only means we can have peace from within and not-without. So, let us remain the masters of our pleasures. Let us no more reduce ourselves to their slaves. Usually, what happens that we experience our mind wanders away from the object of our meditation, as it is not at all a child's play to keep our mind focussing on a particular object of meditation throughout to the exclusion of undesirable thoughts. It is a hard nut to crack to keep our mind fixed on one's desired object of meditation at a stretch so easily at least, at its initial stage. For this we shall have to stop our mind identifying ourselves with all objects of pleasure by and by, if we really want to live no more like slaves, but masters only. For happiness let us live in the world, enjoy it, but let us no more identify ourselves with it. The world is only a necessary means to an end. And the end is peace and happiness. Let us keep it into our minds that charm or no charm, beauty or no beauty in the world fundamentally depends on the onlooker, his motive of work and his values of life. It is our look, which plays the most important part in making ourselves as slaves or the masters of our world or situation. That is why, for a real sane a gold biscuit lying somewhere is like a dust particle and a beautiful girl on the road is only like his own loving daughter. Whether we go higher and higher in our mission or slip away from the desirable path, more depends on our look. Our look too works under the command of our values of life, we cherish. Only the persons, who have the keen and sharp eyes of their '*vivek*', or '*budhi*' (wisdom) or strong power of discrimination, they do not confuse pleasure with happiness. This power is strengthened only through meditation.

We must be very clear on this point that for peace and happiness in life, we shall have to have a perfect union or harmony in the working of our body, mind and consciousness at the earliest possible. Otherwise, they will work in different directions. For this we have to make our thinking, feeling and doing good to be good only. These things are part and parcels of our life long 'sadhana' (meditation).

Meditation is the only course to keep all our ripples or waves of thoughts, that originate in our minds in a day in perfect control by and by. In the world, what it is, the human sharks, the human tigers, the human bagulas, and the like, all are in the habit of disturbing or mudding or spoiling even the calm water of minds of the sane people. In meditation we have our positive thinking or positive attitude of our minds, i.e., if autumn comes in life, can spring lag behind? Or if bad time has come, it must go soon to see good days ahead, as change is the law of nature. This positivity in one's life is the greatest mast with which the meditationist, especially the beginner sails one's ship of life. A seeker of truth (*sadhak*) keeps the boisterous sea of his mind almost calm through meditation.

But we should not confuse our single-mindedness with meditation.

Anyone can achieve single-mindedness in which one sees nothing, hears nothing, smells nothing, does not become conscious even of touch, because the centre of gravity of mind is somewhere else. Do we not have single-mindedness sometime when we fail to hear even the horn of a motorist on the road ? The single-mindedness is easily possible, when our minds and eyes are outwardly, but in meditation our vision must be inwardly.

A person becomes a first class successful criminal, because of his single mindedness. Even the pornographic magazines too can lead us to single-mindedness. Do we not find our wards at home single-minded, when they see a T.V. serial, or when they read a fiction or a story of their own interest ? At such moment they fail to hear even the urgent calls of their respective moms from the kitchen.

Thus, single-mindedness is a state of our minds, when our minds stop wandering away from one object to another. It becomes static more or less, but in outer world. It is concerned with the material world only. While in meditation we focus our respective minds for a period of time for only spiritual gains, which provides us the maximum mental relaxation, happiness and peace of mind, because our vision or our look becomes natural and comes nearer to nature in meditation. From natural I mean that in meditation our thinking (thoughts), our feelings and our doings—all these three work in a union and their energies are utilised in the most desirable way. Obviously, when we come nearer to our natural behaviour, our mother nature blesses us kindly. Consequently, we feel tremendous energy for doing good at such moments in life in our minds.

This is the magic of inward vision only. Because our minds move in and not out in meditation. In intensive meditation our sense organs stop functioning. A sort of brakedown is established between our mind and the so-called outworld, because our mind goes on meditating on a desired object, as it is connected with one's inner-self only. In this context, we are supposed to know the science and art of both attachments and detachments with both the so-called inner world as well as outer world at the same time. We must know the right ordering of our loyalties in life. Let us keep it into our minds that those, who seek happiness and peace in life from the worldly objects of smell, taste, touch, sound, and the like, they are living only in a fool's paradise. They are to get mirage only. Of course, they can have the utmost pleasure from them.

Thus, I humbly feel that meditation is a state of our mind, when we conserve or store our innate mental energy to think worth-thinking, to feel worth-feeling, and to do worth-doing in the world for the good of the people at large. We can clean our minds in meditation. Our mind is not clean and not in harmony most of the time. Through meditation we can keep our inner ecology good.

Mr. Krishna says, "Meditation is the unfolding of the mind and through it, the act of seeing without restraint, without a background and so an endless emptiness in which to see. The seeing without the limitation of thought, which in time, requires a mind that is astonishngly quiet and still" I think by 'mind that is quiet and still,' he means a mind, no doubt, has prior knowledge of the people and the world around, but it is not at all disturbed, or biased, or prejudiced by any authoritative view regarding the subject at hand. All this requires an enquiring mind, which does not work on some presumptions already made. In other words, meditation is not possible by those people, whose minds have been already enslaved by something. In fact, meditation needs complete freedom to think afresh with no prior commitments to any thought, ideology or views, whatsoever. It is only when mind is quite free from such shackles, that the mind works and can properly meditate. Otherwise, mind cannot get peace and proper environment.

We cannot overlook the fact that mind is like a parachute, which works, when it is open. It can only help us in landing at a suitable place, when it is open. So, meditation is a state of our consciousness when our mind is not laden with any pre-supposed notions and thoughts, forced by any authority, whatever. Our mind must be free to meditate, afresh for the good of the people at large. Actually, meditation is not just sitting erect, controlling the breath simply by inhaling or exhaling or wrestling with our errant minds. Everyone can do that by practice sooner or later. But I humbly hold that all the architects of their own destinies are in their meditation, when not only they are in a state of loving a hypothetical God, but all the living gods and goddesses also. A mother is in prefect meditation, when she lovingly makes her children take their food in the kitchen, and a father meditates when he goes to his work, because he cares for his children. Thus, meditation is not escapist by nature, but it is the real 'karma yoga' in action. Here her love and his care is nothing, but pure meditation. Both of them not only love themselves, but others around too. In the same way, when someone throws away the peel of a banana; so that none should slip on it on the way, or if a person just helps a blind to cross over a crowded road, these things can not be done, unless they meditate. Thus, meditation is more concerned with our mental than physical postures. It's more concerned with the planet earth to make it more beautiful to live in and its people better beings. It is to raise all its beings to higher level. When the feelings of real love for all sprouts in people's minds, they don't fall, but rise by themselves. In this non-violent war they are apt to win. Question of their defeat can never arise at all. In the same way, when people do not pollute the environment, but do everything to preserve the nature, they meditate. It is all due to this I humbly hold that meditation is both a science and an art of our conscious, good and natural living only.

One can hold that meditation means 'a state of mindlessness.' But the term 'mindlessness' should not be confused with the term 'unmindful'. It only means that meditation is possible only when our mind is free from all man-made shackles. 'Mindlessness' is not a state, when we live in 'no mind', or a state, when we have no desire, and no goal-oriented life. Desire to achieve higher mission in life or goal always remains there in meditation. In the state of mindlessness, a meditationist is not enslaved by any shackles, whatsoever.

Had meditation been a no goal-oriented state of mind, Osho would never have recommended: "Whosoever is suffering from 'insomnia' should try this dynamic meditation in the night." He adds, ". . . emotions, anger, hate . . . drop them before you go to sleep. . ." He further advises to "have an inner bath . . .". If we do it "sleep will be totally different." Osho is confident of it. Why our sleep will be totally different after this inner bath? Because then we are apt to feel more cool, calm, happy and peaceful. So, let us drop unnecessary anger and hate.

In the context of 'mindlessness' Buddha emphasised: "we have just borrowed, but we do not know anything. Do not nurture any concept just because they were written in scriptures. Who are you ? A Brahmin ? A Shudra ? Remove all these trash and be void of all these things, then only would you be able to know the truth. Buddha could get" Nirvana (freedom), because he kept himself quite free from all these man-made shackles. Buddha rejected even the authorities of the Vedas and other scriptures.

Even Guru Nanak advices: "Meditate on truth. That will give you true light . . ." Obviously, we can never meditate on truth without mind. Of course, without continuous meditations at all times, even when we are busy in our routine-works, we are to pollute our minds with evils. This pollution is apt to disturb our inner ecology. Even in the *Gita,* Arjuna asks Krishna: "O Master of Yoga, how can I know you through constant-meditation?" Even Krishna too says, ". . . those . . . devoted to Me (are) . . . constantly meditating on Me with single-minded devotion."

I humbly feel had Buddha not been able to keep himself quite at bay from these shackles, he would not have been the first revolutionary thinker in centuries to make his honest efforts in getting all the true architects of their own destinies quite free from the age old divine-crutches through his meditation.

For Buddha meditation did not mean other worldly contemplation, or concentration on a hypothetical future world (heaven), but how to get happiness and peace in the present life by removing 'exclusive self.'

But faith in oneself for making of one's life is most essential. Because Buddha believed that everyone is like a lamp for oneself. So, let everyone stand on one's own feet and realise that only by 'doing good to be good' one can be happy and peaceful.

Some people hold that one can meditate only when one renounces this world, because so long, as one is attached here with this or that one cannot have real focus of one's mind for spiritual or higher purposes. Undoubtedly, we shouldn't identify ourselves with each and everything in this world. If we do it, we are sure to become their slaves, and no more remain their masters. But we are living in a fool's paradise, if we think our all attachments in this world are evils, and all detachments are good.

Meditation is both a science and an art, which tells us to know all priorities of both our attachments and detachments at the same time. Where does meditation ask us to detach ourselves with our Lord, if at all He exists? Where does it ask ourselves to detach ourselves with even human-excellence and good? It is allergic to only our excessive identification in this world.

One, who lives for a higher cause in one's life, no matter whether one is a dutiful honest teacher, or an engineer, or a doctor, or a scientist, or an army man, or a researcher in one's lab, or a farmer in the field, or an industrialist or a labourer in the factory, or a writer,or a reader, or a student, or a singer, or a painter, or a true '*sevak*' of the people, wherever one is, actually meditates in one's life. It is meditation in action.

For meditation we need not to wear a saffron robe at all, we need not go to a temple or mosque or church or *gurudwara* essentially. And we need not go to any caves or to reach the peaks of the Himalayas, or to go to Badrinath and the like, or to reach the shore of the Ganges essentially.

Actually, meditation is primarily a way of life, and a particular bent or attitude of our minds. When one, being an architect of one's own destiny, thinks, feels and does good for all, what one can, wherever one is—these are all different states of one's meditation. Actually, we need not to do anything else for meditation, except to change our gear of thinking, feeling and doing for good. From this point of view, one, who's having an '*akhand*' (continuous) '*jap*' or '*kirtan*' like 'Ram-Ram, Hare-Hare' may not necessarily be in a state of one's meditation, because in meditation one not only cares for oneself to live, but earnestly cares; so that others around too may live. So, meditation is not for detaching oneself with the whole world, but with one's own exclusive love or little mindedness and ego. One is called a holy man, because one loves the whole good world, wherever it is, and people know him as a man of meditation because of one's loving mind. Even a beggar, who has nothing to offer to his Lord with him, if he wishes good for all the living gods and goddesses, he too is in perfect meditation. His wish is meditation.

The goal of meditation is pure love of one's mind. One, who achieves this state indeed, no matter one is totally illiterate, or a '*gyani*' or a '*karma yogi*' is in a state of meditation, because all these reach the same destination. Here one's love for all, one's good '*gyan*', and one's good '*karmas*'are nothing, but meditation. One who lives and can die for good, really loves oneself and meditates.

Thus, real meditation is like our carriage, which takes us to the planet of peace and happiness in this human world. It aims at good for all, and evil for none. But that is possible only when we have our twenty four hours inner bath, while doing our own respective works.

Now the hundred dollar question is: can anyone do really good, unless one has immense faith in oneself to be good?

13

Faith in One's Own Making of One's Life—Either Good or Bad—is Like an Anchor

Certainly, each architect of one's own destiny can change the very direction of one's ship of life through one's own steering for the good of one and all, provided one has immense faith in it. It is in this very context, I humbly believe that faith in one's own making of one's life or one's world, either good or bad—is like an anchor.

Faith is like the key-stone or the arch of the edifice of human life. That is why, Swami Vivekanandji too advised us; "They say", "Have faith in this fellow or that fellow," but I say, "Have faith in yourself first"... all power is in you—be conscious and bring it out. Say, I can do everything" ". . . Say . . ." So'ham, So'ham"—"I am He! I am He!" (On page 274 Vol. 6 *Swamiji Works*)

Here Swamiji's advice, undoubtedly, is a great morale booster for all of us. So far we all know the dividened of the 'faith in Him', but now it is an era of the 'faith in us'. If we actually restore faith in our ownselves in making of our own life, what it is, we shall see the magic of this faith soon. This faith is to pour the very life in the dead bodies. No-doubt, there will ever be change in our life, but I am sure this faith, being meaningful and purposeful, is apt to change its very direction for the betterment of the people of the world. Human psychology advises us: let us have faith that no pilot or no driver or no steersman ever likes to have either even minor or major accident, because no one wants to die in one's own hands. So, faith in one's ownself gives us the very sense of duty to make oneself a better human being and, consequently, one's own world too and side by side it sprouts the very seeds of responsibility either to weave or to re-weave the very web of one's life or the world with a normal urge for the betterment of all in the capacity of a human-spider. Today if the very look of the fabric of our lives is ugly mostly, it is all because we do not know actually that it has been entirely woven by all of us either individually or collectively with our own knit-pins. So far due to our fatal ignorance we have been thinking that whether the web of our life is either good or bad, 'its' Master weaver has been He Himself. And, hence, we must accept it, whatever it has been. How fatal this ignorance has been proved! After restoring this faith in one's ownself even, the pilot is sure to commit follies occasionally. After all everyone is subject to error, but natural urge for mending of one's own skill of driving will be quick, having a natural desire for its good results. Of course, if a driver being drunk or rash steers and thus betrays faith, whatever he himself and the society has kept in himself, let the law of the land be strengthened to take its own course then.

So long this restoration of faith in human beings does not become a reality, the major problem is, how can one even think that "I can do everything", when our minds have been poisoned for ages to believe that God has been the sole doer of all things in the world and the human beings are His '*nimits*' only. We have got escapism as the only dividened of this dismal doctrine. May I know: has it made us less egoists and better human beings indeed? Does it not look strange that Swamiji on the one hand holds that "This 'I' and 'mine' causes the whole misery", and on the other he expects from everyone to believe "I am He!" "I am He!" When 'I' causes the misery, how can the same 'I' be 'He'?

Undoubtedly, faith in oneself is the pre-requisite of human life. We cannot imagine even human life, if we have no faith in making of our lives, no matter it is good or bad. Without faith in ourselves for making of our lives, we may say, "we live", but practically more or less 'we are dead like'. Even to see the naked dance of devil, we overlook it, thinking whatever has happened, or is happening or would happen in future, it is for Him to mend it all, and we are quite helpless. We can do nothing, except-prostrating before Him just to worship Him. Thus, the view in question has sucked all faith and strength from our minds, and consequently, we have been suffering from the psyche of 'weak and low' for ages. It is a case of low blood-pressure. Hence, it is more dangerous for our life.

Of course, faith in oneself for making one's life—good or bad—can never mean that one can ever be free to create chaos, anarchy or lawlessness here or there. Where there's Rule Of Law, which means 'Equality before law', and 'equal protection of law,' or in the words of Sir Ivor Jennings it means 'likes should be treated alike', one cannot be allowed to be the law in oneself. Keeping in view these facts, one may or may not have faith in this or that God, there should not be any question of one's ex-communication from one's religion, as belief in this or that religion is only a personal affair.

Thus, faith is good, but blind faith is an anethma to good life. Is it not a fact? Am I trying to produce snakes in the ceiling in the name of blind faith? Can any one accuse me for all this? Have we not been its real victims? Earlier we realise it, the better. Better late than never.

That is why, unlike so many self-proclaimed religious leaders Swami Vivekanandji advised us: "The great thing is to have faith in oneself even before faith in God." (On page 223 Vol. 8 *Swamiji Works*)

What is needed the most is to restore faith in our own steersmenship i.e., the belief that if we have turned heaven into a hell once with our own evil thinking, feelings and doings, we can now turn the same hell into heaven by thinking, feeling and doing good. Only we are supposed to change simply their gear. Swami Vivekanand clarifies: "The Vedanta teaches men to have faith in themselves first . . . a man who does not believe in himself is an atheist." (On page 294 Vol. 2 *Swamiji Works*)

He further adds in this respect: "The old religions said that he was an atheist who did not believe in God. The new religion says that he is the atheist who does not believe in himself". (On page 301 Vol. 2 *Swamiji Works*).

Why is he so emphatic on faith in oneself than in God? Obviously, because faith in oneself means life, activity and momentum. In fact, in its absence our life becomes quite dull and lifeless. We do nothing, except performing this or that ritual or dogma. That is the end of our doings. When we do some wrong, we are in the habit of shifting 'its' responsibility on the shoulders of a poor God, just to save our own skin. This faithlessness has put us on a cross-roads, from where we do not know where to go and where not to. All of us are in a strange dilemma: how to take our day-to day problems? It has blurred our vision even to reach our goal of life by our ownselves.

Swami Vivekanandji thus clarifies further: "If you have . . . no faith in yourselves, there is no salvation for you . . . why is it that we three hundred and thirty millions of people have been ruled for the last one thousand years by any and every handful of foreigners, who chose to walk over our prostrate bodies? Because they had faith in themselves and we had not . . . any English boy will tell you: "I am an English man, and I can do anything." The American boy will tell you the same thing, and so will any European boy. Can our boys say the same thing here? No, nor even the boy's fathers. We have lost faith in ourselves." (On page 190-191 Vol. 3 *Swamiji Works*)

What a statement of bare facts indeed! In fact, the faithlessness in our making of our own life-either goood or bad has been an age old chronic disease, all of us more or less have been suffering from, and our all other talks are its unfortunate symptoms only. Unless, the disease in question is removed, the symptoms in this or that form will always be troubling our blind minds.

For instance, what to talk of celebrating the marriage of our daughters or sons, or construction of our house, or completion of any work at hand successfully with our own heart content, even when we intend to open a petty grocery shop here or there, we having no faith in ourselves, go staightaway to the abodes of God and there we lie prostrate to pray Him to bless us success in our endeavour! We pray our God Ganesh beforehand. The plea of priests has been that they do it just to calm down the gods and goddesses. Is it not a strange plea? One can befool some of the people all the time by advocating that we do it to be lesser egoists. The question is: are we lesser egoists today, because we drag Him in and drag Him out of human affairs simply according to our convenience? Do not we fight still together to prove our own respective gods and goddesses, our own scriptures, our own abodes of gods and goddesses and the like better than others? Do not we pray our own gods and goddesses even for hours together and even then we are ready to digest the living gods and goddesses in the same breath here or there? Do not we ill-treat them? Of course, exceptions may be here or there.

How strange it is that Osho believes: "... whatever you do creates your ego. You feel 'I am doing something' ... And whenever you do something, you start thinking ... of the result ..." I accept the minds of most of us have always been ego-centric, in spite of that we waste our valuable times, in the so called worshipping of the Lord to prove our 'bhakti.' Had we utilised it in raising ourselves by thinking, feeling and doing good, the same world would have been changed altogether. No-doubt, it is the easiest route, what we have adopted, but can we save our sinking ship of life from mere worship? Because for ages it has been observed that "I and me" have been the causes of our miseries", hence, Osho too wanted to flog every 'I' with the same stick of ego. We have already seen, how it is not at all desirable to remove the 'I' from the scene of our lives, and how we are supposed to change only our respective mindset for good.

When the question of faith comes even a doctor says, 'I treat only, He cures'. Not that, he is not an egoist, or the doctor in question is more polite essentially. It's all because we've made this mode of telling things for ages. Is it not all like to say, "We go to work, He works?" When a doctor cheats a patient by removing his kidney without even letting him know about it without any valid reasons, should we then presume that it is not the doctor, but He who cheats? To whom would we like to befool by wearing the mask of humbleness? Of course, no doubt there are very humble doctors too, but they are on tips only. They will ever serve their patients, no matter what happens, and they shall never even imagine to cheat them.

There is no question of difference either we are lawyers or engineers or petty-shop-keepers, or industrialists or farmers or labourers and even petty rickshaw-pullers. All are sailing in the same boat. Being hypocrites we talk of God, and hate our own fellow-beings at the same time. Exception of it might be here or there. How many of us are there, who care that it is our means, which justify the ends?

Unless a doctor has full faith in one's own diagnosis and prescription, the patient's faith too shakes and, consequently, his or her recovery becomes a late affair. Faith can move even mountains. Even a dying person can arrest one's death, at least, for sometime, if one has utmost faith in oneself. It is all due to faith we witness with our own eyes even quacks swimming well in their profession luxuriously, while experts sink as pauper's? Why? Because the former succeed to sustain faith of their patients in themselves, the latter utterly fail in their attempts. This all does not mean quacks are better, than actual doctors.

Of course, perfection is not possible in this world, and no doctor can ever give warranty of the survival of his patient. No one can do it, and no one should do it. But does his hijacking of God in human affairs make him/her more humble by an iron necessity? Of course, a doctor especially must be very polite and submissive in his/her behaviour with the patients. Simply by virtue of our habit we link every happening in our lives with the mercy or blessings of the Lord, not because we essentially want to bury our ego, but the reality is that because the thing like faith in our ownselves has been very cruelly sucked by the wrong doses, administered to all of us by the so-called theists for ages. Is it not enough on the part of the doctor to say that he is treating the patient in the best possible way just to assure him/her for his/her earliest recovery? It is more important for a doctor to be more competent, to be more update in one's own treatment, more considerate and sympathetic towards one's own patient than to drag, his/her God in his/her profession. In fact, it is not any hypothetical God, who cures, but all the desired good qualities of a doctor have a major say in the treatment of a patient. The question of one's survival depends on the nature of the disease, the natural coincidence of the circumstances, and the whole treatment of the doctor, etc. So, what is needed the most is that being quite honest in one's own profession, the doctor is supposed to assure one's own patient that he is treating him/her in the best possible way, just to keep his patient's faith in him intact. Thereafter, no one can say anything about anything with certainty. All round competency and upto date knowledge in one's profession brings almost complete trust in oneself, no matter whether one is a doctor or an engineer or a lawyer or a teacher, and the like. Only a good human can be a good professional.

It is all due to having almost no faith in oneself, generally all the people are in the habit of linking even the question of one's honour-dishonour, success-unsuccess, profit-loss, and life-death, etc., with His sweet or sour will only. Do we not find people telling that whatever the Lord wills, we must accept that happily, as He never does any wrong with anybody? The question of accepting their plea arises only when it is truth. Hence, we never realise that by living merely in such a make-believe world, we do nothing, except putting a premium on our vices. Do we ever realise that it is a human world, and not divine? Most of us seldom seek the truth, but are only after winning one's own point of view, no matter it is wrong or right. We never realise that unless we own the very texture of our lives-good or bad, we shall never be ready to mend it. For centuries our brains have been indoctrinated that whatever fabric of life we have, it is His, and not ours. So, we have left our lives only in the back seat and in the back-gear. When there are both good and evil in this world, how can we accept all is His creation?

Hence, I agree to disagree with Voltaire, who opined that if God did not exist, it would be necessary to invent Him. Does Voltaire think that by merely inventing God human problems would be solved by themselves? I humbly hold that it is not, by inventing God, but merely by earnestly following the principle i.e., 'live and let live', we can solve almost all our problems. Our all problems are man-made, hence, we have to find out their solutions too. Let us invest humbly all our energy in finding their solutions, instead of merely prostrating before Him to do the needful. Even the great saint Sri Ram Krishna Parmahansa holds: "The wind of God's grace is forever blowing, but we have to hoist and unfurl the sails and the rest will be done by the wind itself." Do we not go on hoisting, unfurling the sails and prostrating before Him life long?

Today, when we see people like Christ, Galelio, Socratese, Tolstoy, Lincoln, Gandhi, and the like all over the world, either being exploited or butchered or ill-treated or even raped for centuries in the same world by our own fellow-beings, I humbly feel the opinion of the saint is nothing, but is either only a figment of his lofty imaginations or simply a product of his worshipping mood. Undoubtedly, he has been a great seeker of truth (a '*sadhak*'). Again, I accept that being a small fly, I know nothing about

God or soul. Seekers of truth have always been many and they will always be many. Even the great Buddha, Mahavir, Vivekanand and the like were all 'Sadhaks'. But all of them found truth at different places. While Buddha did accept both God and soul merely as superstitions, Mahavir too accepted God as a mere superstition, but he believed in soul. While Vivekanand believed in both of them. So, let us investigate the truth only as a goldsmith does. Let us be objective, impartial and unbiased, when we go to find the truth. If we are subjective even at such time or if we miss the objectivity, while searching the truth, the truth is apt to miss us, no matter whosoever we may be.

Perhaps, it is all due to his mental agony Anatole France said that he preferred to go to hell rather than heaven, because hell possesses grand people like Galelio and Tolstoy. How can then we ever believe that the wind of God's grace is forever blowing, as Sri Ram Krishna believed? Putting great persons in high esteem does not mean acceptance of everything, what they say.

Let no one think that I am provoking the people to take law in their own hands to create chaos and anarchy in the world. I do not at all aim at turning any one into an atheist (usual meaning a non-believer in God). Who am I to make anyone either an atheist or theist? I humbly believe everyone, being an architect of one's own destiny-good or bad, is apt to steer one's own ship of life and reach this or that shore; everyone is supposed to weave one's own web of life—good or bad—with his own knitpin to be good. I believe the day we attain the truth, we are sure to change ourselves and our world too. Otherwise, our life will remain like a stagnant pool, where only mosquitoes breed and filth or rubbish accumulates.

Hence, my humble submission is that in the illusion of God, we need not surrender ourselves to human tigers or human sharks or human 'bagulas', just to provide them a delicious human soup. Instead of becoming superstitious by believing in a Lord as the just emperor of the whole world, let us strengthen the state-machinery in order to provide everyone necessary protection at the time of need. I believe it is all foolish to wait for God's rescue-operation anymore. I hold that if we may or may not have faith in Him, it would not make much difference, but faith in oneself for making one's life is like a spar upon which the sail is bent. It is only then people's life can ever be navigable for them.

I again believe that there is God or no God, soul or no soul, but unless each architect of one's own destiny makes one's own brute out from one's own nature, the real peace and happiness in this world will ever remain like a mirage only. Of course, perfection here is utopian only. The pertinent question comes to my poor mind again and again as to why even well-read persons, who can defeat any person in their knowledge in the world suffer and live a life of miseries? Clearly, what these learned people have mugged up from different books or scriptures does not enter their own being or does not become a part and parcel of their own nature, and hence they lead a pitiable life. Dr. Radhakrishnan has clarified this point very beautifully here: " . . . you can learn from books, but what you learn from books, does not enter your being, does not become a part of your nature. You are not transformed . . .". Dr. Sahib reminds that even "great men battle with their own littleness, with their own selfishness . . .". So, let us no more behave like a blind person, who was wandering here and there in a dark room just to come out. Proper diagnosis of disease is more important to have a surer cure.

Even the smallest creatures all do—breathing, eating, resting etc. What is peculiar with human beings? We can think, read and write as extra activities. But being humans, if we go on behaving like brutes, and do nothing to build ourselves from within, it all goes in vain. So, building ourselves as good-humans is more important.

By thinking that nothing is possible in this world, except through His sweet grace has been our greatest hurdle. Has it made us less egoists or more humble actually? It has made us escapists only. Let us have our positive outlook to be happier in the prevailing circumstances, particularly, when we know we cannot change the people. Our positive mindset can ease the situation, if we are quite helpless to change them ourselves. Let us be sure that we are not leaving any stone unturned in doing good, what we can, wherever we are to be good. It is only then we may get true satisfaction of creativity, living a purposeful life, living not only for our ownselves, but for others too around at the same time, living a life having almost no chance, when we have convulsion of unnecessary anger, feeling of jealousy, cunningness, vengeance, wave of hatred, and bitterness etc. Let us remember that we are both our best friends and worst enemies. So, let us no more try to fire in the air in blind faith by putting our gun on His poor shoulders.

It is no use to have a negative thinking about others as to what they do and what they do not. Let us no more wear the negative spects to see others around. Let us no more develop the tendency of finding faults or weaknesses in others unnecessarily. Let us have only a positive thinking as to what we can do, and what we can really avoid doing anything which is not in the welfare of the people around, so that we may learn to live on our strength, and no more on others weaknesses or faults. For this let us learn to respond, and not to react to what other people think, feel and do, because we can change ourselves, and not others. An edifice erected on others faults is apt to be collapsed soon. Of course, we must be ready to help others, whatever we can. In case, we cannot do anything in a situation genuinely, we should not feel it much and get our minds tensed unnecessarily. So, instead of peeping into others premises, let us earnestly instrospect our own minds to know what we can, and what we cannot do actually to have almost a painless and stress-free world of our own. But can we do so without having faith in our own selves? So, let us have faith first in our own making of our lives—good or bad.

Let us remember Rome might have been built in days or years even, but to build or rebuild our entire mindset requires, atleast, our entire life. So, we should not be disappointed to see the few positive results of our few efforts. Let us keep our minds more tranquil, quiet than before with our positive outlook and efforts. Let us keep it into our minds that our positive thinking is apt to correct our entire body immunity-system, which remains disturbed, because we have negative thinking—like unnecessary anger, hatred, jealousy and feeling of vengeance. What is needed is a joyful mood in our life, if possible.

The main 'mantra' in this respect to remember is: If we cannot change our circumstances, let us then change our attitude towards them. Of course, this increasing brute in human nature, is definitely the main cause of our main tensions. We can change ourselves, provided we are earnest, but we cannot change others. We can only create awareness, as to how brute in our nature is dangerous for our own beings. So, let us have faith in our own doings of good to change ourselves and our world too. This all does not mean we are to compromise with evils. Quite not. Our positive attitude in life gives us positive energy and it sends positive vibes too for our happiness, because it does not allow the formation of dangerous chemicals, or hormones in our bodies and minds. For instance, if we have feeling of universal love, compassion, kindness, feeling of swim and sink together, we become naturally happy. It saves us from the impacts of dangerous chemicals, which form when we have negative thinking. So, why do we not be happier to see others happy genuinely and feel sorry to see others cordoned by troubles, especially when their own Karmas have nothing to do with them. Let us have no more a burning sensation to see others happier or enjoying life better than ours.

Let us no more be miserly in our due appreciation of others. Of course, we should not be hypocrites in our praise of others—to say something else than actually what we feel in our minds. Better to keep ourselves mum, if it is no use to disclose others weak points. But in case we are keen to know others point of weakness, instead of knowing others good points, we are apt to suffer ourselves. We can never found our own well-built edifice on others weaknesses. So, we are to share others happiness and sorrow as far as it is possible in life to have a meaningful life. We are to ape the good habits and attitude of others. Of course, we should not be the stooges of others at all. In case, we have no guts to say, the right as right, and wrong as wrong, keeping in view that it would all be unproductive, we should not say wrong as right hypocritically. Let us appreciate others whole-heartedly and sow the seeds of happiness here as well as there too, and consequently, make our life worth-living, worth-enjoying full of natural fragrance. For all this faith in one's own steering the ship of life is a prior must.

Nature has always been just with all creatures. In the world of nature justice is never delayed. Nature clears all our accounts of happiness or sorrows within no time. It provides us happiness then and there, when we think, feel and do good. But it makes us full of sorrow, whenever we suffer from hatred, jealousy, or have evil thinking or feeling about others, or do any evil to any of our fellow beings here or there. If there is any delay and justice is seldom met or never received, it is only either in human courts in this world, or in the kingdom of a hypothetical God.

To keep utmost faith in our ownselves means we should not think more about others, as to what they are or what they do. Faith in our ownselves means that we must go on meditating about, what we ought to think, feel and do in a given situation; so that we may not have to repent for our deeds later on. So, it is not the crisis of idea or matter, but the crisis of our positive thinking, feelings, and doings. In order to build ourselves from within especially, we should not mind much others bad commissions or omissions. If we do it, we would not be able to build our own selves. Of course, we must be more careful about such persons, who give us unnecessary tension in life. We shall have to keep the necessary distance with them just to avoid all of them in future. This distance does not mean we start hating such persons or we start wishing evil for such persons in their lives. That will all be unproductive, meaningless and inhuman. Let us have our own way, and let them have their own.

Consumerism has been the main cause of our sufferings. People, who think that it is like a balm to them, are living under illusions only. If we are good from within, let's have faith, we are sure to be free from our main shackles of unnecessary stresses and tension. Of course, we cannot leave the world, but we must not keep the world all times in our minds for peace. World is only a means (necessary) to an end. The end is human welfare at large. Mere worshipping of God, as we have faith in Him, won't help us much.

Faith in oneself also means that we have the good option before us of chanting or singing or looking at inspiring faces for good, or even enjoying buds or flowers in a blooming mood in a green well-maintained decent garden full of springs for our good physical and mental health. Both our mental anxieties and negativity in life leads us to having all types of ailments and even cancerous growth. Music blows over our fear, anxieties, negative thinking or suicidal attitude even from our lives. It acts like a missile of peace, happiness, respite. It has a deep impact on our minds from within. It helps us to be in a joyful meditative mood and makes our depression run away like a foreign element. It makes us full of hope and strength. Even in our moments of acute grief and anger, if we recite our favourite songs, poems, prayers, we dissolve or subside our negative emotions. But this is all possible, when we have faith in making our own life—good or bad ourselves. Does not the poem of Frost infuse new blood, even in dry bones? Some people want to keep themselves always in a weeping mood, and it is strange that they hope to be happier by shedding tears without any reason. Why to invite sorrow?

But let no one live under the mistaken belief that these songs, prayers, poems or 'mantras' can ever change the brutes as men themselves. That is why, Swami Vivekanandji rightly says," we always forget that religion does not consist in hearing talks, or in reading books, but it is a continuous struggle, a grappling with our own nature . . ." (On page 24-26 Vol. 4 *Swamiji's Works*).

It all does not mean to overlook what is actually happening around our world, or lose awareness as to what this world is and how people behave or misbehave actually with their fellow beings. We are not supposed to shut our eyes or ears to know the world, what it is. Let us be careful to avoid doing evil, what we can, and what we must, being humans.

Mistakes and failures are natural in everybodys life. Of course, we must be careful, lest they should be repeated again. Swami Vivekanandji too advises us: "Never mind failures. They are quite natural".

When we talk to have utmost faith in making of our own life—good or bad by our ownselves, we presuppose to have higher values in our lives too. Why? Because the fabric of thoughts, feelings and our doings is mainly designed either beautiful or ugly by the values we, the architects of our own destinies, cherish. As our values are our very thoughts, feelings and our doings in our lives too would change accordingly.

It is due to these values the very behaviour of Ram-Ravana, Krishna-Duryodhana, and Gandhi-Hitler was directly opposite to each other even in similar circumstances. Did not Gandhi and Subhash differ on how to achieve freedom in the same circumstances? Why do we not all cherish higher values in life? Because in spite of knowing the truth, we have no desired will and consciousness to dissolve our higher values into the entire net of our behaviour. So, unless the desired changes in our value-system and will power take place side by side, a change in our individual life and in the entire web of the world, what we as human-spiders weave with our own knitpins, is not possible. So, for a human revolution, the human higher values and their strong will-power to act accordingly are decisive factors. So, what we learn or see or experience good in life, let us make it a part of our own being, let us try to induce it into our nature just to build ourselves as better human beings. We are to transform our good knowledge into our actions.

Peace of our mind is directly attached with our higher values in life. Peace, undoubtedly, is a state of our minds. Even poor people can attain this state, while the so-called affluent people may or may not. In this respect, let us know the view of Dr. Arthur B. Cody, Prof. of Philosophy, California State University. He spoke on "The Crisis of Affluence in the US" at the India International Centre on 9th January, 1973. He said: "I was struck by seeing very poor people in India with happy faces," whereas in the United States, despite the capacity of almost every citizen to have things, there is a terrible loneliness, a great boredom". The recurrent-theme in the US is "there must be more to life than this", which leads to divorces, sexual excuses, mad-buying and purchasing, but still the dissatisfaction continued, he said. The lack of personal dignity and self-respect led to petty thieving, shop-lifting even by doctors, lawyers and teachers . . ." "There is no family life in America," he continued, "no community obligations and no rights or responsibilities between children and adults." Dr. Cody blames money for the "terrible freedom" in so far as it is easy to "buy temporary, immediate solutions of all problems." We never realise peace is not a commodity, and we cannot buy it. We can have it only from within and not without. Can we have peace without having faith and higher values in us? Why to blame money? Why not our minds for our vices? Can we ever shirk from our responsibilities in this respect?

This is all the result of the magic of their values in life alongwith the faith the people of US particularly have centred round 'money' and 'things'—as their real gods and goddesses. Unfortunately, both the values of life and faith of the whole world have been now dangerously infected. Today we find the same values and the same faith being put in the highest esteem of the people everywhere. Today we see people both from the West and the East sailing in the same boat of values and faith in their lives. So, their market more or less has become dangerously global. If there is a difference, it lies merely with the people of the place. Thus, the disease, being chronic and globalised, is common everywhere more or less, but strange nobody, except the few, are taking this cancerous growth very seriously indeed!

The net result of these values and faith is that we can, undoubtedly buy most of the things, we like with our money, what we have, but we cannot buy mental peace. Surely, we can buy the most fluffy mattresses to lie on them at night, but can we buy sleep and peace of mind in the market? Do we ever care and realise that civilisation does not consist in the multiplication of our wants, but in their voluntary reduction? In case we do not care to reduce our wants, we are sure to behave like their slaves, and no more their masters. Then we are sure to talk about God, but behave like devils.

For peace of our minds or to weave a different web of our lives, we shall have to remove the design of 'exclusive self' from our knittings as human spiders. We have no alternative, except to remove our old attitude of getting all our comforts and luxuries fulfilled, no matter 'how' and that too without caring for others around at the same time. Peace can be had only by living a meaningful, purposeful and creative life with a higher mission. If we do not care for peace, peace too would not care for ourselves in its turn. The main output of these dismal values of faith in life will be all-round disappointment and dismay alongwith suicidal tendencies. Human life has a purpose. Man cannot live by bread, comforts and luxuries alone. If we fail to have that purpose in our lives, we are to die not as spiritually-starved, but people having no spiritual appetite. The main trouble of these values and faith is that today, leaving apart some exceptions here or there, we have definitely appetite for pleasures in life, but more or less no appetite for peace, with the result we seek peace in our old attitude i.e., if 'we have one thing to-day, we want more tomorrow'. We are the victims of our own consumerism. Perhaps, we may live for sometime without 'anything' or any 'thought', but not without any apetite for peace. We're to be choked without it and die. Today we have a living death only.

Both peace and happiness will ever remain our mirage, so long we put these dismal values alongwith no faith in ourselves in high esteem. Again, we can have peace from within and not without. Of course, all of us need a cosy and comfortable house and life. But do we ever care that our end of life is peace of mind, and not these glorious bungalows and luxurious life? They are only a necessary means to an end and not an end in themselves. Why to identify our lives with them? Why to be then their slaves and not masters only?

Many Americans are now disillusioned and bored according to a new book '*State of the Nation*'. This illusion will go on increasing, so long we do not have the earnest urge not only for our own living, but for the living of others too at the same time around. The report confirms that the old conception of the people that the more you have these worldly things, the more you have mental peace has been fallacious. The old belief that 'poverty breeds contempt' essentially too is fallacious. In fact, for real peace we need a different mindset, a different attitude of our minds with an utmost urge to achieve the goal, i.e., 'live and let live' side by side. The peace is neither possible essentially in acute poverty, nor in acute prosperity, but within a mindset, which has a definite higher purpose of life essentially. Material progress to a considerable extent too is a must, but for peace to identify our lives with more and more material possession has been a grave mistake, what we have been committing for ages. Let the people neither of the East, nor from the West ape each other by overlooking the goal of life, i.e. peace.

Let us remember that materially glutton people are apt to lose their spiritual appetite, is more or less now a certainty. This shows that the womb of peace is neither the philosophy of 'eat drink and be merry', nor the idea of snatching others properties, but the philosophy of giving and sharing with others around, what we have actually. In case, we have nothing with us to share with genuinely, though we have an earnest desire to do so, we should not mind much our helplessness. But let us note it down that a rudderless ship can never reach its main destination. A rudderless life is no life at all. It is like a life on a unchartered-sea only. Let us have then faith that we can attain peace by building ourselves from within and not by being materially glutton. We cannot have it merely by performing this or that ritual or dogma even.

Mr. Mukand Goswami in his good article 'statistics do not lie, money cannot buy happiness' in the column 'Meditations' in *Hindustan Times* of 18-5-2002 questions: "what is the happiest place in the world?" In this context, he refers to a recent survey and report. "According to the recent research led by the London School of Economics, the happiest place in the world is, would you believe, Bangladesh. Interestingly, the United States came in at 46th place in the world Happiness survey, with Britain at the 32nd mark . . . India came in fifth . . . Thus, although the British have twice the amount of money they did 40 years ago, their perceived quality of life has not improved. In fact, it has decreased, the survey tells us . . . The Gita confirms that 'one whose happiness is within, who is active and rejoices within, is the perfect mystic" . . . Meditation does not mean other worldly contemplation or concentration on a distant future. It means happiness in this life . . . There is no happiness in simply thinking about God all day . . . Is that not the same kind of escapism . . . On the other hand, we know we can be happy with good jobs, lots of money, T.V., pizza, icecream, and by seeing our favourite films."

In fact, rather I myself am amazed to read this report about the happiest place, released by London School of Economics. Why? Because according to my humble opinion the real seat of happiness or peace is not any place, we live at or the jewellery or clothes, we wear, but our mind. No doubt, we can have more pleasure in our lives with better jobs, lots of money, T.V., pizza, burger, icecream, by seeing our favourite films, by having a husband or wife, we like etc. etc. Even merely by prostrating before a hypothetical God throughout the whole day is not the surer road to our happiness and peace. Of course, it has led us to our dangerous escapism from our duties and responsibilities occasionally. If we cannot attain peace of our minds simply by meditating about worldly comforts and pleasures, we cannot attain it simply by meditating about other worldly matters even, but simply by changing our mindset for good. But faith in oneself for it is a must.

In fact, a place never feels happiness or sorrow in itself, and it never delivers us happiness by itself generally. It all does not mean if, hypothetically speaking, we reach near the sun, it would not burn us. I only mean that a place would not grant us happiness or sorrow by itself. It can give us pleasure. In a nutshell, happiness is concerned with our world within and not without. It is a state of our mind. It is more concerned with our mindset, we have made. Hence, nobody can give warranty that every person is bound to be happier in New York or in Bangladesh, or at Ayodhya or Vrindaban or Mecca or Madina, or in Vatican city or at Amritsar or in an abode of God. One may or may not be. Our 'rishis' were happy even when they lacked their basic necessities with them. What to talk of sages, our brave Maharana Pratap lived in the forest on leaves for the country. Even then he was happier, because he had a higher mission in his examplary life to fulfill. Do not we know our sages dressed themselves in rags, never housed themselves in grand bungalows, but only in huts, never travelled by the luxurious cars, but preferred to walk on foot? Did they wear jeans, or listen to Pop music, or participate in rock-en-roll, etc., like us? Of course, so many such things were not there in the existence in their times. My point to stresss over here is that they were very very simple in their habits of life. They cared much to build their minds on desired lines.

By money we can buy pleasure in life, but not peace. It all does not mean the denial of this world at all. Let us live in the world, but let the world of our evils no more make their oasis in our minds. Let us have our necessities, comforts and even luxuries, but let us live here like their masters and not slaves. We should not identify our lives with the world. But can we ever be masters without having faith in our own good steering?

In fact, peace and happiness are more concerned with the quality of our lives, we have, and not with the quality of living. Quality of living may provide us pleasure, but not happiness. We feel more pleasure today, because we can complete our journey of days in hours. So, what is needed is to change our very culture of life altogether, instead of what the Pope once called "The culture of death," if we really want to change ourselves and our world. Let us no more follow culture of death.

Being architects of our own destinies, if we convincingly follow the principle: 'live and let live' in our lives earnestly, we are sure to get peace, because we can be happier and more peaceful by behaving well with all the living gods and goddesses. Let us remember that cockroaches of the gutters too live, but they live and die for themselves. Men too live and do all the activities, what even the smallest creatures do, but they live a meaningful and purposeful life, not only for themselves, but for the life of others around. But to have a life of quality, all of us need to change our mindset.

But for all this faith in one's own making of one's life-good or bad-is a prior necessity indeed. Discontentment in itself as a word is not always bad. Materially glutton are never contented, because Law of Diminishing Utility seldom applies to them due to their peculiar frame of minds, and thus they live like slaves of matter and suffer lifelong. Of course, they may have pleasure, but not peace in their lives. But spiritual discontentment is of an entirely different nature. One who fortunaely has it, lives not like a slave but master only, because his desires are minimum, and he never hankers after them. He does not live for his desires, but he satisfies them only to live. His goal of life is never to satisfy his this or that unending desires, but only to raise the level of his consciousness and to elevate himself at the higher and higher altitude of his life day by day to achieve happiness and peace.

I humbly hold that mere '*Ram naam jap*' is not our essential elevator to take us to the real heaven, but when we have a strong passion to be good men throughout 24 hours a day. When we have our routine work, when we eat, sleep and wake up, the same passion remains quite active in our minds to be good men. The passion unbolts the door of heaven for us. Can we ever forget the immortal words of Christ, who once said: "A camel may pierce and enter the hole of a needle, but I am sure brutes can never enter heaven, whatever it is?" If God is there, can He ever keep His stooges in His kingdom, who keep Ram or Allaha, or God or 'guru' on their lips, but a knife to kill their own fellow beings in their minds? To be good men or to oust the brute, from our minds, we do not need at all to shave our poor heads, or to wear the mask of a 'sadhu'. Without having a strong passion to be good men, and without making our full efforts to satisfy this pious desire in life, we may repeat 'Ram-Ram' or 'roti-roti', practically it has the same significance, and it makes no difference. We can have peace of mind by being happy to see others happy and by feeling pain to see others around in trouble. Those, who behave merely like mendicants, and make their God, if He is somewhere, as a means to achieve some worldly pleasure in life, they get illusion, but neither their God, nor peace of their minds. It is certain that neither we can change our mindset, nor our world, and nor can we attain God even without having full faith in our own captancy of the ship of our lives

Let us be sure that here nothing is pre-determined by the Lord. There is nothing inevitable indeed. Because our life or world is, what we make it-good or bad. Hence, there is no question to accept our old faith i.e., '*Vinash, Kale, Vipreet Buddhi* . . .' If God is there, He cannot be a despot to make blur our vision and put a veil of '*agyan*' on our *buddhi* or '*vivek*' or power of discrimination in a particular situation. It is like putting the cart before the horse. Let us realise that those nations, or those empires or civilisations or those human personalities, who have been turned to ashes, and those who have fallen in their lives it was not because of the wish of some deity, but because of their approach to achieve this or that in life, or to do this or that without applying their poor 'buddhi' or 'vivek' or power of discrimination, what nature has given to them as a privileged gift only. It is only our quack's approach, which declares in ignorance that the main cause of our rise or fall lies with the will or wish of some supernatural force. So earlier we make ourselves responsible that we rise or fall in life not due to the sweet or sour will of some deity behind the curtain, but due to our own good or bad commissions or omissions, the better. It is most essential to show the right light to our own tottering ships of lives at the earliest possible. Let us remember that bad people can never hope to make a good world, and good people can never turn their world into a bad one. It is no use to make God a scapegoat for our own evil behind the bush of '*Vinash Kale Viprit Buddhi*'. Unless we are sure about someone's past, it is all foolish to scratch one's past. Of course, our life or world, what it is may or may not be a one man show for all times.

It is our vicious *buddhi*, which causes our downfall. Good *buddhi* can cause our rise only. Only fools try to shift their own responsibility for their rise or fall both out of their ignorance to the poor shoulders of some hypothetical deity or some adverse situations or human personalities, just to make their own skin safe. It is only fools declare: whatever has happened, is happening or would happen in future too, that is all predetermined by God, the almighty. Even Bhishm Pitama had to accept this reality ultimately, while having conversation with Draupadi in the Mahabharata war. Instead of escaping from his own responsibility for what he did and what he omitted to do, he accepted it as his own fault as a good gesture to give the right turn to the events in history. Again, faith in oneself in making our own life, what it is, is most essential.

But superstition in our life is like a back gear. It is in this context, Edmund Burke, the great historian spoke the truth. He said, "superstition is the religion of feeble minds". Why? Because they weave myths by their nature, wherever they are. I recollect what Oscar Wilde said regarding the people of the world in general. . . . "all of us are in the gutter, but some of us are looking at the stars."

Thus, it is the cowards, weak or superstitious, who say whatever our fate is, is predetermined by some deity, but brave, strong and men of reason will ever declare from their tops, 'They made, they make, and they shall ever make their own fate or destiny themselves'. By removing these 'they' or 'I' or 'me' or 'my' or 'mine' from the scene of life, we shall only kill their minds, while the need of the hour is only to bury the little-mindedness of the minds of 'they', 'I' or 'me' etc. The real womb of our superstition is our ignorance of the universe, the nature and our ownselves. So, let us know all these first. It is this knowledge, which is to bring us out of our woods and give us right direction further.

Our generation is born with worry lines on the foreheads of most of us, since we take birth. The suggestions and solutions, what these religious 'pandits' suggest, are mostly outdated, and sometime they are worse than even disease itself. But if we really want to see a change in our life and the world side by side, we have no alternative, except to change our mindset first. Faith does not mean blind faith. We have to make our faith and outlook both scientific and spiritual.

Huxley, the great evolutionist believed that the whole universe including all planets, satellites, the moon, the earth—all are self-evolved entities. If we throw a ball in the air, it comes down on its own, not because some deity wills it so, but because of the Law of Gravitation of Newton. It is also a scientific fact that due to centrifugal force the planets revolve round the sun at a particular speed and do not collide with each other. According to scientific investigations, the earth has been moving eternally on its own axis with a speed of one thousand miles per hour. The scientists hold that the sun has been burning like a huge ball of fire with a heat of 92,000 F. And if by chance 'its' heat goes down up to 6000 F, it is to cause so much cold atmosphere on earth that everything would be frozen, and in case its heat goes up than the present 92,000 F°, it is apt to cause so much warmth on earth that every living being is apt to be extinct then. So, let us believe in science and not in superstition.

Scientists tell us had the moon not been existing at a distance of 2,50,000 miles away from earth, the tides in the ocean would have been so heavy that the whole earth would have been dipped in the ocean and thus all the living beings on earth too would have been extinct.

Let the theologists no more create or produce divine hands or divine wish behind this extinction. They say God is the cause of all causes in the world. Well, there are people of both divine and devil nature made by themselves in this world in reality. If according to these creationists, God is the cause of good people, who is the cause of people of devil's nature? How can God create devils here, if at all we hypothetically accept there is creation? Let us behave like humans, and not like a trojan horse anymore. One may or may not believe in God, but everyone will have to believe in nature and science. Science does not take anything for granted. It believes in looking at the universe with the spects of why, what, where and who.

Everything in nature looks like a wonder. The very human being is the greatest wonder on earth, but science believes that he is evolved and can never be created. Our brain works like a super computer to conrol our whole body organism. Our heart throbs one lakh times per day and pumps five to twenty litres of blood at times per minute through a 1,50,000 kilometre network of vessels. So, science does not believe in speculations, but facts. People wonder how coal and petroleum are formed in the womb of earth. If we examine a piece of coal minutely, we may see on it the imprint of a stem or leaf, which tells the whole story of its formation by itself. It is a scientific fact that coal was formed by the slow compression of buried forests, which covered large parts of the earth continents in vast fresh water swamps about 30 million years ago. For this coal is called a fossil fuel. As regards petroleum, the word is derived from the Greek words 'Petra' means rock and 'Oleum' means oil. It means oil from rocks. It is said that petroleum was formed and preserved in its crude state in the earth from the dead remains of microscopic marine plants, which settled in muddy sediments at the bottom of the sea millions of years ago. For only ignorant people they are all the creations of God. So, let us no more behave like frogs in the well. For all this faith in science too is essential.

Nobody cares when a small person, made of an ordinary clay like me, says something, but when human giants like Swami Vivekanand too are seen having mystic flights, every one must wonder to see that. Swami Vivekanandji says, "We now see that the various forms of cosmic energy, such as matter, thought, force, intelligence and so forth, are simply the manifestations of that cosmic intelligence (God), as we shall call it henceforth, the supreme Lord. Everything that you see, feel, or hear, the whole universe, is His creation, or . . . is His projection; or . . . is the Lord Himself. It is He who is shining as the sun and the stars, He is the mother earth. He is the ocean Himself . . . In one word, we are born of Him, we live in Him, and unto Him we return". (On page 211 Vol. 2 *Swamiji's Works*)

This all shows that it is a very high flight of that great saint in the ocean of his 'bhakti' only. But can we ignore scientific facts? Science does not believe in seeing nature with glorifying glasses. In the eyes of science, He, himself is man's greatest creation or projection. To draw a grand caricature of God as Swamiji has done here, is of little value in the arena of science indeed.

Human mind can be the highest altitude in the world. It is higher than The Mount Everest even. When Yudhishtir told Yaxya that man did not know even after knowing the truth, he meant that we know the truth, what it was, but we lacked the proper will and conscience to live upto it. In other words, we fail to allow the truth to enter our being. So, let us know ourselves first.

Dr. Chakravarti, the US microbiologist, who came to India to attend 'India Science Congress' in Delhi (as printed in *Hindustan Times* on 7-1-2001) was asked in an interview:

Q: Do you believe that life was created by God or some spiritual power or it is simply the product of evolution?

A: I personally believe in the process of evolution. I think we are creatures of evolution. We develop from simple micro-organism to the state we are in today. Our brain is more complex than what it was a hundred thousand of years ago and will be very different a 100 thousand years hence . . ."

This is all about the magic of evolution, and not the magic of creation. But, you see, who cares for truth and facts in this world? Why? Again, because we almost all lack the requisite faith in our ownselves, while we believe in Him, who has been unknown to us since His conception.

People give this plea that one may or may not believe in that 'God is truth', but one will have to believe in 'Truth is God'. But let us remember that truth may have only eyes, but no feet to walk and no wings to flutter of its own. So, truth by itself can neither create, nor sustain, and nor destroy.

Swami Vivekanandji rightly says that for worshipping the devotees need a mental image. Although I do not know why people worship, except to please Him by repeating parrotwise that He is the creator, sustainer and destroyer or doer of all things in our lives, which He is not actually? Otherwise, no parrots have so far turned themselves into men, simply by repeating Ram-Ram, Allaha-Allaha, God, 'Guru' etc., and no parrots have become less egoists by repeating these names simply. Of course, Swamiji is right to hold: "My brethern we can no more think about anything without a mental image". . . (on page 16 Vol. 1 *Swamiji's Works*) "It does not make much difference whether these images are inside or outside the mind. We are all born idolators . . . who can get beyond it? Only the perfect man, the God man. The rest are all idolators" Temples or churches, books or forms are simply the kindergarten of religion to make the spiritual child strong enough to take higher steps . . . We hear so many talking about God and soul, and all the mysteries of the universe, but if you take them one by one, and ask them "Have you realised God? Have you seen your soul?—How many can they say they have?" (On page 43 Vol. 2 *Swamiji's Works*). I humbly hold that we can see not God, but good in life like Buddha only through meditation. We can be inspired for thinking, feeling and doing good not necessarily through worshipping any image, but through our meditation. No doubt, any image, which inspires us to think, feel and do good in life, should be welcome indeed.

But the tragedy is that these images of God, rituals and dogmas, concerning some religion, are meant for spiritual toddlers to go higher and higher, but not for grown up. What mischief we have been playing is that we behave, as if we are eternal toddlers, because we go on using these divine crutches under our armpits and never want to stand on our own feet. Why? Because we have been suffering from the age old chronic disease i.e., the 'psyche of weak and low.' In fact, with this psyche like a muddle-headed person we feel, as if we have been travelling and travelling, but it is only our illusion. The fact is that we remain permanently static. Today even we are there from where we started our voyage of worshipping God. Our tale is not still straight. It is still curved even after life long worship. Have we become better human beings or less egoists necessarily. No, certainly not. I don't deny its exceptions here or there.

Bertrand Russel in his '*unpopular Essays*' holds on page 92: "We are told that sin consists in disobedience to God's commands, but we are also told that God is omnipotent. If He is, nothing contrary to His will can occur; therefore when the sinner disobeys His commands, He must have intended this to happen . . . If everything happens in accordance with God's will, God must have wanted Nero to murder his mother, therefore, since God is good, the murder must have been a good thing. From this argument there is no escape". "How are we to know what really is God's will?"

Frankly speaking, it has been our age old illusion only that God has been omnipotent and omnipresent. Because had He been so, none of us would have been able to commit any evil anywhere. In fact, the creationists have been caught in their own net, woven by themselves. They have no answer to reply that when the God is omnipresent and omnipotent, why are the evils multiplying in this world?

It is due to this reason Buddha accepted God as only a superstition.

I think the right solution of the problem is: That our life or the world, whatever it is—good or bad—we either individually or collectively make it. And it is only we who can turn hell into heaven, if at all we are earnest and sincere to attain the goal. Implicitly so long we, the architects of our own destinies—either good or bad—allow the rule of our matter over our minds, we won't be able to establish peace in this world. Of course, our mind is the highest stage of the development of matter, but we must remember that mind is more than matter. In fact, mind is the most conscious matter. No doubt, we cannot help in life without matter, but the moment instead of becoming the real masters of our matters, we become their slaves, our life gets into trouble. So, what is needed is that we should not at all act like a pawn in matter's game. Otherwise, we are apt to be matter's slaves.

Keeping this fact in view, we can say that our every Ram-'naam' or every idea or matter or activity is a 'bhog', not 'yoga', if we do not use them in becoming better human beings day by day. If we do not aim at it, they become mere sources of our additional ego only. By 'idea' 'we mean the main-product of our minds. And by matter it means, which occupies space and mass, or material world.

We must not overlook the fact that whenever there is any conflict or contradiction or tussel between two forces, concerning our ideas or matters, it is all man-made; they are not the integral parts either of them. Of course, movement will always be there. The word 'dialectical' has been derived from the Greek word 'Dialego', which means conflict or contradiction or tussel between two opposite forces, but we should not think that such conflict or contradiction is inevitable. Being architects of our own destinies, if we are far-sighted, we can avoid it.

It is no use to hijack God in and out of human affairs simply according to our convenience or whims. It was simply out of our ignorance and fear about this universe and nature, we were forced to conceive God in our minds to infuse the necessary confidence in our minds. But fear is a good servant, but bad master. Whatever evils we have been doing in His name, it is all, because the same fear has become now our master.

Today the same God is being exposed, and the fear of God too is declining, and, consequently, the graph of crimes and sins too is going up and up day by day. In fact, we do not need God-fearing people, but evil-fearing with proper understanding. Today, we have reached a very critical juncture. On the one hand, God is exposed and on the other, we have failed to create the sense, as to why should we not commit any evil knowingly at least. This danger is imminent. Only men-making education and religion can come to our rescue in this context.

In the same context, it is relevant to quote Swami Vivekanandji: "Foolish parents teach their children to pray, 'O Lord Thou has created the sun for me and the moon for me,' as if the Lord has had nothing else to do then to create everything for these babies. Do not teach your children such non-sense". Swamiji's advice is O.K. for foolish parents to follow. But does not Swamiji himself teach us? ". . . It is He who is shining as the sun and the stars, He is the mother earth. He is the ocean Himself . . . In one word we are born of Him, we live in Him, and unto Him we return." (On page 211 Vol. 2 *Swamiji's Works*) To see Swami ji's plea we should not be surprised, if foolish parents teach all such nonsense to their children. The question is: why do we witness such superstitious flights even by human giants? Because we all lack faith in our ownselves alike.

It is all in fear of God the tendency of hijacking of God in human affairs has ben increasing. It is only in fear of God we want to surrender each and everything to Him, except our exclusive self. Have we become less egoists or more humble by this activity? What we need the most is our conviction about the following principle, i.e., 'Live and let live'. This comes not necessarily through prostrating before Him, but through our meditation.

Whenever, we find ourselves cordoned by troubles and problems, We at once try to gaze at stars over our heads, as if they are the causes of our troubles, without realising that we rise, because we make ours rise possible, and if we fall, it is we make our fall possible. It is foolish to put our fate in the dock. There is no fate, pre-determined. We are the true architects of our own destinies—good or bad.

Can we ever forget what Brutus said: "The fault does not lie in the stars over our heads, but in our ownselves."?

The important thing to remember in this respect is that neither we can change the stars over our heads, nor they can ever change our lives. It is all beyond the domain of humans as well as stars to do this. The stars, the planets, the satellites, etc., all perform their usual duties on time as per the schedule, no matter we worship them or not. If there is any trouble anywhere, it is foolish on our parts to seek the cause of it in the stars, instead of in our minds fundamentally. So, our minds are to be overhauled, if we really want to change ourselves and our world.

The love, affection, envy, sympathy and the like are products of good human minds, and the war, hatred, jealousy, vengeance and the like are the products of filthy and vulgar human minds. Let us remember mind is made of the same atom in both the cases. Whether mind loves or hates depends on what mindset or the attitude of mind one has got. Whether our minds are stinky or otherwise, depends on the architects of human destinies. Unless these architects weed out the seeds of hatred, jealousy from their minds, the question of attainment of world peace will ever remain a mirage, no matter how much arms and ammunitions and bombs are thrown away into the sea, or no matter how many armistice we sign together.

If we change our faith from these so-called supernatural entities and instead of asking them to do this or that for ourselves, we are honestly busy in changing our mindset and attitude of life just to change ourselves and the world, it would be better for all of us. But being foolish we go on expecting from these natural phenomenon, living far away from us distance wise to do this or that for all of us. So long the dismal belief is not changed, the expectations from human beings to be better humans is futile indeed. The trouble arises, because we care for the hypothetical God and His abode much more than the living gods and goddesses and their minds—the living temples. Let us then remember what rightly Mr. Kahlil Gibran says about the matter in question: "Your daily life is your temple and your religion. Whenever you enter into it take with you your all."

Here is the right version of Swami Vivekanandji about the will of men, and how much important it is in determining the very fabric of human society. He says, "All the actions that we see in the world, all the movements in human society, all the works that we have around us, are simply the display of thought, the manifestation of the will of man. Machines, or instruments, cities, ships or men of war all these are simply the manifestations of the will of man." (On page 30 Vol. 1 *Swamiji's Works*).

Let us remember that the above statement, what Swamiji has given was only, when Swamiji found himself nearer to the very realities of human life, but let us see how Swamiji changes himself, when he flights in the world of his 'bhakti' only. Here Swamiji talks about in just his reverse gear. He holds: "The second point is that there is a God in the universe. It is not true that the universe is drifting and stands in need of help from you and me. God is ever present therein, He is undying and eternally active and infinitely watchful. When the whole universe sleeps, He sleeps not; He is working incessantly: all the changes and manifestations of the world are His . . . This world will always continue to be a mixture of good and evil . . ." (On page 80 Vol. 1 *Swamiji's Works*).

In the same tune of 'bhakti' Swamiji says the similar things. This is all the magic of faith, what one has got at a particular time. He asks: 'who would live a second, who would breathe a second in this universe, if that blessed one were not filling it?' If He is such a supreme remote-control supernatural power that we cannot live even a second, and we cannot breathe even a second without His mercy, then the question of 'the manifestation of the will of men' in different things and thoughts of this human world, what Swamiji talks about on page 30 Vol. 1 in his own works does not arise at all. We have no choice either to accept 'the will of men' or 'the sweet will of God'. How can we continue with this duplicity in this world? How can we befool all the people all the time by saying two things entirely different from each other? Is it not strange that both these versions of human history are the brain-children of Swami Vivekanandji?

It was Swami Vivekanandji who said: " . . . (they) have fabricated and circulated the most horrible lies about me in this country and behind my back. Americans will never stoop to such meanness." (on page 329 Vol. 8 *Swamiji's Works*).

If really God is caring our lives without any bias, who was ordering those fabricated and the most horrible lies for circulation about this great human giant? Who was trying to stab him in his back like this? Does it not look quite strange that still Swami Vivekanandji holds the same view: "Now let me tell you—still there is a God, no joke. He is ordering our lives." (on page 330 Vol. 8 *Swamiji's Works*). Of course, we must pay due heed to him, when he advises us: "Stand on your feet and be men". (Swami Vivekanandji). I humbly hold that had we not used these divine crutches under our own armpits, we would not have behaved like eternal handicapped as we do.

Now the real bone of contention is if there is a God in the Universe, as Swamiji holds, and He is ever present, eternally active, infinitely watchful, working, incessantly without even a wink of sleep, and if all the changes and manifestations of the world are His and not men's, then where have these red-bloody pages of human history come from? How is it then under His nose even in broad day light human's exploitation, human's rape, human's butcheries, human's ill-treatment by their own human fellow-beings have been going on for ages in His kingdom? Some people may try to behave like that stupid ostrich by telling us that there is neither good, nor evil in this world, but thinking makes it so. It all does not mean we can ever deny the fact that the world will always remain a mixture of good and evil. May I know from Swamiji: whether these bloody pages of human history too are the manifestations of His Leela or play, as it has been depicted by His *bhakts*? Let us remember the way these *bhakts* treat the men, they have definitely turned men into His Master's pets, but not pets into men indeed.

It is our foregone conclusion that God may or may not need any human help, but we humans cannot help without helping each other in making our mutual lives—good or bad. If by chance we get a golden opportunity to help our brethern here in this or that respect, why to feel it a matter of any ego? Why do not we take it as a good opportunity to turn the brute out of our minds? Why not we feel obliged for the person, who has given us such an opportunity to set another good brick or stone slab in the construction of the edifice of our own lives. Let us learn this simple maths of our peaceful and happy life then at our earliest possible.

Money can buy us a decent bed and all types of pleasures possible in life, but not necessarily a sound sleep, books, but not necessarily mind to understand them, property and food, but not necessarily appetite, medicines but not necessarily health, a cosy house, but not necessarily home, all comforts and even luxuries, but not necessarily human culture, and human excellence. Let us decide: whether we are in a mood to die as evil men to leave the world a worse place to live in than before? Good or bad decision will ever be ours, because we are all the architects of our own destinies.

Let us accept the realities of our lives. That our life is full of odour these days. Why is it so? Because bad people are everywhere and, unfortunately, they have got the major say in making our life, what it is today. In fact, heaven never asks us: "what have you?" or "what do you wear?", or "what do you read or write?", but "what do you do?" "How do you think, feel and do in this world?" Heaven has nothing to do with the question: "What clothes do you make your Lords wear", but with "what clothes of your own thinking, feelings and doings you make the living gods and goddesses—your own sisters and brothers wear"? Thus, both heaven or hell is the product of human mind and human faith.

In this context, I dissent with Swamiji, who says "The path to truth or path of truth" is a contradiction. Truth is not distant. How can there be a path to it then? Truth is with you already . . ." (Swami Ram). I dissent. Becuase to know the path to truth is one thing, and to follow the path of truth in life is another. So long we do not follow the path of truth on this or that pretext, this distance remains. There are miseries in our lives, because we keep the truth quite distant from our actual life. We say something and do another. Why? Because our actual belief or faith lies with our doings, not with our sayings. So, there will ever be a path to truth, so long we do not track our lives on the path of truth. There is chaos in our life, because we have no-doubt, material investment, but we have investment in men at a very low-key.

From the angle of faith today our entire world needs again a Renaissance of the 14th century, when people came to realise that it was not any deity, but men were the true architects of their own destinies—good or bad. We need a simultaneous Reformation as well. But why both these? Because we are all to realise that with same mind, but with a different attitude, we can build a new world. My humble submission in this respect is that it is only through human revolution we can have a true revolution of wider meanings in the world.

In this context, it is again relevant to quote Swami Vivekanandji, who says, "until man's nature changes, the physical needs will always arise, and miseries will always be felt." (On page 53 Vol. 1*Swamiji's Works*).

The thing, what is material, and what is spiritual—is all based on our faith. Swami Vivekanandji clarifies: "what is material, and what is not? when the world is the end and God the means to attain that end, that is material. When God is the end and the world is only the means to attain the end, spirituality has begun" (on page 66 Vol. 6 *Swamiji's Works*). When we take God as good only, we can remove all our confusion.

It is no use to feel helpless anymore. We need not either to weep. Here is the life-giving dose of truth for all of us, what Swami Vivekanand wants to prescribe. He states: "We have wept long enough. No more weeping, but stand on your feet and be men. It is a man-making religion that we want . . . It is man-making education all round that we want. And here is the test of truth—anything that makes you weak physically, intellectually and spiritually, reject as poison; . . . Truth is strengthening . . ." "Give up these weakening mysticism and be strong". (On page 224-225 Vol. 3 *Swamiji's Works*). But I humbly hold that so long we go on believing that it is the God, who makes our life, what it is -good or bad- and so long we escape to own the baby-world, no matter the baby is beautiful or ugly—we are apt to feel paralysed physically, mentally and spiritually. By hijacking God in human affairs, instead of becoming less egoists, we become more escapists and inhuman even, because this whole philosophy makes us learn how to love the hypothetical God, no matter what happens to the living gods and goddesses. The biggest proof of it is that in the same house, where we prostrate before God to worship Him, especially the elders feel, as if they are parasites on their shoulders. Of course, exceptions are there. It is due to this hypocrisy we see homes for elderly people or Ashrams for elders' are being built just to face the problem of homeless in their homes in this modern world. All this brings us back to the old question: how can anyone love the God by hating the living gods and goddesses at the same time? But who cares for them, when our mind is full of fear of the so-called almighty God? Here it all does not mean I justify all the evil deeds, what these elders also do.

The devotees of God are proud of having their association with 'satya' here or there. When we sometime ask them as to 'where are you going? They respond with a great pride that they are going to '*satsang*'. Of course, it is a matter of great pride, if our association with 'satya' becomes permanent. But the question is what does the 'satsang' mean? Literally 'satsang' means association with 'satya' or truth. The question again arises: what is *satya*? Does 'satya' essentially mean not telling lies? Or does '*asatya*' mean essentially telling lies? Of course, we should not tell lies, at least, for our own selfish interest or gain. But telling the truth is not an end in itself, but only a means to an end. And the end is human welfare at large. Thus, the welfare of the entire humanity is the greatest truth, we must aim at. We are supposed to protect the welfare of all beings as far as it is possible. If we are trying to have the welfare of the people of the whole world through our thinking, feeling and doing, we are serving the cause of '*satya*', and we have the association with '*satya*' too. Otherwise, we are not.

This shows we should not mind, and we should not be fanatic regarding telling lies or truth. There is nothing eternal in this world, except the passion for the welfare of all beings as far as it is possible. This is the greatest 'Satya', we must always seek for. So, there is only one yardstick to decide a particular action of ours whether it is 'Satya' or Asatya'. To know it we must know whether that action in question serves the beings as a whole or not. If it does, it is a good means, to that good end. From this point of view mere recitation of Ram-Ram, Allaha, God or '*waheguru*' is not necessarily '*satsang*'.

In this context, let us remember that for some people like Gandhiji telling the truth can never be compromised, while for persons like Bertrand Russel telling the truth can be sacrificed for the welfare of the beings, as it is more important than the telling the truth. For Mr. Russel the welfare of the beings, was a greater 'satya' to be a better human being. Mr. Bertrand Russel holds rightly that he does not think he would have been a better human being, had he not lied in disclosing the facts about the very exact whereabouts of a fox to a hunter once in a forest. I also appreciate the approach of the philosopher in the context. Although we should not forget that Gandhiji too loved all human beings without any discrimination. It is all due to this fact, Gandhiji had withdrawn his Non-Cooperation Movement just to know some British police men being burnt alive at Charichaura. Only their line of approaches (the means) to achieve the end i.e., the welfare of beings, the greatest satya, were different. Like Mr. Russel, Gandhiji too would not have been happier to see the fox in question being killed by the hunter.

Sometimes rigidity, instead of becoming a blessing, becomes a curse. So, we should not—have our rigid approach to attain 'Satya' in life. Like Kabir, the great poet here too we see a different line of approach for achieving 'Satya' in the following couplet:

'Masjid to banali shabbhar mei
Iman ki hararat walon nei,
man apna purana papi hai
barson mei namaji ban naa saka'.

From this point of view it is nothing, but a gross blind faith, when a 'yogi', who lived in a cave, welcomed an animal, which bit him as only the 'Messenger of God'. Can a messenger of God ever even imagine to bite a 'yogi'? Does not the blind approach of the said 'yogi' in question put a premium on the vices of the people? (The case of this 'yogi' was referred by Swami Vivekanandji in his lecture). When we know nothing about God, how can we presume the messanger in question had come from Him?

Even Gandhiji wrote in '*Young India*' in 1924: "I do not say eschew violence in your dealings with robbers, or thieves or with nations that may invade India." He believed: "Where there is a choice between Cowardice and Violence—I advise violence." Gandhiji gave his consent to send Indian army to oust the '*mujahids*' (infiltrators), who entered Jammu Kashmir from Pakistan for the first time just to snatch Jammu and Kashmir by force from India. So, on this point Gandhiji was quite clear in his mind. How can we consider those 'mujahids' or people like Osama bin Laden as 'messaegers of God? The world is in a greater danger from fanaticism today.

So, let us beware of the dangerous paralytic effects of the age old philosophy on our mindset, as it has turned lions into simple mice, and a mighty nation into a sick nation, which has lost faith in itself. It is not at all an exaggeration to say that its effect on our minds and bodies have been more damaging than even cancer or AIDS and the like. It has atrophied us completely.

Beware of the false claims of these believers that the view 'His Master's pet dogs on a long leash' has made them more humble and less egoists. Is it not a fact that those, who prostrate before their divine Master out of sheer fear, are the same persons, whose minds start burning to see their fellow brothers and sisters even a bit happier? Of course, the few exceptions may be here or there.

Like the creationists, who believe whatever God does, does right, even in Italy people viewed: "Mussolini is ever right." When children used to come back home from their schools in Germany, their parents hailed them by telling: "Hail Hitler." Even Swami Vivekanandji had faith: ". . . In every being He lives, through all minds He thinks". How can ever God live in everything and thus think through Osama bin Laden's, or Veerappan's or Ranga-Billa's minds too? Let us remember Hitler and Mussolini might have become people's gods there, but god can never live either in Hitler or Mussolini or Osama bin Laden or Veerappan or Billa Ranga. No matter there is Vedanta or no Vedanta.

It has become quite common that while we love God, but hate the living beings. Swami Vivekanandji rightly regretted: ". . . in modern India the spirit of religion is gone, only the externals remain. The people are neither Hindus, nor Vedantists. They are merely don't-touchists; the kitchen is their temple and *Handi Bartaon* (cooking pots) are their 'devta' (object of worship)." (On page 439 Vol. 3 *Swamiji's Works*).

Let us believe that a hand in help is better than two hands together. Swamiji advised us: "Have faith in your destiny" (on page 445 Vol. 3 *Swamiji's Works*). To have faith in one's destiny means that our destinies—good or bad—are never born or pre-determined, but are actually made here by all of us concerned. Can anyone deny the fact that here both Ram-Ravana, Krishna-Duryodhana, and Gandhi-Hitler, who were contemporaries made their own destinies themselves quite differently, simply by their own commissions or omissions? Even if we accept it hypothetically that there is creation, then the question arises how can a Lord, being the sole-creator creates both Ram-Ravana, Krishna-Duryodhana and Gandhi-Hitler? No sensible person can ever believe that it was only His 'Leela' or play. We cannot accept them as His 'puppets'. Who would accept this belief that a Ratnakar became a Balmiki, a great saint, because of His 'Leela'? May I know how many roles does the Lord play? Let us remember so long a dog does not know that the bone it licks is its own and the blood it sucks too is its' down, it goes on and on relishing it under mere illusion. The point to ponder over here is, if Arjuna was Krishna's '*nimit*' in the battle field, then whose 'nimit' Duryodhana was? Did not He fail to apply His remote control on Duryodhana? Otherwise, why do we call Him as an almighty?

Krishna might have said in the *Gita* that He has been creating endlessly, but scientists believe that no one, no matter how big one is, can ever create anything out of nothing, as there is no creation, but evolution only. Had He been the sole-creator, why did He create a human world, which has been painted with human red-blood too? How can the world ever be His projection only? Because it contains both good and evil. Some people have faith that God created only good, and men created evil. Should then we believe that there are two creators—one, who creates good, another creates evil, if at all there is creation? Being bewildered most of us believe that there must be some creator of this complexed world. But the question is if there must be a creator of all creations, then who created the Lord Himself? In fact, the whole belief regarding creation is against the law of Cause and Effect.

Jacques Monod, the French Nobel laureate in his book "*Accident and Necessity*" published in 1972 believes that man is the result of an accidental genetic mutation in the process of DNA replication in biological evolution, and consequently, there can be no purpose in his creation. This is all for those, who stand by science and reason and no more by any superstition and illusion.

I earnestly believe that no-doubt we cannot create a world, but if we almost all inculcate the habit of thinking, feeling and doing good, what we can, wherever we are, we can definitely build a better world in which everyone will follow the principle 'Live and let live at the same time, and, consequently, we can change the world, what Marx aimed at.

It is my firm faith that had we, instead of making God the very nucleus of all religions, made men, the very axle or centre of them, perhaps, we could have saved the humanity from so many unnecessary troubles, disasters, we have been facing for ages. Perhaps, then we could have the very pace of our growth faster towards good.

Let everyone of us realise that perhaps heaven would not fall over our heads, if by chance we do not remember that 'Om' through these rituals or dogmas, but the human world would become like a keg of explosives or would be turned into a volcano and, consequently , it is apt to emit 'lava', if at all we forget the very message of that 'Om' in our actions.

Let us be clear on this point that no religion is an end in itself, but only a means to an end, and the end is human welfare at large. If it does not serve this purpose, it is like an unnecessary load on the back of an ass. Swami Vivekanandji too endorses this view: " . . . the aim of this institution is to make men. You must not merely learn what the Rishis taught. Those Rishis are gone and their opinions are also gone with them. You must be Rishis yourself. You are also men as much as the greatest men that were ever born—even our incarnations . . ." (on page 447 Vol. 3 *Swamiji's Works*).

Let us listen the sane advice of Swami Vivekanandji: "Therefore, " . . . you must stand on our own feet. You must have the new method—the method of men-making". (On page 448 Vol. 3 *Swamiji's Works*)

But the moot-question is: how can we have the new method—the method of men-making, unless we restore the lost faith in our own captancy of this ship of our lives?

Swamiji advises and believes: "work out your own salvation." "I cannot help you. No man can help you. Help youself" (on page 478 Vol. 3 Swamiji's works). It is a good advice. These words can be well-digested only when we have utmost faith in making our life-good or bad by our ownselves.

So, let us believe that Buddha like Ram was also from the same earth. Of course, both were great humans, but they did not hail from any divine world. So, let us have faith in men. To boost up all humans, Buddha like

Ram too said: " . . . I am a man amongst men". (page 527 Vol. 3 *Swamiji's Works*).

In fact, Buddha did not believe in erecting any wall of mysticism around Himself. He believed in the Doctrine of Equality of all men. Swami Vivekanandji quotes Buddha: " . . . work out deligently your own salvation. Each one of you is just what I am. I am nothing but one of you. What I am today is what I made myself." (on page 528 Vol. 3 *Swamiji's Works*). Fanatics may dub Buddha as an atheist, as he had no faith in His existence. But how can we do so, when he had immense faith in himself?

Thus, Buddha believed in perfect human will. He believed the path of one's salvation is to be made by oneself. Everyone is like Buddha. Whatever Buddha was, he was not born, but he was made by himself. If we restore such faith in our ownselves, it is only then we can prepare ourselves to change ourselves first, and then change the world as well. Let us have faith that everyone can be a Buddha by one's own commissions or omissions.

Buddha endorsed the view: 'Our life is, what we make it—good or bad.' He did not believe in the subjugation of any views, no matter where they come from.

Hence, Buddha advised us: "Believe not because an old book is produced as an authority. Believe not because your father said (you should) believe the same. Believe not because other people like you believe it. Test everything , try everything and then believe it, and if you find it for the good of many, give it to all". (on page 528 Vol. 3 *Swamiji's Works*).

Of course, we must give due respect to all, no matter what we believe and what we not.

Swami Vivekanandji had honest dissent with Buddha and he complimented Buddha too in these words: "I do not agree with many of his (Buddha's) doctrines. You may not. But in my opinion—oh, if I had one drop of that strength!

"The sanest philosopher the world ever saw. Its best and its' sanest teacher. And never that man bent before even the power of the tyrannical Brahmins. Never that man bent . . . weeping with the miserable, helping the miserable, singing with the singing, strong with the strong, and everywhere the same sane and able man". (on page 528 Vol. 3 *Swamiji's Works*)

The question is where did Swami Vivekanand ji dissent with Buddha? It is the most important thing to know the difference in their views. In Swamiji's own words: "And, of course, with all this I can(not) understand his doctrine. You know he denied there was any soul in man . . . that is, in the Hindus sense of the word. Now we Hindus all believe that there is . . . in man we call 'Atman', which is without beginning and without end. And (we believe) that there is something permanent in nature (and that we call Brahman), which is also without beginning and without end. He denied both of these. He (Buddha) said there is no proof of anything permanent. It is all a mere mass of change, a mass of thought in a continuous change is what you call a mind . . . So, is the life, so is all body, so is all mind." (on page 529 Vol. 3 *Swamiji's Works*).

The question is: Do we Hindus believe in both in God and soul on the basis of our own experiences or on the basis of merely what make-believe world forces us to do so?

Buddha did not accept anything by virtue of the reason that others like him believe in this or that, unless he found it believable. I humbly feel Buddha's views regarding soul and the so-called Brahman were closer to Scientific truths. According to the 'Law of Motion' matter is in a state of perpetual change. There is nothing static or permanent in nature. There is nothing eternal. There is nothing which has beginning or end. Had Brahman been really the remote control super natural power there would not have been any wickedness in the world. Buddha was not ready to accept God's permanent character even. No one can ever be beyond the 'Cause and Effect'. None can be put behind the thorny bushes of the theory of time, space and causation.

Swamiji might hold that Buddha's views regarding God and soul were negative in character. In fact, Buddha did not believe in speculations. His views were quite positive, and based on great reasoning. It is a different thing that majority of the people in India did not accept his views due to the lack of understanding, and their irrationality, unfortunately, because it is easier to prostrate before God to please Him, than to oust one's 'exclusive self' from one's mind. If a pathological report regarding some suspected disease is authentic and negative side by side, there is nothing to worry upon, but the more important question is: whether the report is in the ultimate interest of the patient or not. My humble submission in this respect is, had most of us accepted his views, the lives of both individuals and the people as a whole would have been astonishingly different today. A negative report means that it is a warning bell for us that if we are not any more careful for the disease, it can be fatal. He denied God on facts. The report uproots our illusions.

It is all due to this Swami Vivekanandji complimented Buddha for the great 'motive', what Buddha had behind his revolutionary views. Swami ji accepted it quite honestly with the catholicity of his mind: "But I can understand the motive behind that Oh, the gignatic motive! The Master says that selfishness is the great curse of the world, . . . Have no God; have no soul; stand on your feet and do good for good's sake—neither for fear of punishment, nor for (the sake of) going anywhere. Stand sane and motiveless. The motive is: I want to do good, it is good to do good . . . I warm to think of this tremendous giant . . . And I have not yet seen any other strength like that. We are all born cowards . . . And there he stood: "Do good because it is good . . ." (On page 529 Vol. 3 *Swamiji's Works*)

If we do not believe in any God and soul, heaven won't fall on our heads, but if we fail to curb our 'exclusive self', it is apt to ruin us completely. Let us beware of it.

I hold what a worthy compliment Swami Vivekanandji had paid to Buddha for his epoch-making views! In fact, Buddha was a matchless great human giant ever born in the entire human history of the world. How? Because, what I earnestly feel is that Buddha honestly had endeavoured to remove all the age long meaningless and purposeless divine-crutches from the armpits of each one of us: so that none of us might feel anymore the necessity to wait for Him to descend on the earth with His rescue—crane to uplift the already age long bogged down humanity quite deep in 'adharma', and consequently, we might feel earnestly free to remove the blood-red patches from the fabric of human history ourselves by weaving a better web of our lives with our own knitpins simply as human-spiders.

For Buddha no person, whosoever one may be, is required in this so-called age old tradition of worship of God to perform this or that ritual or dogma, but only to make really one's sincere efforts to remove one's 'exclusive self' from one's own mind, which has been the main cause of age old human miseries. In fact, Buddha's motive was to see everyone of us standing on one's own feet and humbly realise that one's life, whatever it was—good or bad—was not made so by some hypothetical deity, but it was made by everyone of us concerned. According to Buddha what was urgently needed was not to prostrate before any God for one's own upliftment, but to remove the 'exclusive self' from everybody's life by one's ownself. Buddha's main concern was: let everyone of us 'do good only to be good'. This all shows that we are neither born cowards, as Swami Vivekanandji thought, nor we are born brave, but we are made, what we are, by all of us concerned. We become cowards, since birth, because of our dismal indoctrination. Removal of these age old divine-crutches was certainly a great motive, what Buddha had in his very revolutionary mind, and it was really a gignatic task he had performed for the first time in the whole human history of the world. None before him even imagined to do that. Buddha's life shows and proves that in the world, what it is, here no one can work without any motive, no matter the motive may be good or bad. What we need is not to remove the motive, which is like a spar on which the entire sail of the ship is bent, but the bad motive only. Thus, in Buddha's rejection of both God and soul, there was definitely a gignatic motive, he had. Buddha was matchless in his rejection of both God and soul.

Buddha was quite different from all other pioneers in so many ways. We have been talking of soul, while Buddha talks only of character. Swami Vivekanandji quotes Buddha in this respect: "And what remains of man? . . . Not the body, not the soul, but character . . . All that have passed and died . . . Tremendous doctrine." (On page 530 Vol. 3 *Swamiji's Works*).

In fact, Buddha did not believe in giving, any unnecessary temptation, whatsoever to us like the hypothetical Vaikunth', the heaven. He wanted people to do good for good's sake only, and not for attaining the Vaikunth', the heaven. For him both heaven or hell are here in the world. Both are the brain-children of human beings. Some people hold God is nothing, but bliss which can be experienced by us within our ownselves and not outside. Alright, the moot point is: how can we experience bliss inside, unless we architects of our own destinies—good or bad—change our mindset and earnestly follow: 'live and let live'—our 'dharma'?

Is it is not our common experience of life that here when one departs from this world for ever, we usually talk of the person concerned? We talk about the thinking, the feelings and the commissions or omissions of the person. If by chance one is found good on such screening, one is put in higher esteem. On the other, if by chance one is found an evil person, one is put in the lower esteem. It is these one's commissions or omissions which are the components of one's character. While we know nothing about one's soul, we know a lot about one's character, even when one is no more. Thus, one's character becomes eternal, no matter it is good or bad. Buddha preferred to call them as one's character by virtue of this reason. It is only in this context, or through one's eternal character one can live even beyond one's death. It is due to this reason one who can donate one's blood or one's organs to the needy, one lives with a greater esteem beyond one's death too.

Practically speaking, it was Buddha, who stirred our minds tremendously by snatching the steering-wheels of our ships of lives for the first time from the hands of the so-called God's hands. It was Buddha, who handed those steering-wheels over to all the human steersmen ultimately to steer their own ships of lives themselves either to their left or to their right, being the true architects of their own destinies—good or bad. Thus, Buddha was the first pioneer to show us how could we change ourselves first and then our world too. But so far we have failed in our mission. Why? Because we have not restored the faith in our ownselves. We have been beating the same old-track due to fear and escapism.

Buddha told the age old cowards, the fatalists, the escapists, the shirkers and the parasites, how could they change themselves as brave persons. It was the prescription how to be courageous, unprecedented in the whole history. It was unprecedented, because it contained no usual coin, or flower or petal or any idol, etc., to be good men.

Like Buddha Swami Vivekanandji too believed: "To believe blindly is to degenerate the human soul. Be an atheist if you want, but do not believe in anything unquestioningly . . ." (Swami Vivekanand) Buddha too had advised us: "Do not believe in what you heard." "Do not believe in doctrines because they have been handed down to you through generations; . . . do not believe because some old sage makes a statement; do not believe in truths to which you have become attached by habit, do not believe merely on the authority of your teachers and elders. Have deliberation and analyse, and when the result agrees with reason and conduces to the good of one and all, accept it and live upto it." (On page 216-217 Vol. 4 *Swamiji's Works*).

Thus, Buddha honestly attempted to save us from degeneration further.

Swami Vivekanandji too wanted all our road blocks to be removed by us. He advised: "Come, be men! Kick out the priests, who are always against progress . . ., because . . . they are offsprings of centuries of superstition and tyranny. Root out priestcraft first." (On page 10 Vol. 5 *Swamiji's Works*). Let us remember in course of changing the world, we cannot make everybody happy with us.

I earnestly believe that our life is like a great '*yagna*'. Everyone who works here honestly, no matter where one is, performs a great 'yagna'. Pouring 'ghee' on fire is only a ritualistic 'yagna'. The real yagna is done by those only, who earn their livelihood quite honestly. It is certain the day when most of the people become honest workers, when they earnestly start following the principle 'live and let live', the greatest 'yagna' will start. That will be the real beginning of the change of individuals and a simultaneous change of the world too. It is to purify both our inner or outer ecology. But as the faith in our ownselves in making-good or bad is lacking, it has been the greatest hurdle in our ways.

When rubbish or filth is not given almost any birth in one's mind by oneself, one being the real steersman of the ship of one's life starts sailing it towards the sea-shore of peace and happiness automatically with the feelings of 'oneness of all' or universal love. The philosophy of oneness means that we are all one, or the same blood flows in everybody's veins, no matter whosoever one may be. So being so, everyone must be treated equally before law and everyone must get equal protection of the law of the land. While Rule of Law is a legal phenomena, the philosophy of oneness is a social phenomena. Both mean the same thing more or less.

The philosophy of oneness does not mean that if there is God, He must exist both in sane as well as brutes. If God makes His Oasis in sinner's minds too, then who makes one's oasis in sane's minds? Because where brutes or wicked live, God cannot live there. I fail to comprehend Swami Vivekanandji's plea that even the most wicked person is his Christ. That is a different thing that we are all the combination or a mixture of both good and evil. None of us can claim that he is all good and there is no evil in him or her. But how can we see God in Ravana, Duryodhana, Hitler, Ranga-Billa, Veerappan and now Osama bin Laden? Had there been no difference, why did great Ram fight Ravana? Of course, we are all embodiments of both good and evil. There is only the difference of degree and not of kind. When Ram fought Ravana, did He fight God too, if at all God lives in wicked persons?

One becomes godly or demon like by one's pattern of behaviour, one's nature and qualities. I do not think there is any such thing like innate or inherently one's divine or devil. Why do not we accept a brass, a brass and as diamond as diamond only?

If we really want to make our life a heaven on earth we need the most is the re-making of human nature. Our centres of learning must work as refineries of human nature, besides fulfilling other excellent objects. It is the men-making education and men-making religion that purify human nature. Who am I to have a blue-print of such education and religion?

It is said Advaita philosophy believes that man is essentially divine by nature, no matter one is sane or insane, and God dwells in the minds of both. If a human scorpion too is divine, why does it then bite 'its' own fellow-beings? If there is nothing like good or evil in the world of wilds, should we then ape the wilds in this respect? Of course, if a dog has a good quality of faithfulness to its master, we must envy that quality of a dog. Although, I have an allergy against any blind 'bhakti' by anyone.

But those people, who are in the habit of glancing over the human world and human nature merely with the angle of what they ought to be and not what they are actually, they commit a grave error in their judgement, and, consequently, their prescriptions for human miseries too become dangerous for the health of the patients. So, let us no more try to erect human edifice on wrong foundation.

I humbly hold that man is neither essentially good, nor evil by nature, but what one makes oneself. It is all due to this fact, we come across not only great Gods like Ram, Krishna, Mohammed, Christ, but evil men like Ravana, Duryodhana, Hitler, Veerappan, Ranga-Billa and now Osama bin Laden too in the entire corridor of human history. What is Veerappan? Has he not shot dead hundreds of humans? Can we ever see God in Him? Can we ever call him divine by nature? What were Ranga-Billa? Were they divine by any angle of vision? The question is: what is divinity? It is a quality, which restrains us not to harm or hurt or injure anybody without any genuine cause. But when a person behaves like a scorpion or 'bagula' or a tiger, he is to bite another person, harm him without any genuine cause, because he has made his nature of a devil. How can then we shower our love over them? Because they are not divine, but devil.

Let us no more live in a fool's paradise. Let us remember everything, what is extracted even from a gold mine, is not all gold. So, let us remember that if one has the potentiality to be good, one has also the potentiality equally to be evil or demon like too.

Hence, the view of Swami Vivekanandji that "The more I live, the more I become convinced everyday that every human being is divine" (on page 186 Vol. 8 *Swamiji's Works*) is not convincing. I humbly feel that it was all an assumption of a great saint, not based on facts. We cannot overlook the fact that no doctor can write a right prescription on a wrong diagnosis. If human nature is all divine, and not demon, then why has there been an eternal war going on between divine and devil forces even in one's mind? Once, Sardar Patel, our beloved ex-Home Minister too sounded Gandhiji, his mentor: "You see good in everybody. Indeed you see good, where there is no good". How right that iron man was proved at so many times, history is a witness to it! Gandhiji believed that human nature is essentially divine. Did Nathu Ram Godse not represent evil? After all no one has a right to kill anyone, whatsoever in a civilised world, no matter how genuine a cause for it one has got. Where there is a Rule of Law, one can never be permitted to take law in one's own hands.

I humbly hold the views of both Machiavelli and Hobbes regarding human nature were only lop-sided, because society consists of both types of people, who represent good and evil at all times in human history. In this respect, Dr. Radhakrishnan was nearer to truth. He rightly says, "... it is wrong to assume that human nature is static and unchanging. Human nature has changed in the past and it will change in the future".

I know bad persons too can have certain good qualities with them. But can we ever put a robber, who helps the needy out of his loot, in our high esteem? Can we ever pat a tigress, who kills even an innocent passerby to satisfy one's own appetite and her own progeny? Of course, a tigress has a right to satisfy her appetite, but can we ever ape her? So, if at all God exists somewhere, He can never like to live in devil's minds. In fact, men become devil like only when devil's thinking reigns their minds and not good or divine qualities. When I am ready to snatch others' due to fill in my belly, my house etc., or when I am ready to rape or to satisfy my carnal desires; when I do eliminate my brothers or sisters just to freely exploit their absence, it is not my body or eyes or belly is at fault, but my filthy and vulgar mind. If my same mind, moves and works on higher channel of life, credit goes to the same 'I' and the same mind. So, it is not the poor 'I' that is to be removed from the scene of life, but I have to remove the filth of my mind. Had God been living even in Devil's minds, He would not have allowed them to misbehave with their fellow beings. So, I honestly dissent with the Advaita philosophy particularly on this point. Keeping all these facts in view my faith in God's existence has been shaken completely. Whether there is God or no God, soul or no soul we have firm faith that only good men can make a good world, and bad men make it a bad one.

In fact, it is beyond my comprehension, what Advaita philosophy propagates here; "... In every being He lives, through all minds He thinks." (Swami Vivekanandji). When I look towards persons, who have always applied only their back-gear in human history, my doubt whether He lives in every being, becomes quite natural and firm. Everyone knows that if we think good, we also think evil too. Even hard core criminals too think good occasionally. How can then we agree with Swami Vivekanand's view that through all minds He thinks, and in every being He lives? How can a God ever think through all minds? How can we presume that He thinks through the minds of both Ram and Ravana, Krishna and Duryodhana, Gandhi and Hitler at the same time? How can He live in both beings? If He lives and thinks through Osama bin Laden's life and mind, then who lives and thinks in Swami Vivekanand's mind? Of course, a Gandhi becomes a Hitler only, when, instead of being a messiah of 'Satya' and non-violence, he becomes a war-monger. Let Swamiji remember that it was he, who believed that 'where there is wickedness, God cannot live'.

Undoubtedly, all of us have the same mind, made of the same atom. But, you see, everybody's mind works on different channel according to the values, one cherishes. Swami Vivekanandji goes further in the flights of his 'bhakti': "God in every person—working through all hands; sees through all eyes; walking through all feet, and eating through every mouth, thinks through every brain." From this statement it appears then this world must be a world of angels or gods and goddesses. The fact is that if at all He is there, He cannot work through wicked's hands, cannot see through wicked's eyes, cannot walk through wicked's feet and cannot think through wicked's brains. Let us talk of facts and no more about the make-believe world. What is the use to hijack Him in both Gandhi's and Hitler's brain? Why to hijack Him in a Cobra's body? If he lives in Cobra's bodies and minds too, I do not believe in such a God then.

Let us no more be ridiculed by the people. The moot point is if He is everywhere and works through all brains, how then the evils make their oasis in human minds? How can a God think bad about anybody?

We cannot escape from our own responsibilities for what this world or our life is—good or bad? Whether the child is beautiful or ugly, the sense demands from us to own him/her; so that we may then bring up the child properly. Let us accept the fact that the world is our own babe, if at all we want to change it. It is not an illegitimate child at all.

When Ratnakar used to loot the passersby, he acted like a devil, but when he prevailed upon his evil desires, he became a Balmiki, the great saint. The mind was the same, the person was the same, but person's working's channel of brain was entirely different. Is there any sense to see God both in Ratnakar's as well as Balmiki's minds? We do great injustice, if we do it. Why did Ram fight Ravana then, if God is everywhere? Can God ever fight with God?

Why to hijack God either in Ratnakar's or Balmiki's mind unnecessarily? Why to create unnecessary confusion? If God works behind Balmiki's or Buddha's or Vivekanand's mind, then question again crops up, who works behind Ratnakar's or Osama bin Laden's mind? In order to remove all confusion, why do not we accept the reality that through all hands, or brains, or feet, eyes, ears, mouths it is only these architects of human destinies that work and nobody else? And it is they who make their destinies either good or bad, and not any God at all. Why to go on mystifying all this unnecessarily?

In fact, the main cause of this confusion is that, instead of becoming our servants, our fear of god has become our master. Because on the one hand Swamiji holds: "In every being He lives, through all minds He thinks", and on the other he paradoxically holds: "No one is to blame for our miseries, but ourselves." Is it not all contradictory and inconsistent? When He works through all brains, then the blame for all human miseries too must go to God and not to human concerned? But it would be the most tragic *modus operandi* of our escapism from our own responsiblities? I feel our blind *bhakti*, fear and faith in God have been the main causes of our problems. They are the greatest hurdles in our way to take the right judgement. Fear is a good servant, but bad master. What a paradox! That we have lost all faith in our ownselves on the one hand, and we glorify God simply in blind faith, on the other.

Again, if Swami Vivekanandji holds 'God is the greatest monitor and controller of the world', but when we witness with our own eyes evil living along with good in human minds, how can we accept the said plea of Swamiji? How can we accept his plea: 'for whatever exists in it (the world) has all come from the Impersonal (God)?' How can God ever be held responsible for the sinners or saints? How can both good and evil be manifestations of the same God? Or are there good God and evil God too? But how can there be an evil God? God and evils are contradictions in terms.

Did not we make responsible the God for the very cause of malaria even at a time merely out of our own ignorance and fear of God? It is strange: if we fall down from our roof-top and by chance survive, we at once drag our Lord even in our survival. And if by chance we die, we again drag the poor Lord in our death too, saying it was our *fate-accompli*, predetermined by God according to our past actions. The question is: if God is the sole monitor and controller or doer of all things in our world and we are His '*nimits*' only, then let us know, who has pushed us down the floor? Logically, being mere 'nimits' we cannot fall down on our own. Unless we own all our activities, we shall never be able to mend the very fabric of our lives. The question is: has this blind bhakti, or blind fear of God, or ignorance made us better human beings indeed?

Human nature is dynamic and not static in character. All persons can change their evil mindset, if at all they want to be good indeed. In fact, human nature is, what one makes it. If we accept Swamiji's plea: "Man is divine," the question is if we are all divine, then where do the devils come from in His kingdom? The fact is it is neither essentially good, nor evil. That is why, there are good and bad people here in the world.

Actually, our fear of God, our blind 'bhakti' and ignorance about the universe and nature have been forcing us to see even ghosts of God everywhere and making us superstitious unnecessarily. For instance, the

Swami Vivekanandji too rightly holds further: "The Vedanta also says that the cause of all the apparent evil is in ourselves. Do not blame any supernatural being, neither be hopeless and despondent, nor think we are in a place from which we can never escape unless someone comes and lends us a helping hand." If Vedanta believes in this truth too, then why to talk as if we are only His 'nimits' and He is the sole doer of all things in our lives? Why do we believe we are only His Master's pet dogs on a long leash? Whatever He does, does right? Do these things not cause us depression in our lives? Why do we talk that we can only prostrate before God? We can do nothing more and nothing less? Why is this hypocrisy? Why do we not accept the truth that our mere enlightened self and not exclusive self' is the saviour of the sinking ship of our lives? Why do we hijack God in human affairs? Has it made us more humble and less egoists or better human beings? Let us no more try to behave like that stupid ostrich. Nobody seems to be careful about what Emile Zole says, "while truth is buried underground, it grows, it chokes, it gathers such an explosive force that one day it bursts out, it blows everything up with it." So, earlier we accept the truth that the cause of both good or evil is in ourselves, the better.

What we need urgently to do today is to change our mindset only. Let us be pure humans only. We are to change our attitude only. The Newtonian Law of action-reaction is more appropriate to apply in the world of matter, but it cannot be applied in the world of humans. Instead of knowing how to react, let us know being humans, how to respond in a given situation? Otherwise, there will all be chaos here.

Swami Vivekanandji too rightly says, "All knowledge that the world has ever received comes from the mind; the infinite library of the universe is in your mind . . . The falling of an apple gave the suggestions to Newton and he studied his own mind . . ." If it is true that all knowledge that the world has ever received comes from our minds only, why does then Swami Vivekanandji profess that 'God cannot be known through our minds or through any senses? The knower can never be known, and so on and so forth. Why to mystify or glorify the Lord? In case we can know Him through the soul, science does not accept its existence.

It is all due to this undue glorification of God, that men have developed the psyche or the mentality of 'weak and low', which has dangerous consequences.

Here Swami Vivekanandji's version of miseries in the world is most reasonable. He says. "The cause of all miseries we have in the world is that men foolishly think pleasure to be the ideal to strive for." "A fool may buy all the books in the world and they will be in his library: but he will be able to read only those he deserves to".

What a paradoxical thing it is that on the one hand Swamiji took even the wickedest as his Christ, and on the other, he recommends: "It is the duty of the householder not to pay reverence to the wicked; because if he reveres the wicked people of the world, he patronises wickedness: and it will be a great mistake, if he disregards those, who are worthy of respect, the good people . . . he must not go out of the way making friends everywhere, he must watch the actions of the men he wants to make friends with and then make friends." So let us no more try to fire in the air. Our blind 'bhakti' is our greatest shackle. It is due to lack of faith in our ownselves we become inconsistent and paradoxical in our approach.

The age old fanatic view '*kan, kan mey* '*Bhagwan*' too has been sprouted in our minds due to the same fear, blind 'bhakti' and ignorance. As it is said that all roads lead to Rome, but in the world of blind 'bhakti' all roads lead to 'Bhagwan'. To know whether God or demon lives in an atom (Kan), let us know what an atom is. According to *Oxford Dictionary* an atom is the smallest unit of an element that can take part in a chemical change. A molecule of water (H_2O) is made up of two atoms of hydrogen, and one atom of oxygen. An atom is neither the abode of God, nor of demon. If we take God by good and demon by evil, let us understand that the real abode of both of these is not an atom but our poor minds. Both the use or abuse of atom perfectly depends on the beholders of minds. Do not we human beings use the same atom either in construction or destruction? Is not our mind, which is the highest stage of the development of matter, the real womb of both war and peace? No atom, whatsoever, does any construction or destruction on its own. Do we not know that the minds of both Gandhiji and Hitler were made of the same atom? Do we not know that their minds worked on different channels? Do we not know that while Gandhiji was essentially the 'messiah' of 'Ahimsa', 'satya' and peace, Hitler believed 'war was a necessary instrument to keep the nations alive'. This amply shows that neither the seeds of war, nor the seeds of peace sprout in one's mind themselves. Which seeds sprout mainly depends on the beholder. This all proves that it is not, the 'atom' (Kan), which is in the dock, but our minds only. Of course, it is O.K. if 'Kan Kan me Bhagwan' means all are equals, because the same blood flows in the veins of all. But let us remember no atom has its own will or consciousness. It has neither its' own feet to walk, nor wings to flutter. Atom bombs too did not fall on Hiroshima and Nagasaki in 1945 on their own, but they were dropped by some humans. Was God there in these bombs? Had God been living in every atom (Kan-Kan), He being the almighty, all-pervading, as it is known, would not have allowed Mr. Truman, the President of USA to order to throw away those atomic bombs on these poor cities of Japan. Of course, Truman patted the back of his poor men on this cruel duty by assuring them that God was with them at that time. Thus the view '*Kan kan me Bhagwan*' was exploded as a myth only. In this context, let us know what Milton viewed about it: "The mind is in its own place, and in itself can make a heaven hell, a hell of heaven." Of course, it is O.K. that we should preserve nature and should not act against nature and maintain an ecological balance. But it is all illogical to see 'Bhagwan' in atoms.

In this context, let us then remember the old saying '*Is ghar ko aag lag gai hai, ghar ke chirag se*'. Why to make the poor atom a scapegoat for our own follies? Some psychiatrists hold that the vast neurotic misery of the world could be termed as neuroses of emptiness. They hold men cut themselves off from the roots of their being, from God, and their life turns empty, inane, meaningless and without purpose. They hold that when God goes, meaning goes, goal goes. When meaning goes, values go and thus life turns dead. I humbly hold this is nothing but is akin to a quack's diagnosis of the disease. In my humble opinion the main cause of these neurotic miseries in this world is not because most of us have cut ourselves off from the hypothetical God by and by, but our life turns empty, inane, meaningless and purposeless, because we have made our exclusive self' as our only modern deity or in other words the nucleus of our lives. Now we have changed our deity simply. Formerly most of us lived for a hypothetical entity, known as God, but today we live exclusively for our 'self'. If today we are living a meaningless and purposeless life, formerly too we were living a life, which had no purpose at all. Has 'He' made us more humble or less egoists and better human beings? Mere prostrating before Him is not like a machine, which produces good men indeed. Today we have no high mission in our lives. We are living like a frog in the well. Do we not live like a dog in the manger? Our goal of life is not actually peace, but pleasure and that too by hook or by crook. Our values of life are centred round the ideal 'eat drink and be merry' most of the time. Do we ever care for our means to attain our good end? Let us remember the fact that even today the majority of the people the world over still keep their link with this or that hypothetical God intact. So, in a nutshell, it is not essentially when God goes, meaning and goals go in life. God is still there more or less intact. But when high mission in life goes, meaning, purpose, goal of life and values too—all go en bloc. There is all-round darkness. Obviously and naturally, we feel, as if our life is almost dead. So, we should no more live the life like on an unchartered-sea. We are all human beings. We cannot live only for our bread and personal pleasure in life. Of course, they too are important things in our lives, but they are not the end of our lives. The end is peace and happiness, which can only be attained by having a very high mission in life. That mission is not only 'to live', but 'let live' also at the same time.

Today we are living a materialistic life only, because we make the so-called God only a means and the world's pleasure only as our end. Do not we make shopping with Him too, when we prostrate before Him, just to get this or that worldly pleasure in return from Him? Can we ever live a spiritual life when our worldly pleasures become only our end, and God becomes a means to an end? In a nutshell, '*Om*' is no more to be kept on our lips, but the very message of 'Om' is to be kept alive in our minds at all times. In other words let us follow Buddha's message then: "do good to be good only. Let us hope then for the flood light after the tunnel, because of this creativity in life, and because of our living with a mission in life.

Undoubtedly, the philosophy of Advaita propounded in the Gita in the words of Swami Vivekanand ji i.e., "...the truth as given in the Gita. 'He who sees everyone in himself, and himself in everyone, thus seeing the same God living in all, he, the sage, no more kills the self by the self.' Know through Advaita that whomsoever you hurt, you hurt yourself; they are all you..." (on page 425 Vol. 3 *Swamiji's Works*) is the highest stage of the development of spiritualism , provided it sprouts in everybody's mind the universal brotherhood or '*Basudheva kutumbkam*' or universal oneness. It is based on the old principle of 'live and let live'. It means we must love each other without any bias, whatsoever, thinking the same blood flows in everybody and everyone has the same right, like us, to live. So, everyone must be treated according to the spirit of Rule of Law. If we follow the same spirit in our lives it will mean our overpowering of spirit of killig or hurting others wthout any valid cause.

But frankly speaking, to the extent, what it preaches; 'He who sees everyone in himself, and himself in everyone' is very appreciable, but beyond this when it preaches, 'thus seeing the same God living in all' it becomes rather meaningless. How can God ever make His Oasis in Gandhiji's and Hitler's or Veerappan's or Ranga-Billa's or Osama bin Laden's mind at the same time? Treating them according to the Rule of Law is OK, but seeing God, if at all He exists, in brutes too is beyond my poor comprehension. Had god been living even in Ravana's or Duryodhana's minds respectively, Ram would not have ever fought a 'dharmayudha' with Ravana, and Krishna would not have prepared Arjuna to fight war with Kauravas as his duty. I humbly feel it is only our wrong use of this advaita philosophy of oneness. How can we see God even in Human cobras, human sharks and human scorpions and human 'bagulas'?

After all a cobra bites even that hand, which feeds milk to it. Oneness of all is O.K., but oneness of saints and sinners is a dangerous pill, which 'Advaita' wants to administer to us. Can we ever imagine even to see God in Osama bin Laden, the most cruel terrorist in the world? We cannot make a wicked person as our christ, as Swami Vivekanand ji did. It will be the great injustice and inhuman, if we put Gandhi and Hitler on equal footing or in our same esteem. Let us no more live in a fool's paradise. A God can never fight God. He fights with devils only. The glorification of God is the effect, because we have lost all faith in our own navigation.

Today we have reached a cross-road, where two alternative lights i.e., simple fear of God and faith in oneself with conviction or understanding—both are more or less no more visible on the polls or at the most they appear to be flickering. How long can we get anything accepted by the people merely out of fear? When the myth is exposed, you cannot keep it intact. Of course, when you lack proper conviction or understanding, you cannot revive your faith too. So, to revive one's faith in one's making of one's life—good or bad—is, undoubtedly, the most ticklish problem of the modern day world. Earlier we solve it, the better. Otherwise, there is an imminent danger for the survival of human beings.

But in this world, what it is, old habits die hard. This world still consists of most of the believers. Non-believers like me are only in microscopic minority. While believers have immense faith in Him, they lack the requisite faith in themselves. Let no one believe that all believers in God are sane and all non-believers in God are insane. What I humbly feel is that Swami Vivekanandji too is not an exception in regards to this habit. Rather I am astonished to go through, what Swamiji believes in. He says:

"If all understand one day for one minute that one cannot become great by the mere wish, that he only rises when He raises, and he falls, whom He brings down, then all trouble is at end." (On page 285 Vol. 6 *Swamiji's Works*). The statement is the product of lack of faith in one's making of life, what it is—good or bad by oneself. It is not out of one's humbleness. Has the age long belief that 'He is the doer of all things,' made us more humble or less egoists? If yes, why are our miseries multiplying?

He adds further and reaches the very climax of his blind faith in Him, when he wrote the following to one of his friends from Chicago in 1894 in his letter. He wrote: "He makes the dumb eloquent and makes the lame cross mountains" (On page 283 Vol. 6 *Swamiji's Works*). It means He is all-in-all and He is all and all. In spite of being all powerful, why is there so much wickedness and hypocrioy? How can God and wickedness co-exist?

The above two statements of Swami Vivekanandji, are testimonials in themselves to prove that Swamiji might have said that man is the master of his destiny', but he actually believed in an age old view i.e., 'we are all His Masters' pet dogs on a long leash'. Of course, he has used these words nowhere in his lectures, but this is the implication of what he actually believed in. This clearly shows that Swamiji's all talks of restoration of faith in men themselves as architects of their own destinies are all futile, because his above statement makes humans complete puppets in His hands. The view in question makes everybody clear that according to Swamiji's views too everything is pre-determined by Him, and there is nothing in individual's hands-neither one's rise, nor one's fall. Everything depends on His sweet or sour will only. There is no question of free-will of humans. The view is in complete negation of the view that man is the architect of one's own destiny—good or bad. It implies that He too can be arbitrary in His decisions, because He has assigned to Himself the sole prerogative of making one's rise or one's fall in His own hands. I humbly believe so long we go on granting lease after lease of life to this dismal and dangerous view, we are not going to oust the brute from our nature and thus Marx's dream to change the world too would remain merely his dream-pipe.

But it is all befooling, deceptive and dangerous to believe, 'that he only rises, when He raises, and he falls, whom He brings down.' It is strange to believe that human wish is immaterial before God's wish. The believers may put their old plea that whatever He does, does right, because He does on the basis of our own past activities. The question is: who knows about one's past, if at all it is there? If they are right in their views, should we then derive this dismal conclusion that here in this world one, who suffers, it is all exclusively due to one's own deeds? Let us remember here those who look ahead of their times, they suffer here the most. Has it not all happened with Ram, Mohammad, Christ, Gurus, Galelio, Socratese, Kabir, Lincoln, Gandhi and the like? May I know why did Galelio, who discovered that the sun, and not the earth was the centre of the solar system, suffer? Is discovery of truth a crime? Was he even ex-communicated from Christianity, because of His wish or blessings? Was Christ nailed, because of His own deeds? If not, then why to drag Him in and drag Him out of human affairs according to our own convenience? Of course, one must deserve before, what one wishes to be.

In fact, human history has been full of human's '*zulum*' due to the fear of God. Here are some instances:

It was in the early 16th century Charles Darwin's (1809-1882) Theory of Evolution (like Galelio's discovery) too went against the Christian's belief regarding the origin of life. These contractors of religion denounced Darwin too for holding that we are descended from apes. When Bishop Welber-Force was unable to clinch the issue scientifically, he almost asked in desperation: 'O Key, Prof. Huxley, (Who supported Darwin in a public debate) finally please tell me, which side did you descend from the ape-father's or mother's? T.H. Huxley, in fact, refused to find any solace in the prevailing religion, as he was drowned in grief over the death of his beloved son.

I feel when all these unfortunate human's *zulums* were pent up in Friedrech Nietzsche's mind, he declared that 'God was dead'. Whether God was dead or alive, I know not, but my humble faith in His creativity of this world was further badly shaken, when I came to know that Socratese too was forced to sip the cup of poison, simply because he too wanted to track the path of truth. One of the charges against Socratese was that he disbelieved in the gods of Athens. Another charge was that he was corrupting the youth of the city. Socratese said before the judges: "If your purpose to acquit me on condition is that I abandon my search of truth, I will say: I thank you O Athenians, but I will obey God, who, as I believe, set me the task, rather than you (judges) and so long as I have breath and strength I will never cease from my occupation with philosophy . . . I know not what death is—it may be a good thing, and I am not afraid of it. But I do know that it is a bad thing to desert one's past and prefer what may be good to what I know to be bad," "This plain-speaking of mine is the cause of my unpopularity," said Socratese to judges. Socratese was finally condemned to death by drinking poison. Socratese heard his punishment calmly and like a great human teacher, he said: "But now it is time to depart for me to die, for you to live". "No one can kill me . . . Have all my teachings been in vain . . . ?" His teachings are definitely immortal.

Owing to celebrations, his execution was delayed by a month. He was kept in prison loaded with chains. Crito, one of his most faithful follower came to the prison and told socratese that he made all arrangements for his escape. Socratese smiled and refused to act on his advice by telling that he would rather die than to live by disobeying the laws of his country in the true spirit of the Civil Disobedience Movt., launched by Gandhiji later on. Can God, if he exists, ever be the cause of these heinous crimes against humanity?

What a hypocrisy we have been playing in the very corridors of human history time to time with all the great human teachers ever born in the world? No sooner did the Athenians bury the Socratese, they started repenting for what they did with him. Because it is these Athenians, who gave Socratese, one of the wisest men on earth, the cup of poison to die an unnatural death, when he was busy seeking the truth, and it is the same Athenians too who established his statue in his memory, when he was no more physically. I do not know how many more such precious lives this world is wanting to end in such an unfortunate way. Then how can we believe 'that he only rises, when He raises, and he falls, who He brings down? When I look towards the actual '*zulum*', what we have been committing against even our human giants, my faith in His creativity is further shaken.

Did we not give poison to Swami Dayanandji, and nail the Christ for no fault of their own? Here I remind an Urdu couplet, which shows under what illusions we humans work. It is also in that series:

'Muddai lakh bura chahe to hota kaya hai,
wahi hota hai, jo manzur-e-khuda hota hai . . .'

Only out of illusions, persons can hold that whatever has happened or is happening, or would happen with the people of the world must be blessed by God.

Goswami Tulsidas too expressed the same view out of his 'bhakti'.
'*Hoga vahi joo Ram racha rakha*'. . .

Let us remember that human welfare does not lie in such glorification of God. It is not in tune with the view that we are all the architects of our own destinies—good or bad.

Did all these unfortunate episodes in human history occur, because God pre-determined or willed them? I think God, if at all He exists, can never be a party or an ally, when we commit evils. It is only His fanatics, who link the 'Tik'-'Tik' even in an automatic watch to the will of their Lord. Fanatics due to their little mindedness are often soaked in violent and unreasonable enthusiasm and excitement in blind beliefs only.

It is this universal divinization has made even our petty activities like sneezing and yawning based on mere God's will. It has made our life a complete mess and a bundle of confusion only. Let us remember that the fear is a good servant, but bad master. Only men-making religion can provide oxygen to such mentally paralysed humanity.

Voltaire once remarked that if we have no God, we shall have to invent Him. I do not know why? What led him to say so about Him? I feel our centuries old association with such a God clearly warns us that our such artificial respiration of God to put Him into life again can make us at the most God fearing, and not evil-fearing people. We can be evil-fearing people only when we have conviction, rocky-will, conscience and understanding that without following the principle 'live and let live' side by side there is every danger to the extinction of this human world even. May I know how many persons, who have been repeating Ram-Ram parrot like, have been liberated in their lives without following Ram's message in their lives?

I humbly believe that this unnatural fear can produce nations of slaves or escapists, and not nations of the architects of their own destinies at all. If the same slavish mentality goes on for another century, these nations are apt to be doomed, because such people are born crippled and they cannot walk on earth even without their divine crutches. In place of curbing our ego from our minds, the dismal thinking has paralysed us both physically and mentally. Only in our ignorance we have made the planets, stars and satellites wear the mask of divinity.

The fact is that the sun is like a huge ball of fire, which causes light in the moon and stars. Although the sun is several light years away from earth, there cannot be life on the planet earth without the sun. It is the warmth of the sun and not any Lord, that causes the shine or the light on the earth. Swami Vivekanandji linked the very colours in the wings of the butterflies and the blossoming of the rose bud to the will of a hypothetical God merely out of his 'bhakti'. The scientific truth is that the colours in the wings of the butterflies happen to be, because of their genes only. God's will or no will has nothing to do with them. As regards fragrance in the flowers, it is said because of the presence of nectars (glands), which contain different kinds of scents, the flowers give us different fragrance. Further, there are thorns along with these roses. They are the protective devices of nature, provided to rose plants. Moreover, these thorns check transpiration as well. We yawn, because we need more oxygen. We sneeze, because some foreign element goes in, which is not acceptable. If some fruits are sweet, while others are sour, it is because they synthesise different kinds of proteins due to the presence of different kinds of genes and different heredity. If we have a particular shape of our eyes, ears, brain, height, intelligence, or dullness, it is because of our different genes. So, let us no more hijack Him in and out of human affairs merely out of our convenience or ignorance.

May I know does an electric bulb in our house shine due to God's sweet will or due to the electric-current which passes through wires? If the bulb shines due to God, where does He go, when there is a black out? Can we ignore the facts that the *filament* of the bulb is heated, when electric current passes through it, and as a result of it, the hot *filament* emits light? It is a scientific truth that an adult human being has as many as 600 trillion cells in the body. They develop. Is the God working behind their growth? Let us not to try to bolt all the doors of scientific discoveries by dragging Him in human affairs. Being fanatic we have made God like a butter which we can put in between our two slices of bread, and we can put in our 'dal' too out of mere ignorance. Let us no more apply the back gear in the arena of science too.

We have a well-known example of Ratnakar before us. Did he fall down in his life due to his own '*agyan*', or because the Lord brought him down, as Swami Vivekanandji believes? Later on he became the Balmiki, a great saint. Was it all because he realised his own follies or because the Lord raised him to that high stature, 'as Swamiji thinks?

If one rises, if He raises, and one falls, whom He brings down, and our wisdom or '*vivek*' or power of discrimination or follies have nothing to do with our own rise or fall respectively, then I do not believe in such a hypothetical, whimsical and arbitrary God indeed at all, because it snatches the very fundamental right of determination of one's own destiny—good or bad from the people. This divine-determinism of Swamiji is dangerous indeed. It is nothing but the same old Divine Origin theory of universe, which has been thrown into the dustbin of history long long ago. Determinism is a dangerous pill, because it reduces humans to the level of slaves. I am not a determinist, because I do not believe in human history being merely like a snowball rolling down the hill according to the dictates or wishes of the object, which determines it. I believe, being architects, humans determine their own history.

The view is apt to reduce all humans to the level of docile animals. It is apt to turn all humans into escapists, fatalists, cowards, shirkers and parasites. The view is apt to put premium on our vices only and that too in the name of God. This determinism has the most dangerous germs of stagnation. It closes all doors and windows from outside.

If everything including one's rise or one's fall was to be decided by the Lord only, if it was exclusively Lords' domain, then what was the necessity for the revolutions, which have shaken the outer surface of economic, political and social structure of the entire world? Even before expressing this view Swami Vivekanandji expressed in other words. 'Even a blade of grass cannot grow, and we cannot breathe even without His mercy'. So, this view is like the old wine in the new bottle only. The unfortunate priests of Somnath temple, when it was looted by a foreigner, were the offsprings of the same age old poisonous philosophy.

If Ram, Mohammad, Christ *gurus* and the like had risen to the peaks of The Everest in their upliftment, and the persons like Ravana, Duryodhana, Hitler and Mussolini had gone down upto the sea-level in their downfall, was it because the Lord had installed a divine lift to take the concerned people upstairs as well as downstairs respectively? Let us beware of such myths attached with Him. Earlier this sandy edifice of Lordship is collapsed, the better.

The view in question is pregnant with all the deadly viruses of confusion, which can make all the human beings like dumb, deaf, lame and lunatics in their first attack, and in their astonishingly second attack on the believers minds, this view is sure to get it certified by them that their Lord is so great that He can make the dumb eloquent, lame cross a mountain and even make lunatics talk like sensible persons, who can change even human genes and produce human clones in His lab etc., as if their Lord is the first wonder of the world.

Is it not strange that Swami Vivekanandji too believed in the view: "He who makes the dumb eloquent and the lame cross a mountain. He will help me. I do not care for human help?" (On page 328 Vol. 8)

In fact, it was the faith in Him, which was the most potential thing, which could infuse blood even in the dead veins of humans and make dead like alive. But the fact is a fact. Had God been at all helpful to Swami ji, when he was undergoing his character-assassination out of mere jealousy by the people, he would not have been disturbed. Ultimately, not any deity, but wise people in US and India helped Swamiji to come out of the woods. Where did He go at that time? Were they His '*nimits*'?

Is God a magician that He works with some Alladin lamp to make all such wonders?

When the faith eclipse our vision, it turns masters into slaves.

Even Gandhiji believed: "He can live without water and air, but he cannot live without God, as He is the creator of this world and the master of it." Even Gandhiji once declared that you can say 'no' to 'God is Truth', but you cannot say 'no' to 'Truth is God.' Let us remember, firstly that whatever Gandhiji's God is, He cannot create anything out of nothing. Secondly, even if 'Truth is God', Truth might be having His own eyes, but has no feet to walk, and no wings of His own to flutter or fly. It is due to this reason Truth remains lying buried quite deep in the graves of books in the world, and, consequently, the unfortunate history of human miseries and sufferings goes on and on repeating again and again. So, the greatest need of the hour for the architects of human destinies is to be ever alert and awake; lest no bloody patch should come on the web, what these human-spiders weave with their knit—pins in future. I doubt earnestly whether Gandhi's God can ever be the master of this wicked and hypocritic world. Faith is, undoubtedly, such a potential missile to remove all obstacles on the way, but blind faith, wherever it is, is such a dangerous missile, which kills even its' beholders one day soon.

If we are really nobody to wish even to rise, then it is obvious that we humans have got only the lollipop of the so-called human freedom or free will to make or unmake our world, whatever it is good or bad. We have been waiting for the Lord with the hope that He is to descend on this planet earth with the divine rescue-crane to uplift the downtrodden or the centuries old bogged down humanity from the huge pond of 'adharma', but now we have lost all patience and realised that it was only a 'gimmick' of theists. It was only the pious will or wish of all His pet dogs simply. The trouble becomes more serious, when instead of making them rise, their God becomes the major cause of their own fall, or escapism or degeneration only.

So, there is no question of shelving our pious wish of turning our hell into heaven. Let us be brave, arise and awake ourselves from within and sleep no more, till we as human spiders weave a better and better web of our own life or the world with our own knitpins, at least, in future. Wait for none. Time is passing. A lot of rubbish water, we have already flowed under the bridge of Sutlej, and more will be flowing, if we are not more serious and careful for this passage. We are only to throw away our 'hypnotism of weakness' now into the dustbin of history for ever.

In fact, the philosophy in question is more dangerous than even cancer, AIDS etc., because its deadly viruses can never be traced anywhere. It can never allow us to rise in our lives, and, consequently, it is apt to make our permanent fall or doom a hundred per cent certainty. So, earlier, we see it off from our lives, the better.

Swamiji is hundred per cent free to hold: ". . . God is everywhere preached in every religion. The Vedas teach God . . . God is . . . preached in the Gita. Hinduism is nothing without God." (On page 12 Vol. 6 *Swamiji's Works*) I do not think it is correct to say that Hinduism is nothing without God, because Sanatan Dharma which is the correct nomenclature of Hinduism, embraces even the so-called atheists, who do not believe in the existence of God. On the other, they have utmost faith in themselves. It is due to this toleration Sanatan Dharma is still alive and shall ever be alive, because it stands for certain fundamental human principles, which must govern everybody's life, no matter who so ever one may be. Moreover, religion is realisation. It is not in books or scriptures essentially, but it is being. God is not an essential part of religion. It is essentially concerned with the mutual bonds among different social animals. Both Buddha and Mahavir did not believe in the existence of God. Had God been an essential part and parcel of a religion, Buddhism and Jainism would not have been considered as important religions like others. I humbly believe that it is not God, but human goodness and human excellence or good human conduct which are the keystones of a religion. That is why, Buddha stressed on 'to do good to be good' only.

In fact, the protagonists of remote control super natural view are apt to be caught red-handed in their own net, woven by themselves, because it is they who fail to explain the pertinent question that if God is the sole creator of this world, where have these blood-red pages of human history come from?

Darwin has already proved that there is no creation, but evolution. Carl Sagan points out as to how life actually came on earth by demonstrating that 'when a mixture of methane, ammonia, water and hydrogen sulphide gas is irradiated by a long wave-length ultraviolet source, amino acids (the building blocks of proteins) are produced.' But this dose is meant only for those, who stand by science, and not superstition or any illusion.

Let us remember what William Shakespeare says, "The web of our life is of a mingled yarn, good and evil together." Obviously, the web must be woven by the people in the capacity of the human-spiders only. When the web has bloody patches, how can we accept it that it has been God-ordained? The days of mentioning to external causes for both our rise or fall, fortunes or misfortunes, honour or dishonour, defeat or victory, benefit or loss in life must have been gone now too far. The God cannot be held responsible for our circulatory, or digestive or respiratory or any other natural systems in the body. If rains come or there is drought somewhere or there is famine or flood or earthquake or cyclone in any part of the globe, there are scientific reasons behind them. If two elements of Hydrogen and one element of oxygen mingle together and make water (H_2O), where does the Lord come into the picture? The days and night occur, not because of the mercy of God, but because of the rotation of earth related to sun. Due to revolution of earth with respect to sun climates change. Solar or Lunar eclipses occur due to the particular positions of the Sun, Moon and the earth in respect to each other in the firmament. The colours in nature occur due to particular property of different substances to absorb and reflect different wavelength in the spectrum of light. Do not all-these scientific facts blast deadly the age old Remote Control supernatural view as a mere myth?

Primarily it is we, who are the real causes both of our rise or fall individually, as Swami Ram too holds: "All your falls, all your injuries, all your hurts, all your anxieties, and troubles are due to some weakness within you. Remove that and fight not with circumstances, do not blame your fellowmen, throw not the blame on the shoulders of others, but remove your own weakness. Bear in mind that whenever you fall or suffer or are troubled, it is due to some weakness within you . . . fight not with gravity. What is the weakness within? It is the dark pitch of ignorance which makes you look upon the body, the senses, as you. Get rid of it . . . and the power itself you become . . ." This view is against the view what Swami Vivekanandji holds that "he only rises when He raises, and he falls, when He brings down . . ."

I do agree with great Swami Ram that whenever we fall or suffer or are troubled, it must be generally due to some weakness within us. He is perfectly O.K. upto this level. But to say emphatically that causes of one's rise or one's fall must always lie within one's ownself necessarily, will be farther from the whole truth. Of course, if the cause of disease lies within oneself, one must remove the cause. There is no alternative to it. But it is a big 'if'. We all know that our world, what it is, is not at all a one man's show. So many hands are responsible sometime in having the world-scenario, what it is—good or bad. Particularly, all the great human giants have to suffer in this world. Let us remember the facts. That our fortune sits, when we sit. It rises, when we either individually or collectively rise, but it is certain that 'things' of Marx and 'thoughts' of Hegal or the hypothetical God do not play as umpires. Yes, the 'things' and thoughts do help us in the game what we the architects of our own destinies play, as both never grow like weeds in the fields or the ocean or like the hair on our heads. Of course, we can never rise, unless we remove our own weaknesses or little-mindedness generally. Truth is truth, no matter who likes and who does not.

I further hold humbly had God not been a mere age old myth, there would not have been any doubt regarding the existence of God even for a single moment in the unconscious mind of Swami Vivekanandji, who witnessed a naked dance of some Britishers here in India before her independence. In reality, doubting His existence, Swamiji put the following straight forward question to Mary Hale in a letter written by him on 30th of Oct. 1899, more than a hundred years ago.

Swamiji related a pathetic real tale in his letter: "There has been a reign of terror in India for some years. English soldiers are killing our men and outraging our women . . . we are in a terrible gloom . . . where is the Lord? Mary, it is hopeless with us, unless there really is a God, who is father of all, who is not afraid of the strong to protect the weak, and who is not bribed by wealth. Is there such a God? Time will show." (on page 476 Vol. 8 *Swamiji's Works*).

Even if we accept God is good or Truth, our bretheren Mohammadens and Christians say that there is a gentleman called 'Satan'. How can we accept that there are two gentlemen working behind us? That is why Swamiji said: "Now, who is responsible for all this good and evil, if God is ever the good? The Christians and Mohammadens say there is a gentleman called satan. How can you say there are two gentlemen working? There must be one". The fact is that it is we humans who are responsible for good or evil, no matter we are sane or insane.

Buddha too expressed: "God is only a superstition invented by the priests. If there is a God, as these Brahmins preach, why is there so much misery in the world?" (On page 98-99 Vol. 8 *Swamiji's Works*). Buddha said, "There is no Brahman, no Atman, no soul . . ." (On page 22 Vol. 7 *Swamiji's Works*). So long we go on repeating parrotwise that God is the sole doer of all things in life, we are simply his *nimits*, the evil-doer too is apt to go on saving his own skin under this umbrella by befooling: "I am acting as I am being directed by the Lord . . . (On page 127 Vol. 7 *Swamiji's Works*). So God has become rather his shield or saving-device to protect him.

Just to avoid this age old confusion Buddha and Mahavir do not accept His existence: "How can it be that there is a God?" "It must be a mere superstition". (On page 12-13 Vol. 6 *Swamiji's Works*). How wrong it is to believe that Buddha was an incarnation of Lord Vishnu! Because Buddha accepted God as only a superstition. Of course, he believed in re-birth.

If Swamiji's view that he only rises, whom He raises, and he falls, whom He brings down is correct, then God must be held responsible for this reign of terror in India or for killing our men and outraging our women, but I feel that only fools can accuse God in such a way. If anyone even tries to attribute any degradation to God, it must be observed as the outburst of a nonsense person. Of course, one can doubt His existence.

In fact, both our rise or fall in our lives are our own brain children either individully or collectively. History has been a witness to it. It is on the basis of his meditation just to remove the dark clouds of confusion regarding God, Buddha rejected to accept both God and soul. While Mahavir believed in the soul. It is strange that Swami Vivekanandji had turned all the real architects of their destinies into mere puppets in Lord's hands. He says, "Always remember that we are but puppets in Lord's hands" (On page 246 Vol 6 *Swamiji's Works*). If really we are puppets in God's hands, then his view that 'there is no fate—and man is the master of his own destiny', is only a myth.

I humbly feel Swamiji's natural dilemma: 'where is the Lord' or 'Is there such a God'? depicts its own tale. But his own religious Sanskar's and how an age old pouring of Remote control Supernatural view into our minds had, perhaps, eclipsed even a catholic mind of such a human giant, are only matters of great wonder for a Lilliputian like me. In fact, the view of Swamiji is apt to extend the life span of the divine shackles, which have been the greatest hurdles in the ways of our thinking, feeling and doing as architects of our own destinies. Consequently, we shall go on leaving the question of our rise or fall on God's will only and thus we shall ever be failure to change ourselves first to change our world. Is not the view 'God is the sole doer', our biggest shackle?

So long Lord's fantom fear and His blind 'bhakti' reigns our minds, we shall never be clear in our views regarding God. We shall ever remain paradoxical and inconsistent.

Hence, to avoid any confusion regarding who is responsible and who is not for our deeds—good or bad, it is always sensible to own the responsibility for both our good or evil deeds, whatever they may be, so that we may be easily ready to undo, what wrong we have been doing so far at the earliest possible. It is only then that we can claim to be the true architects of our own destinies. In fact, the right wombs of good as well as bad impulses, where they conceive, are our own minds. If we really want to change ourselves to change the world, we have to cease hijacking God in human affairs for all times to come. Instead, we have to invest our whole energy and resources to change our mindset; so that it may be in a position to follow the principle: 'Live and let live' simultaneously. Our salvation from 'dukh' (miseries) lies not in escapism, but in owing our very parentage of the baby-world, no matter the baby is beautiful or otherwise. Those advocates, who declare that we can do nothing, except prostrating before the Lord, as He is the sole doer of each and everything in the world, they suggest only an easiest and escaping route from our entire responsibilities for the web of our lives, whatever—good or bad we have been individually or collectively weaving with our own knitpins as human spiders. Beware of them.

If we change our gear of thinking, it is O.K. Otherwise, the people like Swamiji's friends are apt to make God a scapegoat for one's own wickedness. That is why, Swamiji's friend rightly involved God in his wicked impulse by telling: "But it is He who is giving me the wicked impulse? (On page 275 Vol. 7 *Swamiji's Works*).

But in order to have a face saving device Swamiji responsed him: "No, by no means. It would be blaspheming the Lord to think in that way. He is not inciting you to evil action, it is all the creation of your desire for self-gratification." Thus, Swamiji too dragged his Lord out of human affairs out of his sheer convenience. When you drag Him in, how can you drag Him out? When 'I am directed by His will', the Lord must be responsible for all impulses that conceive in our minds, no matter they are good or bad.

Swamiji in order to find no alternative before him suggested us a strange solution. He says, "Rather say that He is causing the good work to be done, while you are responsible for the evil action." (On page 275 Vol. 7 *Swamiji's Works*) I humbly hold that it is our sheer folly to compartmentalise all our impulses into these two: (1) self-regarding impulses of actions (2) Divine regarding impulses of actions. It is a dangerous inconsistency, we find in Swamiji's approach. Swamiji holds: 'we are all the puppets in Lords hands, and on the other he says, "the truth is . . . that no one has created you . . . you have created yourself . . . Therefore, the . . . aspirant should begin with the dualistic standpoint, that the Lord is causing the good actions, while he is doing the evil." (On page 275 Vol. 7 *Swamiji's Works*). Are there two creators, if there is at all creation?

When we are all the puppets in His hands, how can we accept Swamiji's plea that no one has created you . . . you have created yourself? Of course, it is most truthful to believe 'that no one has created you . . . you have created yourself . . .', because we are architects of our own destinies. It is untruthful rather to believe that we are puppets in His hands.

The idea of Swamiji seems to be not founded on good grounds, when he says, ". . . if one sincerely believes that the most wicked impulse is also prompted by the Lord, rest assured that one will not have to do those mean acts for long." (On page 276 Vol. 7 *Swamiji's Works*). The example of Osama bin Laden is before us these days. He has been sponsoring the most dangerous terrorism in the world in the name of his

God or 'Jehad'. In His name only he has got his net of terrorism spread throughout the world. In fact, these wicked impulses of ours have been breathing freely in His name.

In fact, when we believe that our wicked impulse is also prompted by the Lord, we are apt to believe and throw away our own responsibilities here or there either in confusion or otherwise. Hence, Swami Vivekanandji says, "We human beings are very slow to recognise our own weaknesses—men in general lay all the blame of life on their fellow-men, or failing that, on God, or they conjure up a ghost, and say it is fate. Where is fate; and who is fate? We reap what we sow, we are the makers of our own fate . . . we make our own destiny . . . when you find yourselves suffering, blame yourselves, and try to do better . . . say . . . this misery that I am suffering is of my own doing . . . Take the whole responsibility on your own shoulders, and know that you are the creator of your own destiny . . . Therefore, make your own future . . . (On page 224-225 Vol. 2 *Swamiji's Works*)

When Swamiji teaches us that it is He who makes our rise and it is He makes our fall, how can he expect from all of us to blame our ownselves, when we suffer in this world? Of course, it is the truth of all truths. The fact is that we talk in a great confusion. Instead of making God, had we made ourselves the true makers of our own destiny, we would not have given our own sufferings any leases of life again and again. This blind 'bhakti' is the only cause of our whole confusion. Unless we come out of this dark tunnel, we cannot see the light. Swamiji's puppets in Lord's hands have no minds of their own to see their own weaknesses themselves. How can these 'puppets' ever even imagine to create their own destinies or future? Unless we reject the dismal view of human puppets in Lord's hands, we cannot accept, that we are the true creators of our own destinies—good or bad. Either we accept the truth, or live in utter darkness of confusion. No more hypocrisy will do any good to us.

We talk of religion, but we have confined our religion into the four walls of what is to be eaten and what not on a particular day; what rites or dogmas are to be performed and how. All our talks regarding religion are nothing, but speculations. Swamiji rightly says, "To the students of religion almost ninety-nine per cent of the books and thoughts of religion are mere speculations. One man thinks religion is this and another, that . . . when they could not reason out, they said, Believe." (On page 429 Vol. 7 *Swamiji's Works*).

Due to those speculations Buddha's views were more practical, rational, scientific, more appealing and more worth adopting indeed.

robot? To know this fact in advance, instead of rising to fight, no sensible brave soldier would ever like to go to the battle field to fulfill simply this formality of fighting. I do not know how was Arjuna, Krishna's 'Bhakat' and 'sakha' (friend) ready to fight ultimately. A soldier is a solider, but not a puppet. If he comes to know that it is the job of the commander to put all the soldiers of the enemy to death, and not his actually, then instead of becoming bolder, he is apt to become a permanent coward and an escapist, or a fatalist and shirker.

To prepare Arjuna ready to fight the war and fulfil his duties by Krishna was alright. But to pour into Arjuna's mind that he was neither a saviour, nor a destroyer of anybody in the war, he was only His 'nimit', an instrument, it was Krishna's strategy to get even brave soldiers morally degraded unconsciously. Of course, Krishna's aim was not this, but to prepare Arjuna to fight the war without caring for the results of the fight. People believe that Arjuna went to the battle field on Krishna's insistence, and fought in the war ultimately. But the question is when the motive of war was already fulfilled by Krishna Himself, I do not know being motiveless how Arjuna had gone to the battle-field and with whom he fought there? It was, in fact, a strange play, played by Krishna. It was strange, because on the one hand, Krishna told Arjuna to know clearly that he was not to kill anyone in the war, as all have been already killed by Him, and on the other, Krishna wants to use Arjuna simply His '*nimit*' in the war in these activities of killing or 'leela'.

We must remember that no soldier ever goes to the battlefield without any motive—good or bad. No soldier follows 'work for work sake' principle in the war. I believe that being hypnotised by Krishna, Arjuna failed to ask His master as to what remained there for him to fight, when everybody was already killed by Him in advance. Arjuna must have been bewildered and became like a puppet in Krishna's hands.

The question has been very pertinent. The question is how can one ever work without a motive, if one is not a lunatic, who only wanders here or there even without any purpose? Motive is like the wheel of any work or activity. If there is no motive, there will be no activity or work. No motive, no work has been the age old rule of the world of activities. Of course, when we adopt bad motive, it causes its bad results, and when we adopt good motive, it causes good results.

It is certain that we must know where to attach, and where not to attach ourselves at the same time. We must be well aware of this fact that even a baby plays for joy without knowing its motive. But motive is there. If one's motive of prayer is to attain money, then one leaves praying, if one gets money even in the midst of prayer. On the other, if one's motive of work is purification of one's personality, and if by chance one gets God in the midst of this work, he would not leave it. He will go on trying for purification of one's mind. Once, Ghalib, the great too ceased to worship in its midst, when he was tempted to see a bottle of wine.

Certainly, the soldiers have no free-will, how to fight the enemy in a war. They are to follow their commanders, who decide the whole strategy of war. But in case only the commander fights and not his soldiers, as he is the doer of all things, then the commander cannot escape from the responsibility either of victory or defeat in a war.

If a commander hopes to make his soldiers more brave, but less egoists, or better human beings by disclosing in advance that the soldiers are only his '*nimits*', as Krishna did, I humbly feel, then the commander concerned is living merely in a fool's paradise only. Again, I humbly feel it is most unpsychological to snatch the very right of doing anything or the right of free-will of doing anything from the people of the world in the hope that they would be less egoists by tempting them to feel as if being 'nimits', they do nothing, except to prostrate before their Lord. Had it been a reality, there would have been only humans, and not brutes, moving in this world.

In such a case, the 'nimits' are apt to lose their own responsibilities either for their good or bad fabric of lives. A greater loss indeed!

Instead of seeing them more brave or less egoists, every such commander will make them more escapists. Krishna's sermon to Arjuna might have been a boon for him but it has been proved for others practically a poison, as it yielded only a bumper crop of mere escapists in the world. Today the real siblings of the priests of Somnath temple (when it was looted) are found moving in every family, and in every petty lane of the world. Do they do anything to build themselves from within, except prostrating before their beloved Lord? Do they really take the living gods and goddesses as their equally beloved? Am I exaggerating? After all, eating, resting and sleeping even four feet animals can do. Can we build ourselves from within merely by prostrating?

By nature in fact, we all Indians are mystic in our behaviour. Even great Dr. Radhakrishnan pleads! "If you can define God, He ceases to be your God." Really, a strange logic of a great philosopher! Should then we ever like to see the ashes of 'agyan' lying on us?'

Jesus too preached us 'The Sermon on the Mount' to save us but, you see, we cannot forget the most unfortunate chapter of living human's history that in His honest efforts of saving the world, we crucified Jesus, the great, our saviour on the nail due to our little-mindedness only. Nobody knows how many such honest human saviours, we have already crucified under His nose in His kingdom and how many more we need? Does it not clearly show that it is not some deity, but human spiders, who weave the web of their lives—good or bad with their own knitpins? When the real architects of their own destinies work like tools in a divine machine, they have no alternative, except to work with the 'psyche of low and weak' only. For them to change their brutish nature and their world is beyond their imagination even.

We think our religion begins and ends with our prayers. The prayers we usually chant: *'Jai Ganesh, Jai Ganesh, Jai Ganesh deva . . .', and 'Vishia vikar mitao, pap haro deva, Swami pap haro deva . . .'* definitely increase our blind faith in the deity, but they instead of making us less egoists or more humble necessarily, suck all faith from our minds. Has He removed our evil tendencies? The old saying that the tale of a dog remains twisted even after 12 years is more relevant in the context of this belief that we His Master's pet dogs on a long leash keep our tale of evils twisted even throughout our lives.

There is a *puranic* tale, which narrates how once a peripatetic saint, known as Narad posed before the so-called Lord Vishnu, known as our saviour or sustainer an humble question: "O, Lord, name your greatest Bhakta". Narad believed that Lord Vishnu's reply would be, "Of course, yourself, Narada". But beggars are never choosers. It is true had wishes been horses, even beggars would have tried to ride on them. On seeing Lord Vishnu quite mum or non-plussed, Narad asked the Lord: "Why this hesitation?" I am, by all means, Your biggest 'bhakta'. Am I not chanting your name all the time. "Narayana, Narayana—your attribute?" Lord Vishnu had no alternative, but He smiled to have the arrogant claim. why? Because in Lord's eyes only that person could claim to be His 'bhakta', who always thought, felt and did good, whatever one could, wherever one was, and not that person, who chanted only. "Narayana, Narayana" all times in a day. This is not at all to put the saint in question in the dock in any way.

The moral of this tale is that a person, who follows His real message or teachings in one's life is His real 'bhakta', and not necessarily a person, who simply prostrates before the Lord and chants 'Narayana; Narayana'. It is in this context, it is said that a hand in help is better than two hands together. In fact, our good thoughts, good feelings, and good doings are our real prayers. If we follow honestly 'live and let live', that is the greatest prayer we can do. That is the greatest meditation we can do.

It is told Narada was dumb-founded, as it was a strange thing for a saint like him to see his ego completely shattered. In fact, one prays and wishes the best, who thinks, feels and does the best not only for oneself, but for all at the same time, what one can, wherever one is to be good only. When we wish in our prayer "all the best for all out of pure universal love, our prayer too acts like a balm and a baladona plaster. Of course, prayer can never be a better substitute of a good medicine or our good action. For pious prayer every place is a temple, and every living person is like a living god or goddess. We may or may not pray to God, but if we do not pray or wish for the living gods and goddesses out of pure love, our prayer is a sheer wastage.

So, let us no more make God as an escaping route from our responsibilities. Pure prayer and pure wish sprout only in pure minds. In case our minds stink with foul or filthy thinking, feelings and doings, they are to see only rubbishness. We can say 'No' to God, but we can say 'No' to good at our own peril only.

The whole emphasis of Buddha was on doing good to be good only. While Krishna kept the role of doer of all things to Himself in the Gita, Buddha told his disciples: "Let there be no false bondage, no dependence on me, no false glorification of the passing personality . . .". Thus, Buddha did not want to treat any human as his pet or '*nimit*', and, consequently, Buddha had no long or small leash in his own hands to decide people's destiny himself even when he was at his death bed. He wanted: let people work out their own salvation themselves. In fact, unlike Krishna, Buddha did not believe in his own monopoly of works. Actually, Buddha made all people free from the age old bondage of a hypothetical God to realise that it is not Buddha, but they themselves are the real architects of their own destinies—good or bad. Let us remember Krishna imparted the lesson of 'passive-karma yoga', instead of 'active-karma yoga' to Arjuna. According to Buddha, if people have been bogged down in the marshy land of 'adharma', they need not wait for any divine-crane for their upliftment, as they are to uplift themselves. Let us remember this remarkable difference in the approaches of these two great human giants.

How correct Swami Vivekanandji is to tell the truth: "The vast majority of people do not understand the meaning of this doctrine . . . Buddha . . . made man stand on his feet."! (On page 102 Vol. 8 *Swamiji's Works*)

Swamiji added: "Buddha's idea is there is no God, only man himself." (On page 101 Vol. 8 *Swamiji's Works*)

Buddha's doctrine was: "why is there misery in our life? Because we are selfish. We desire things for ourselves—that is why there is misery.

It is our misfortune that we failed to understand his entire doctrine. He was the first revolutionary thinker in the entire history of the world that he stood for the good of men. What an unfortunate thing it is for all human beings that God was conceived for men, but men made themselves meant for God! He diagnosed the human disease (miseries) on the basis of his most scientific analytical studies and gave his patent prescription (the removal of exclusive self). Thus, Buddha was the first human giant to impart us the lesson of active Karmayoga. To help human beings in the right perspective was Buddha's only religion. No-doubt, the climb, he suggested, was very steep and hard, but if we want to reach the highest altitude of spiritual attainment, we have no other option.

Let us listen to the voice of science and not superstition. Prof. H. Narasimhaiah in his book *Science, Non-science and Paranormal* says: "There is no evidence of the working of any supernatural force". (on page 163-164). But, unfortunately, most of us have only close minds. Mind is like a parachute, which works when it is open.

In fact, the unfortunate inertia and passiveness on our parts to understand Buddha's doctrine has caused us our unfortunate cordon by our age old miseries from all sides. We never realised that without eliminating the 'exclusive self' from our minds, we can never dream even for our salvation, no matter how many times a day we lie prostrate before Him.

Let us understand the language of reason only. Dr. Narasimhaiah says in the same book: "There seems to be more truth in the statement of Voltaire that man created God than in the belief that God created men . . . There is no creation. Everything is evolution."

If there is more dangerous type of negativism, it is in our belief, which teaches every baby with his/her milk here that this world is '*mithya*' (illusion or dream) or full of sufferings or '*dukhas*'. We are taught that we are all to go from this world one day, it is no use to beautify our world. We are here only for a transitionary period. Ultimately, our goal of life is to reach Vaikunth, a hypothetical heaven. The truth is that the world or our life is neither good, nor evil in itself. It is what, we make it. In fact, our birth or the so-called death are nothing, but two important stages in our evolution. Let us then highlight the positive side of our lives. Of course, we should not behave like slaves of this world, but only its natural masters. Why to seek the very filth or rubbishness of this world? Why not try and try earnestly for spiritual attainment, living in the world? Why to be escapists then? Is it not a truth that being hypocrites we go on dubbing the world as '*mithya*' or dream or illusion and even then we behave like the slaves of the same world? Do these foolish philosophers leave anything using from this so-called illusory world? Why do they not leave it and go to a hypothetical heaven? Vedanta is for us. We are not meant for Vedanta.

Merely taking a dip in the sacred water of the Ganges would not purify us. Had it been a fact, all the fish, which remain in the water 24 hours, would have been the purest beings in the world. These rituals or dogmas, what we usually think as the real passport to heaven can never be the better substitutes of our good thinking, feelings and doings. Let us remove our age old illusion: Our main goal of life is not to attain God, but to be good men by doing good only. Buddha became a Buddha not by prostrating himself before any hypothetical Lord, but by elevating himself on the higher altitude of his thinking, feeling and doing, known as meditation for 'nirvana'. Since our miseries and sins are the main products of our own evil thinking, feelings and doings, it is usually our good thoughts, good feelings and good deeds that can purify us.

We are still living in the world of superstitions. It is not correct to believe as Swami Vivekanandji does that "every human being is divine" (on page 186 Vol. 8 *Swamiji's Works*) Let us be practical and say man is neither devil, nor divine essentially, but what one makes oneself. Otherwise, where do these evils come from?

"Numerous studies have shown that astrology is not a science", says Jayant Narlikar, an Astrophysicist. Still we find ourselves lying deep in superstitions! It has been pointed out by 186 scientists from all over the world and 19 Nobel laureates, including Sri S. Chandrashekhar, an India born scientist that "the time has come to challenge directly and forcefully the pretentious claims of astrological charlatans."

Let us believe that there is no such thing as fate, predetermined. Because Buddha was not at all superstitious, Swami Vivekanandji paid very rich tributes to Buddha in these words: "I am the servant of the servant of the Buddha." How good it would have been, had we instead of surrendering ourselves to a hypothetical Lord for our moral upliftment, surrendered our 'exclusive self', at least, by and by earnestly from our lives to attain 'nirvana'—the complete freedom in our present life like Buddha!

Swami Vivekanandji further praised Buddha rightly: "Even when dying, he would not claim any distinction for himself. I worship him for that. What you call Buddha and Christ are only the names of certain states of realisation. Of all the teachers of the world, he was the one who taught us most to be self-reliant, who freed us not only from the bondage of our false selves, but from dependence on the invisible being or beings called

God or gods. He invited everyone to enter into the state of freedom which he called 'Nirvana". (on page 105 Vol. 8 *Swamiji's Works*)

Really speaking, Buddha was matchless in so many respects. He was more clear headed in the sense that he made sincerely everyone of us an important unit to bring revolution to everybody's door by oneself through surrendering one's own most dreaded enemy i.e., 'exclusive self' without depending on the usual mercy or blessings of an unknown and invisible, called as God.

That is why, I truly feel that Buddha was matchless in the sense that he was one of the most truly epoch-making human giants in the whole world. I bow before him with my highest esteem. But there is one difference here. I do not bow before him, as people do this customarily before their God to get themselves uplifted by Him, but because I treat him as one of our greatest 'gurus' ever born in the world to suggest us ways to remove our miseries. I bow before him to get inspiration from him to get uplifted by my ownself.

Buddha's main teaching was that everyone of us without any distinction was potential to realise good in one's life simply by removing one's 'exclusive self'. In short, his message was: 'do good to be good'. He told that everyone can be free, if everyone tries earnestly to remove one's little-mindedness or little self. So long as we do not do it, we are all slaves of our little self. His second message was that none of us need to wait for one's upliftment for an invisible and unknown hypothetical power, known as God. In fact, Buddha had no faith in any divine power, but only in manhood. In Buddha's view, if one removes one's exclusive self from one's mind, one gets freedom or state of 'nirvana'. How right it was! In fact, what we all need is to change our bad spar, if it is there, to be a good navigator.

Just to boost up one's faith in oneself Dr. Radhakrishnan made it clear! "If anyone asks why we suffer, we need not point to the stars above, or say that God has punished us. We have to put it down to our iniquities, our disloyalties and our deviations from the ideals, which we profess. We have the best ideals inscribed and embodied in our constitution, but how many of us are carrying them out properly?"

So, we may or may not have any faith in God or soul, but let us have faith in our destiny, made by our ownselves, no matter whether it is good or bad. Prof. H. Narasimhaiah holds in his famous book *Science, Non-science and Paranormal*' on page 312-314; "Man is the master of his destiny, the architect of his future. He makes his own hell and heaven, and he makes it here and now . . . Humanism is opposed to . . . determinism, predestination and fatalism. Humanism examines everything in the light of reason . . . Humanists do not believe in making petitions to God through prayers or rituals."

Hence, in the words of Swami Vivekanandji: . . . "the Buddhists will stand up and declare—not only is it illogical, but immoral, for it teaches man to be a coward and seek assistance outside, and nobody can give him such help. Here is the universe, men made it; why then depend on an imaginary being outside, whom nobody ever saw, or felt, or got help from". (page 412 Vol. 3 *Swamiji's Works*)

I humbly hold it was not negativism, but realism, what Buddha represented, no matter who chews, who swallows, and who digests his doctrine in the right perspective, and who does not? Buddhists clearly warn us: "By constantly repeating, "we are very impure, Lord makes us pure," the result will be that you will hypnotise yourselves into all sorts of vices . . . if your ideal, your aim and goal is to go to the place called Vaikunth, where God lives, and then stand before Him with folded hands—it is better to commit suicide than do that." (on page 413 Vol. 3 *Swamiji's Works*).

Unlike Krishna, Buddha nowhere assured us to wait for Him for our salvation. Buddha told us: "work out your own salvation." "I cannot help you . . . no man can help you. Help yourself. (on page 478 Vol. 3 *Swamiji's Works*)

Ghalib, the great Urdu poet too says the truth:

"Humko malum hai Jannat ki hakikat lekin,
Dilke bahlane ko Ghalib, yah khyal achha hai."

[We know the reality of heaven, but in order to console one's heart, this is a good (thought).] In fact, we need not God-fearing people, but evil-fearing people.

I hold Buddha made his honest efforts to remove the age old hypothetical divine crutches from everyone's armpits and, consequently, made even a lame stand on one's own feet merely by changing one's very 'psyche of weak and low' altogether. He made everyone mentally free from the so-called divine shackles or dependance to do good, to be good, to change one's own destiny, and one's world oneself without waiting for an unknown. Of course, Buddha's doctrine was not supposed to be digested especially by the class of priests, and the so-called believers in general easily.

But it was beyond any doubt that it was the matchless contribution of Buddha, the great human giant to the entire humanity. We need not convert our religion to follow Buddha, but only to change our selfish attitude. It is we, who shackle our minds with this or that little-mindedness, and it is we who can unchain our minds, because it is we, who raise ourselves high, and it is we, who make us fall.

That is why, I truly believe that, Buddha was not only the so-called 'Light of Asia', but the tallest Light House' in the midst of the whole human ocean indeed. Buddha did not fail, but it was we the small human creatures the world over who have failed him to understand him and his immortal teachings in the right perspective. Now being foolish, inhuman, uncivilised and disloyal, some of us have definitely dismantled Buddha's statues with dynamite at Bamiyan. I treat it as inhuman to dismantle religious places of others too. Civilised world cannot imagine that some of us can even degrade ourselves to such a medieval barbarous act even in this 21st century. In fact, when fear does not remain our slave, but becomes our master, we too become inhumans and brutes even in the name of God.

Of course, Buddha was deadly against people worshipping him as a deity. People's usual petitional prayers too were allergic to the great human 'guru'. But we should not be much tensed to see such heinous crimes and sins, as Buddha, in fact, does not live in his idols or statues, but in the realisation of his matchless teachings. Real Buddhism is not worshipping, but being. Only foolish believe that a religion survives only through idols or statues, and it can die too, if they dynamite them. Let us realise Buddha was not only the name of a great human teacher, but he was a great institution for the removal of human miseries. Buddha can never die, because of his most precious immortal principles. But let us listen to Kabir: Let us blow off the husk, accept the grain only, where ever it is.

Long live the Buddha. Earlier we understand him and his teachings quite objectively without any bias, the better. If we really find that they can give the desired tonic to strengthen the sick humanity, accept them whole-heartedly not by building another Buddha's temple or erecting his statue here or there to worship him, but by removing our 'little self' from our tiny minds. That would be the greatest tribute to this great human giant indeed. Buddha does not need to build any memorial for him. If we human beings earnestly build ourselves as pure men, that will be the greatest memorial of the great Buddha indeed. Earlier we do it, the better. Better late than never.

Being humans we are not supposed to accept anything, no matter where it comes from, unless the thought is reasonable to build the huge edifice of humanity. Keeping it in view, I find there is a great inconsistency in the following statements of Swami Vivekanandji. Due to immense faith in the Lord, Swami Vivekanandji claims rightly on the one hand: "when we suffer, it is because of our own acts. God is not to be blamed for it." (on page 319 Vol. 1 *Swamiji's Works*) But on page 285 Vol. 6 in *Swamiji's Works*, he says something directly opposite to it. " . . . that he only rises, when He raises, and he falls, when He brings down . . ." Again, on page 125 Vol. 3 in his works, Swamiji again in a critical mood says something real. "We are the effects, and we are the causes . . . If I am unhappy, it has been of my own making . . ." The question is when He is the sole cause of both our rise or fall, how can we accept that we are the effects and we are the causes of our own making? Is it not all speculative and paradoxical? Of course, the truth of all truths is that we are all the effects and we are the causes of our own making. But how can we accept the untruth that he only rises, when He raises, and he falls, when He brings down? Earlier we cease to drag Him in and drag Him out according to our convenience, the better.

Here is another statement of truth by Swami Vivekanandji again: "From my childhood I have heard of seeing God everywhere and in everything, and then I can really enjoy the world, but as soon as I mix with the world, and get a few blows from it, the idea vanishes. I am walking in the street thinking that God is in every man, and a strong man comes along and gives me a push and I fall flat on the footpath. Then I rise up quickly with clinched fist, the blood has rushed to my head, and the reflection goes. Immediately, I have become mad. Everything is forgotten, instead of encountering God I see the devil. Ever since we were born we have been told to see God in all. Every religion teaches that—see God in everything and everywhere. Do you not remember in the *New Testament* how Christ says so? . . . but it is when we come to the practical side, that the difficulty begins." (on page 151 Vol. 2 *Swamiji's Works*) What a great truth Swami ji has told! So, it is all futile to be speculative about God. It is no use to fire in the air in the name of God anymore. So, let us accept the truth then that God is nowhere and if at all He exists, He cannot make everybody's mind His oasis.

When Swamiji puts himself out of the mood of worship, he is found standing dipping in the Ganges of truth. He says, "We are the makers of our own fate." (on page 224 Vol. 2 *Swamiji's Works*). "Take the whole responsibility on your own shoulders, and know that you are the creator of your own destiny." (on page 225 Vol. 2 *Swamiji's Works*)

But see the paradoxical change in Swamiji's yourself, when he talks as a staunch bhakat of his Lord. He says, "It is all really in sport; the universe is His play going on . . . If you are poor, enjoy that as fun; if you are rich, enjoy the fun of being rich; if dangers come, it is also good fun; if happiness comes, there is more good fun. The world is just a playground: . . .

built by any divine entity, but they were the products of evolution, which has ever been going on automatically by itself in the universe. We have no right to misguide, at least, now the new generation about these stars and satellites, etc.

If you do not know the way, you are asked for by a passerby, it is always safer to say 'I do not know', rather to misguide him/her. I would like to be apologised for this view. President Truman boasted: "This is the greatest thing in history." Was it really great, because President Truman too played with God, who lives in every atom? Or because his men did the greatest heinous crime alongwith him against humanity?

Thus, this Swamiji's philosophy puts a dark curtain of gloom on the faces of the so-called makers of their own destinies actually. Swamiji forgot easily that there are individual, social, economic and political factors behind one's poverty or one's affluence, one's life of miseries or happiness. To link them all with the blessings of a hypothetical Lord, Swamiji, in fact, gave people's attention and their hard-earned energies and resources to a wrong turn. Being disgusted then, some of us might feel, as if we are sailing on an unchartered sea. Let us remember for the real architects of their own destinies, there is nothing to be disgusted. Only firm determination is needed. Let us be humans, and no more brutes. The hundred dollar question is: How can 'Swami ji's chess-men' change themselves and then change their world too, what Marx aimed at? Chessmen never change, but they are changed by somebody else.

What a fun it is! On the one hand Swamiji declares: 'The universe is His play going on', and on the other, he claims: "This is the Law of Karma. Each one of us is the maker of his own fate . . . We, we and none else are responsible for what we suffer . . ." What a horrible inconsistency we see here! We are in a dilemma: what is true and what is myth? His both versions cannot go together. Now we have no alternative: either we have faith in Him and simply behave as His Master's pet dogs on a long leash as before, or have immense faith in our ownselves and behave as perfect architects of our own destinies—good or bad. But let us no more behave like hypocrites. Be ready to face the music, what we play.

On page 100 Vol. 3 in his own works, Swami Vivekanandji again says boldly, but in a worshipping mood: "The whole world is a lunatic asylum . . . If you are mad after money, I am mad after God . . . I think my madness is after all the best." My humble submission in this respect is that madness, no matter what colour it is, has never been a good thing, because the moment one becomes mad after this or that, one becomes a slave of that, and, consequently, one's *vivek*, or '*buddhi*' or power of discrimination to decide what is right and what is wrong in a given circumstance too disappears. It is almost a state of no light, but heat only. It is only in their madness of the so-called god, the terrorists are bent upon finishing human civilisation and humanity itself in the name of the so-called '*Jehad*'. They do not know that 'Jehad' is mainly meant to remove little-self and one's evils from one's minds. Let us see what even saints like Swami Vivekanandji say something merely in blind faith. He says, "If you ask, you are a '*sanyasin*', so why do you trouble over these desires?"—I would then reply, I am Ramakrishna's servant, and I am willing even to steal and rob, if by doing so I can perpetuate his name in the land of his birth . . ." (on page 241 Vol. 6 *Swamiji's Works*). It was all in the context of building a temple to perpetuate the name of his 'guru'. It proves how dangerous it is to be mad after this or that.

From this we can very well imagine how madness here which is the very off-spring of blind faith, is dangerous! I know Swamiji believed that 'means justify the end', and thus I know such a great Swami can never go to steal or rob for anything, whatsoever. But it shows how our mind shows red-light, when it has blind faith in this or that. Actually, this world needs not madness of God, but an innate earnest desire to be good men indeed. We have fought enough wars in the name of religion in the world merely out of our madness: Have we become better human beings today? No. so, this world is not like a lunatic asylum. Here we do not need mad people but people with a mind to follow earnestly the principle: 'Live and let live' side by side. Brutes only want to live alone. They do not bear to see others living around themselves. We are all humans. Let us then follow peaceful co-existence, to be happier and to have a more calm mind of our own. We can forget that we are real architects of our own destinies, at our own peril only. Of course, madness after money or this or that is equally dangerous.

It is only in blind faith, when one's reasoning stops responding well, one takes the help of past Karmas to believe. Swami Vivekanandji too gives his plea in this respect: " . . . it is not the fault of God . . . but how can this difference of some being born happy and some unhappy be explained? They . . . Not in this life, but they did it in their last birth . . ." (on page 124 Vol. 3 *Swamiji's Works*)

It seems to be like following the same wolf, which told the lamb: 'If you have not called me bad names, then your father must . . .' Do we know anything about our past authentically? If not, why to try to scratch our past, if there is any? Why do we not live in the present to make it a better and better one; so that we may have our future the best one possible. Let us no more try to escape from our responsibilities. Because causes of one's happiness or unhappiness in life are many. There may be individual, social, economic and political reasons behind one's present. Moreover, nobody is born happy or unhappy here. The real causes of one's happiness or unhappiness are mainly concerned with either one's individuality or heredity or environment.

It is relevant to quote Swami Vivekanandji in this respect: "If you make a plea of Karma by saying that men die through Karma, then it becomes a settled fact that it is useless to try to struggle for anything in the world . . . it can be said (then)-the mother-cows through their own Karma fall into the hands of butchers and die and we need not to do anything in the matter. (on page 451 Vol. 6 *Swamiji's Works*)

This all shows how we have been misusing Karma theory. Let us remember there is no greater 'Tirtha' (holy spot) than the mind of an innocent good man in this world. If he too suffers, it is not essentially due to his past, if there is any, but due to the unfortunate circumstances, what we have made here. Here every great man has to suffer, because he is ahead of his age and time. We simply escape from our own doings, if we justify one's present on the basis of one's past.

Here is the befitting reply to those, who remember God both when they wake up in the morning, and when they go to their bed too, but forget the men around them throughout the day. Swami Vivekanandji says, "I do not believe in a God who cannot give me bread here, giving me eternal bliss in heaven". (on page 368 Vol. 4 *Swamiji's Works*) When He does not exist, the question of giving to anybody this or that, now in this life or in the life to come does not arise at all. It's only our age old illusion.

Swami Vivekanandji too realised the realities of this world ultimately, when he spoke: "I almost lost my patience when I see these underhand dealings. This is the world—those whom you love best and help most try to cheat you—." (on page 372 Vol. 8 *Swamiji's Works*). That is why, I humbly believe that one's happiness or unhappiness depends on the world, what we, the architects of our own destinies, make it. It has never been the off-spring of any deity. When we experience here that 'those whom you love best, and help most try to cheat you', how can we say man is essentially divine, or God lives in all? By simply firing in the air we cannot turn our hell into a heaven on earth. Let us accept the ground—realities first.

Let us bear in our minds that religion does not consist in our tall talks, or sermons or volumnous books or scriptures, or temples, or doctrines, or discourses, or in going on a pilgrimage or holding a huge 'satsang' with all pomp and show, or delivering long lectures or prescribing some do's or don'ts, performance of this or that ritual or dogma, but in earnest realisation only. Let no reader be under the illusion that merely reading of good things or virtues or good books is religion essentially. If I am writing '*Architect of Human Destiny*'?, I must not live under the impression that I am essentially doing some religious work. May be or may not be. Religion is realisation. Religion is neither learning, nor reading, nor writing, but being. Who does not know that we should not tell lies without a valid reason? Again, who does not know we should not steal? Again, who is not aware of that we should not harm or hurt or injure others without a genuine cause? But knowing of truth is not enough. It is not religion? It is all useless like a load of sandalwood on the back of an ass, if we have no earnest will or conscience to live up to them? It is only due to this reason religion is known as the art of right action. Knowledge of good is not essentially religion, but when our good comes into our humble actions, that becomes religion. Religion is transformation of good into our being.

The very implications of this nuclear age is: either we can live together, or die together. No alternative. In this context, let us remember if religion is only a system of faith in God, and if it is mainly associated with His worship, then Buddhism is not a religion. Buddha never believed that we can gain 'nirvana' (perfect freedom) or purity in our lives either by seeking refuse in the Buddha or by having mere faith in Buddha or by worshipping Buddha as a deity. Buddha was against God. He believed in manhood only. He was clear-headed on this point particularly that it is not within the power even of himself to wash out the impurities or the dust or the filth of the minds of others. He nowhere claimed to have such unusual divine powers.

In the Dhammapada Buddha says:

"By oneself alone is evil done; by oneself is one defiled.
By oneself alone is evil avoided; by oneself alone is one purified."

So, none of us is supposed to worship Buddha as God at all. If we remove our 'exclusive self' or little-mindedness from our minds, that will be the greatest tribute to that great human giant indeed. We can have Buddha's image in our minds; we can have Buddha's idol on our table, as we have the photos of our elders, hanging on the walls of our sleeping room, just to get real constant inspiration from them for virtuous life. But by doing this, let no one understand that Buddha is going to change our destinies for good. We are all makers of our own destinies—good or bad. Buddha can take us to the pool, but he cannot make us drink.

According to Buddha: " . . . He honours me best, who practises my teachings best."

Let us remember Buddha nowhere claimed the monopoly of knowing the truth. Hence he recommended: "Intolerance is the greatest enemy of religion". Buddha always advised his disciples not to get angry, discontented or displeased even when others spoke ill of him. How relevant Buddha is especially in this context today in this most intolerant world!

It is true Buddha had not expressed his views about some problems that perplexed humanity, because they were irrelevant to his noble mission and they were unnecessary to one's emancipation. His mission was the emancipation of the people from their miseries. So, Buddha embraced all people without any bias. According to Buddha the cause of human-sufferings is craving or attachment. But the question is if we want to live, can we live life on this earth or in this world, what it is without any attachment or craving or desire at all? Actually, what we all need the most urgently is to have our earliest proficiency in the art of both attachment and detachment at the same time. We must know what it is to be attached, and what it is to be detached at a particular moment by us. I think Buddha became the Buddha, because he was the most proficient artist in this respect. Buddha knew well the art of giving the right ordering to both attachments as well as detachments in his life. That is why, he got 'nirvana'. He was against excessive attachment only to make life almost painless and stressless for all.

But we find great paradoxical inconsistencies in Swamiji's approach, because on the one hand he says, 'world is neither good, nor evil in itself', which I think is the most factual statement, Swamiji has given. But on the other, Swami Vivekanandji says just the opposite of it. According to him, "Is it such a bad choice in this world to think not of matter but of spirit, . . . not of man but of God? That intense faith in another world, that intense hatred for this world, that intense power of renunciation, that intense faith in God . . . I challenge anyone to give it up. You cannot . . ." (on page 221 Vol. 3 *Swamiji's Works*). Let us remember God was conceived in humans mind for humans, and not vice versa. The question is why is there such intensive faith in another world? After all, we cannot say there is all around evil and evil in this world, and no good. Moreover, is it not truer to say that our world is neither good nor evil in itself, but it is what we make it. Why is then the intensive hatred for the world? Why to think not of man but of God? Will we be the better human beings merely by thinking of God? Why do not we remember, what Buddha prescribed for us to be better human beings? Buddha's prescription was: "Do good, to be good."

My humble submission is: we may or may not think of God, but we have no choice, but to think of men. Because, we have already made our God, but we have failed to make ourselves. So, let us follow Buddha to do so. We cannot love God, if at all He is there, by forgetting the living gods and goddesses? Let us live in the world as humans and not brutes. Let us no more allow our vices or our evils to make our minds their easy oasis to live in, if we earnestly want to change ourselves to change the world. For this all we shall have to restore faith in our own steersmenship. Let us try to remove all the possible causes of world hatred first. If we do it, peace will enter our minds on its own. If our minds are calm, we shall love the world not as its slaves, but its real masters only. We may or may not love God, that would not make any difference. Let us love men and their world. If we do it, we shall feel the difference ourselves. So, let us follow earnestly the old principle: 'live and let live' to love men and the world too. Let us no more wait for Him for our own upliftment. Let us only rely on our own efforts for our emancipation from our own miseries. He cannot help us, no matter whether He is somewhere or not. It is only a matter of pride, and not at all of any ego, if we build our ownselves, and do not depend on any. This is the proper way for our spiritual as well as material world to develop.

Of course, in building our ownselves our motive of work must be good and not evil. In fact, in this world we do not work without any motive, no matter if one is sane or insane. The difference lies in their good or bad motives respectively. In this world, if we say 'no motive, no work', there is no exaggeration in it. This principle is common, as it applies to all.

Even Swami Vivekanandji too accepted this reality. He says, "Man works with various motives. There cannot be work without motive . . . Some people want to get fame, and they work for fame. Others want money, and they work for money . . . Others want to get to heaven, they work for the same." (page 31-32 Vol. 1 *Swamiji's Works*)

Swamiji adds further: "work for work sake. There are some . . . who work for work's sake, who do not care for name, for fame, or even to go to heaven. They work just because good will come of it." (on page 22 Vol. 1 *Swamiji's Works*) Swamiji overlooked the fact unconsciously to say 'they work just because good will come of it.' Obviously, they too are not without any motive in their lives. Of course, their motive is higher.

Even Osho accepted the truth, when he said: "I am alive only to see a few of my plants blossoming, a few of my trees bringing fruits. I have devoted my whole life . . ." He adds: "Now my only remaining work is . . . to turn your eyes towards the truth." Here osho's 'I' and 'my' are working on a higher altitude of life. Hence they are good—instruments.

Thus, work for work's sake seems to be an ideal simply of fairy tales. Even Swamiji himself worked with motive. He says, "I have been running all the time between Boston and New York . . . In Both my success is more than ordinary . . ." (on page 64 Vol. 5 *Swamiji's Works*). Of course, swamiji was on a very high mission, and naturally every human wants to make his/her mission a grand success, because success acts like a calmpose or a balm. Swamiji accepts this fact again by telling: "Last Sunday's lecture was very much appreciated . . ." (on page 370 Vol. 8 *Swamiji's Works*). This all shows how our good motives boost our morale.

This makes it amply clear that only the lunatics loiter here or there without any motive or purpose even. Others cannot work, because motive is like a spar upon which the sail of our ship of life is bent. The fact is that if you remove the motive from life, you shall see the work at hand too is removed from one's life. So, what we need is not to remove the motive from work, but to remove our selfish motive only.

Had there been a fool-proof system, which would have provided everyone's due to everyone, perhaps, there would not have been any thought of result or reward of work in one's mind. Hence, it has become a part of human nature that if 'there is no reward, there is no work' in this world. There are people who go to their beds hungry even after shedding their sweat throughout the day. Does any God come to their rescue in this respect? Instead of making efforts to deliver justice to all, people try to justify one's poverty or one's unhappiness or one's richness or happiness on the basis of one's past Karmas, just to put a lollipop in their mouth. Work without motive is seen only in books and not in our practices.

Marx would not have needed to propose: 'From each according to one's capacity, to each according to one's work/need in his *Eldorado*, had there been even a divine entity to provide one's due for one's work. Only in extreme attachments on one side and extreme detachments on the other side of the fencing we see injustice is done by us here or there. It is not our attachment or detachment, but extreme attachment and extreme detachment, that emits 'lava' in a family, or in a country or in the entire world, because both turn us into slaves or brutes. In extreme attachment with their own religion or God, the terrorists talk of 'Jehad', and do all inhuman activities today.

Let us remember man can be the greatest of all beings and these living gods and goddesses are greater than any God. Swami Vivekanandji too endorses this view: "The older I grow, the more I see behind the idea of the Hindus that man is the greatest of all beings. So say the

Mohammedans too . . . This earth is higher than all heavens." (on page 94 Vol. 5 *Swamiji's Works*).

In Swamiji's eyes this earth is higher than all heavens. Why to see heaven in the sky then? Why do we not turn our own planet earth in heaven by our own good thinking, feelings and doings? If we adopt this religion, it will be the first right step in the right direction. Rituals or dogmas may be necessary to some extent, but they are like husk of religion. If this earth is higher than all heavens, then why to have craze for Vaikunth, the heaven?

It is our good motive of work that goes on giving us oxygen, and, consequently, fresh breathing in our lives too goes on. It does not allow any choking at all. So, our good motive inspires us for living with a sense of purpose. It gives meaning to our lives, and a subsequent feeling that, at least, we would not leave the world a worse place to live in by our own doings. That is why, it is rightly said that 'work is its own reward'. Hence, one feels rewarded even in one's unfortunate failings here in the world, because one feels rewarded only in purposeful living, no matter there is success or unsuccess in this human world.

So, I humbly believe that Karma theory, which professes: 'work, but not with any motive or with any desire of getting some reward or fruit, leaving it to the will of God', is nothing, but a sheer myth. I feel it is Swami ji's figment of imagination only to view it that "we are simply working out His will and have nothing to do with rewards and punishments . . . seek no praise, no reward, for anything you do". All know that if there are good people, there are people with their filthy minds. Are then all the people like Osama bin Laden, Veerappan, Billa and Ranga and the like, who have their filthy minds, working out His will too? Here Swamiji's people are only His Master's pet dogs on a long leash, and not like architects of their own destinies. If we accept that the sane persons are working out His will, then question that at once crops up, is whose will have the insane persons been working out in this world? Moreover, nobody knows where does He live, if at all He exists. Does He ever reward or punish the good or wrong-doer respectively? Then no faith in Him is possible. Only blind-faith one can have.

It is a matter of great pain that we Indians are more interested to have mystified talks, no matter there is sense or nonsense. Why do we not cease to hijack God in human affairs and believe that no matter there are sane or insane, all work out their own will only? Moreover, Swamiji's thesis, i.e., 'working out His will' is anti-thesis of human free-will. In case, if all work out only His will, how can we be responsible for the evils in this world? Then how can we be ready to reweave a better web of our lives as human spiders?

Let us remember only criminals and sinners are to thrive under the divine umbrella of this will. The innocents will ever remain crushed. In an age of escaping responsibility this Swamiji's thesis, i.e., 'we are working out His will' will be only a god's gift for them.

Earlier, we accept the right solution that being the architects of our own destinies, we have been working out our own will, no matter our will is good or bad, the better. There is no ego in this truth. How long can we go on riding on blind-faith?

We should neither follow that yogi of Swami Vivekanandji in a cave, because the yogi took even an animal's bite on one of his arms granted as Lord's will, nor the priests of Somnath temple, who remained only passive spectators of the looters, who looted the temple. Being escapists they thought that their duty only was to worship the Lord, and it was the Lords' will to make them safe and survive. What a fantastic world of their own that yogi and the priests in question actually lived in! Thus, the thesis 'we are simply working out His will' is simply a product of an age old superstition. Let us talk sense and no more try to rub the salt on the wounds of the victims by pleading this thesis before them. I humbly feel that the yogi and the priests both were the victims of divine hypnotism only, as there are crorers of people of such mindset in the world still-today. These talks are irrelevant today. Instead of taking us forward, they can apply only a back gear.

When a wasp or an ant bites us, it is its nature—why to drag Lord's will in such petty matters? The wasp or an ant is to bite, no matter one is sane or insane. Being foolish when we have no escape, we at once try to scratch one's past just to justify, what has happened, or is happening or would happen with oneself as an inevitable one's *fate-accompli*. How foolish we have been to make every happening in our lives wear the mask of divinity! Have we not made ourselves fools of the first order in this act of God's glorification? Have we become less egoists, and more humans merely by indulging in such false sense of divinity? Being foolish let us no more make our bodies like a delicious soup for the brutes. Let us no more try to live in a fairy world. Does it not all prove that we have been living simply in a make believe world for centuries, and our such beliefs are heretical only?

How strange it is that Swami Vivekanandji had accepted all the thieves, the murderers, all the unjust, the wickedest, the devils as his christ! Once, a disciple of Swamiji asked him rightly (on page 327, Vol. 5 *Swamiji's Works*):

Question of the disciple: "God may be in the love of the mother for her child; but, Sir, this idea is really perplexing that God is even in the thieves . . . It follows then that God is as responsible for the sin as for all the virtue in the world".

Swamiji's reply: "That consciousness comes in a stage of highest realisation, when one sees that whatever is of the nature of love or attraction is God." I humbly feel Swamiji avoided the pointed question of his disciple and gave only an evasive reply. Love is divine. Alright. But can we change the tigers to a vegetarian simply by feeding it a vegetarian diet or by putting Christ and the wickedest on equal footing? The question is that consciousness does not arise, when we see God in every being, no matter good or evil. Whether we are sane or insane, God must be responsible for all our acts—good or bad then. But these presumptions are myths. When there is no love in the minds of wicked persons, there is no sense to see God in persons like Osama bin Laden or Veerappan.

I humbly opine that now we need no more to behave like that stupid ostrich in the sand dunes. If a cobra came to that yogi and yogi took it, as if it was "a messenger came from beloved," should then we take Mohammed Gaznavi, who looted the temple of Somnath and now Osama bin Laden, who has terrorised the whole world by his inhuman activities and such people, who work against humanity as "Messengers from the beloved?" How long can we live on the feeling that 'everything that comes to us, comes from the Lord? Let us no more make the Karma theory a mess. In this hypocritical world even the wickedest persons pose themselves to be messengers of God, just to live safe in His Oasis'. Should we accept their whimsical hypothesis? Did not the theory of Divine Origin accept the wicked king even as the representative of god? Did not we explode this untruth?

What an inconsistent approach it is! On the one hand, Swamiji professes rightly that whatever miseries come to us, they are all man-made and we must seek their causes in our minds, and on the other Swamiji puts his devotional seal on the yogi's view that 'everything that comes to him, comes from his Lord'. In fact, that Yogi's philosophy is the offspring of our old philosophy, which teaches: "who can live a moment, breathe a moment, if this all powerful one does not will it?" (on page 107 Vol. 1 *Swamiji's Works*). Let's remember it has neither 'freedom of action', nor 'freedom of option' for the real architects of their own destinies. It has been a first class hypocrisy, which we have been playing on our ownselves

Of course, I can never support Duryodhan for what shameful and cruel acts he did, but I appreciate that he accepted the transparent truth, at least. What he said was:

"Jaanaami dharman na cha me pravritti
Jaanaami adharman na cha me nivritti,"

(I know what is 'dharma', but it does not attract me, I know what is 'adharma', but I cannot give it up).

This is the crux of all our problems. All of us know what is dharma, or what path we should adopt in life. We all know too what is 'adharma', but we have no will to give it up. We never realise that it is the cause of our suffering. For all this we have to strengthen our will to oust 'adharma' from our lives.

It seems, as if more or less we have all been standing on the cross-roads here, and we have suffered from the stroke of the delusion of poles (दिशाभ्रांति). We do not mind this delusion even. Why? Because, we believe the sole-doer in the world is the Lord. We are simply His Master's pet dogs on a long leash. At the most we can worship Him. What a degradation it has brought!

Swami Vivekanandji had a clarion call for all of us and said: "Stand on your feet and be men and extend the hand of help and strength to your fellow men." But how can we restore this faith in our ownselves, when Swami Vivekanandji wants to get us convinced that 'Lord God is the Governor and maintainer of the human world?' He is the doer of all things. Has it not sucked all faith from our minds?There was a time, when people did not know anything about the universe. Hence, people invented the God. But today the era of God is over for all times to come. Now it is an era of manhood. So, let us know ourselves to change ourselves and to change our world too. Thus, knowing or building ourselves is more important than knowing God.

It is in this very context, Sri J. Krishnamurthi says, 'You are your own 'guru and your own pupil'. "Be a light unto yourself."

The fact is that most of us are not at all religious, but we have been posing to be religious simply by performing this or that ritual or dogma mechanically. This religion is purposeless and hence it has no life at all. It is nothing, but wasting our time, energy and resources. Simply, we are becoming more egoists, because we feel that we perform this ritual or that dogma unlike others.

I wonder how Dr. Radhakrishnan on the one hand says rightly: "There is nothing inevitable in human history. The very fact that we are human beings means that we have the power not to be mere servants of nature, but shapers of the world," and on the other he holds "that from which all things are derived, by which they are sustained . . . that is Brahman, that is the ultimate reality" . . . When according to Dr. Sahib Brhaman is the creator, sustainer and destroyer i.e., Trinity-three-in-one, how can we be the shapers of our world? How can we sail in the two boats at the same time? Let us accept either of these two. Either we are not the shapers of our own world, and consequently, everything is derived and sustained by Brahma. Or if everything is derived or shaped by Him, then the talk of that we are the shapers of our own world or destiny is nothing, but a mere hypocrisy. When Dr. Sahib makes Him "responsible for the movement from matter to life, life to mind, mind to intelligence, intelligence to spirit, what role for humans remains to play? Let us remember that 21st century is not the time of God, but of men, not of such blind faith or superstition, but of science and reason, as our future lies with them. Why do we not talk from our own experiences honestly? Why do we simply repeat, what we have read somewhere parrotwise?

The world is in an unprecedented crisis. Everybody feels so. Is it pre-determined by some deity or is it all man-made? Let us remember that the crisis is not reverting back simply if we remember 'Om'. The belief that everything is derived and sustained here by Brahman, is the belief of a myth-prone society only. Hitler got sixty lakh Jews killed in Germany. His average per day killing was 500 Jews. Stalin too got lakhs of people killed in Soviet Russia. To know of all these massacres in the history of the human world, it is very difficult to believe that everything is derived and sustained here by Brahman. All seems to be an age old concoction or simply a projection. Should we take it for granted that these victims had suffered, because of their past Karmas alike? Swami Ram Krishna Parmahansa had to suffer from throat-cancer, Sri Vinobaji too had to suffer from stomach-ulcer. Should we then seek the cause of their sufferings in their past lives? In case, yes, then how? Of course, it all does not mean the denial of the law of cause and effect. But we must remember the decay, disease and ultimate death are natural in everybody's life, no matter whether one is sane or insane. They are parts of evolution in our lives. Why to drag Him in?

People say and declare that there is God in everybody. But so long there is wickedness in the world, how can God be there? Dr. Radhakrishnan says, "There are many today, who fed by the results of modern science and technological developments are prepared to disregard the reality of a Cosmic supreme. Cosmonauts the other day went round about the world and said that they had searched everywhere, but they have not found God . . . God is not up in the skies sitting like a despot. He is not outside of us. He is within us." . . . But anyone can say that God is here or God is there without caring for the proof. Dr. Sahib holds: "If you can define God, He ceases to be your God." It is like saying that if you go for searching someone, he would not be yours. The question is: when we cannot define Him, how can we know Him? People want to make everything mysterious; so that it remains ever beyond their knowledge.

Another obvious question is how can we take it for granted on the basis of mere hearsay that Cosmic Reality is within all of us, when we witness with our own eyes that in the world innocents suffer under His nose? If there is really a Cosmic Reality, He must be felt, or experienced, or known by us. Hundreds of soldiers have been butchered in the non-declared Kargil war between India and Pakistan in 1999. Should we take it for granted that their death was pre-determined by the same Cosmic supreme on the basis of their past deeds, and in their case He was quite helpless to sustain or protect them? If we do it, would it not be the gross-misuse of the Karma Theory indeed? For me, it is fully a divine drama, staged by humans. It is all a myth. Earlier we realise that our life is, what we make it—good or bad, the better. Was God there in the minds of those Pakistanis, who inflitrated in Kargil? Why do we live in a fool's paradise?

Dr. Sahib says, ". . . He is not outside of us. He is within us" . . . Does he hold this view on his own experience of life, or more on the basis of hearsay? If He is within all of us, and when we, being little-minded fight with each other, does it mean, God fights with God.? Or devil fights with devil? Why do we befool our own fellow beings? Now it is more than enough.

It is only on the basis of scriptures we have been condemning people doing work with a desire of some fruit or reward or motive. May I know, what is unnatural, or immoral, or unethical in it, if one works with a motive? Desire of fruit of one's work has been the greatest motivating force of all our actions. It is evil, when we desire, which is not our own or for which we really do not deserve. Of course, we should never be slaves of the desire of fruit of our work, but only its masters, and being so we should not identify our lives with the fulfilment of the desire of fruits by hook or crook. Because if even our due desire for fruit is not fulfilled here in this world, or if we do not get our due, we should not be disheartened, or crazy or restless to get it, no matter what happens. We must remember that it is a human world and not divine, and unless all people change their tigerish nature or unless all of us follow 'live and let live' earnestly in our respective lives, we cannot change hell into heaven. Leaving the work of distribution of fruits for one's work—either sweet or sour—in the hands of a hypothetical entity has been proved only a mirage so far. Have we really become less ego-centric by having a faith in Him for all this? Earlier we realise that the ideal: 'work for work's sake' is against human nature and human psychology, the better. Of course, everyone must calm down one's mind, if one fails to get one's due in this world, thinking it is a human world and not divine. Hence, to be a slave even for one's due to get it, no matter what happens, is not at all advisable for a sensible person. It is our sensible thinking only that can cool down our minds, and it is our senseless thinking that makes us restless, when we do not get our own due. That is why, for a seeker of truth a constant 'meditation' is advised in one's life. It all does not mean we must keep our hands tied behind our backs, not to get our own due in this world. Let us take the help of the law of the land in a welfare state. Full justice in the world will ever remain a mirage only, so long as all the architects of human destinies do not change their brutish nature. Hence, to have a motive in life, is not bad or evil in itself. What is evil is to have an evil motive. We are supposed to change our evil motive only. Motive is like a spar, if we remove the spar on which the sail of the ship of life is bent, how can we sail the ship then?

Do we know how a capitalist used to compose his labourers, who did not get their due rewards? He pleaded with them that poverty was their *fait accompli*, and starvation was the reward of their past Karmas, and thus he used to make himself quite safe behind the thorny bush of the Karma theory? Was it not a fraud, played by him to confuse them under His nose even?

On 11-9-2001 thousands of Americans were feared dead in multiple terrorist strikes in US cities. Should we accept it that all of them must have done some wrong in the past or present and, consequently, all had to suffer so much? On 31-8-99 an earthquake came in Turkey and as a result of it several thousand persons had died. Was it all because all these people too must have done some wrong in their past or present? Is an earthquake necessarily related to our past or present deeds in any way ? Is it not related to some natural or geographical reason or to some ecological imbalances created by us? We know when there is an atomic blast, it disturbs the natural or ecological balance and thus it causes tremors in the earth. But the question is Karma theory has no explanation to tell us why those people suffer, who have nothing to do with any such blast? In this world so many people die in a railway accident or in an aircrash either due to human folly or due to the development of some snag in the machinery.

Some years ago in the remote past due to our ignorance we used to relate malaria-fever with some displeasure of the unknown and not with the bite of female anophelese mosquitoes. Should we not come out from the tiny capsules of our superstitions?

Attributing increasing frequency in earthquakes to underground nuclear explosions and depletion of coal, oil, gas and other fossile sources of energy is no more now a guess-work, but a reality accepted throughout the scientific world. So, let us no more make Karma Theory a mere mockery or an idea to be ridiculed by the people. Let us no more misuse it. It is better not to hijack that hypothetical cosmic supreme in human affairs, if at all He is there.

If the God is the sole creator of this world, why did He then create evil persons like Nadirshaw, Changez Khan, Hitler, Mussolini, Osama bin Laden, Veerappan, Billa-Ranga and the like? They not only kill insane, but sane people too. In fact, Nadirshaw and Hitler, Ram and Gandhi were not born, but were made here by themselves. The very idea of a creator-God is unscientific.

Do we not know as to how many health-giving bacterias we swallow, chew and digest daily, when we take curd? Do we not kill thousands of microbes, while performing our daily activities? Do not the research scholars make experiments on the bodies of mice, frogs, monkeys, deers, cats in their labs for the welfare of mankind? Should they not be rewarded, because they do so much researches for the welfare of humanity, or should they be punished, because so many animals die, because of these experiments? Should we cease to use disinfectants and even then hope for our survival? Even vegetable or milk, what we take daily, have lives. Should we then stop taking them and still hope to survive? Perfection in this world is utopian only. There is the question of lesser evil before us. Should we stop breathing, because so many microbes die, while we breathe daily. In short, it is all foolishness, if we think that we suffer because of the death of these microbes.

Prof. Narlikar says, " . . . but as soon as it (astrology) concludes that those planets are going to affect someone's life, because he was born on a certain day, it has no scientific backing." "You depart from science as soon as you start reading something very sinister from an eclipse, like it is affecting human life." "I look upon astrology as a pseudo-science" . . . (Narlikar). He adds: "Superstitions are born out of ignorance of how nature functions. Science is dedicated to the unravelling of the mysteries of nature. I give one example, early human societies ascribed divine powers to planets . . . This assumption arose from ignorance of what planets are and how they move. Now that astronomy has answered most of the questions." (Narlikar) It is merely our superstition, if people believe in a destiny, pre-determined by divine or astral forces beyond their control.

Actually, it has been our age old practice to link anything with the divine, which we cannot know or explain out of ignorance. At such occasions we at once jump on to our insistence to believe. It is in this respect, my humble submission is, if Karma theory is correct in its application, then a butcher, or a murderer, or a rapist, or an exploiter must have been either a leper or blind or lame and the like in their next birth, if it is there. But have the propounders of this theory got such an authentic record with them? Let us remember if a mosquito has a right to live, so is the case with a lizard, which swallows it to satisfy its appetite in this interdependent world. The whole world of wilds is based on the principle: 'Survival of the fittest'. Can we apply Karma theory to their world? If not, why not? Let us remember it is all futile to go on discussing these matters. If we do it, we are sure to find ourselves in a lunatic asylum only.

In fact, in the realm of nature there is a provision of an automatic reward or punishment by itself. If we plant a *babul* tree, we cannot get mango fruits from it. In the same way, if we prick needle into the body of somebody, we may or may not get momentary pleasure by doing this heinous crime, but we cannot get happiness or peace of mind. So, in this respect, nature has ever been judicious. Of course, it is beyond nature's domain to hang the assassins, rapists and exploiters.

People ask us to do our works with the spirit of *'nisham-karmayoga'* i.e., without desiring for the reward. Alright. Their plea is that if the Lord is pleased with us or shows His mercy, even a pint of mud can be turned into gold. And in case He turns away His merciful eyes from us, even fertile land is turned into a barren one. I wonder how magical, whimsical and arbitrary their God is! Have we ever witnessed Him with our own eyes, sitting and wiping the tears of downtrodden, who have become victims of human '*Julums*' only? This means we have no free will in His kingdom even and our show will ever remain flop, unless He wills it. How far is it consistent with the same Law of Karma?

Science believes in facts and not fictions. Swami Vivekanandji rightly asserts, when he says, "when we suffer, it is because of our own acts; God is not to be blamed for it." (on page 319 Vol. 1 *Swamiji's Works*) But we cannot overlook the fact that all our sufferings in life are not the effects of our own personal doings. Do we not know a drunken rash driver kills innocent persons here or there? Again, we cannot overlook this fact too that this world is not a one man show only. Thus, by offering the master-keys of our own both pleasure or pain, victory or defeat, profit or loss, honour or dishonour, life or death in Lord's hands, we have become a source of ridicule. Whenever, I see any person doing such things in life, I feel as if I am being dragged into a dark tunnel from where it is impossible to come out to see the light.

This glorification of God, is, in fact, inconsistent with what Swami Vivekanandji says here that 'we are free therefore . . . the human will stands beyond all circumstances . . .' Somewherelse it is Swamiji says that God's will is supreme. Hence, it is beyond our comprehension as to which view of Swamiji's is true and which is not. I am definitely a Lilliputian before the great human giant, but is it not a fact that Swamiji holds: 'we cannot live or even breathe without His will?

Let us remember, happiness or unhappiness is also a state of our minds. There are people, who are happy even when they lack their basic amenities with them, and there are people here, who are unhappy even when they roll here in wealth. Socratese was happy even when he was ill-treated by his wife. One day Socratese was serious in his mood. On asking, he told the reason of his being serious. He told that as his wife was not well on that day, he did not get an opportunity to test his patience.

Due to natural calamities people suffer a lot in this world. In this world bad things happen to good people even, is a proof in itself that the web of human life has purely been woven by human spiders with their own knitpins, no matter whether the web is good or bad.

It is an age of increasing contradictions—an age in which life and death, happiness and sorrow, affluence and poverty, peace and war, good and evil go together. Are they all divine-planned or man-made? Our life is dialectical or Hegelian. We can minimise strife and struggle, if we are earnest. We cannot remove them perfectly.

We pose to remove our 'I', 'our family', 'my mom', 'my child' and and 'my this' or 'my that' to get the false certificate of renunciation. It is false, because with some exceptions, those who do it, they are actually found clinging themselves to 'my god', 'my goddesses', 'my Bhagwan', 'my Allaha', 'my guru' in the same hypocritical breath! Thus, if somewhere our clinging dies artificially and hypocritically, it takes birth somewhere else. Only our family or world changes. We remain the same as before, as our minds or mindset do not change. With this change of our mask, our little-mindedness, does not go necessarily. Thus, our life remains fragmented. Do such people think in terms of whole necessarily? Only 'Thou' replaces the 'I'. The ego, which was attached with 'I', 'me', 'my' or 'mine' formerly is now attached with 'Thou'. That is why, people feel pleasure in 'holier than thou' attitude, or in the attitude that 'my god' or 'my Allaha' or 'my Bhagwan', or 'my guru', or 'our scriptures', or 'our holy places' are greater. We do not think in terms of 'live and let live'. Why do we not think that others too are our own? We can become holy only when we think of the whole.

It all does not mean I believe in one God, if at all He exists. I have no allergy, if there are as many gods and goddesses as there are humans. What is needed the most is same inner eyes to look towards all the architects of their destinies without any discrimination. So, renunciation of our 'I' or 'family' won't help us. In case, we do it, our life will come to a grinding halt. Hence, if at all we are earnest, let us then renounce our little-mindedness, or the filth or rubbishness, or garbage of our minds only. If we do it, everything will be O.K. soon.

Being worldly, we cannot help having 'Kam', 'Krodh' 'lobh', and 'moha' in our lives to some extent. Of course, their excess is dangerous. Hence, when we use them in our lives, we have to move with our greatest awareness, as to what is to be done and what is not. We have to keep our inner eyes quite open at all times to give light to our ownselves. With this awareness our heat of *Kam, Krodh*, *lobh* and *moha* is turned into exceptional light, because it will be the creative use of our energy. So, earlier we live in the light of awareness, the better. The more there is light in our being, the happier we become in the same world. Here '*Kam*' means cravings.

Thus, it is nothing, but a myth woven by ourselves as Swami Vivekanandji holds: "Man is born poor or blind—what is the reason? He had done something before he was born that way . . ." May I ask who says that man is born poor or rich? It is the circumstances of a man in which one is born, which make one either rich or poor. The fact is that if here one is poor, it is because the cause lies with oneself or with one's circumstances—economic, political or social and the like. Here nobody comes and nobody goes laden with wealth. Even Sikandar had to go from the world with empty hands. If physically handicapped children are born that shows the cause lies with one's heredity or genes or environment. By dragging God into these affairs we can misguide ourselves only.

It looks very strange to view that God distributes rewards or punishment here. Sri Vivekanandji holds: "For those, who believe in God . . . they give up the fruits of work unto the Lord; they work . . . for Him. . . . Let us . . . think that we are only servants obeying the Lord, our Master, and that every impulse (ripple) for actions comes from Him . . ." First of all, it is crystal clear that whether we believe in Him or not; whether we work for Him or not; whether we give up the fruits of our works unto the Lord or not, He neither rewards, nor punishes us for our good or bad deeds. Secondly, we all know that being humans we have impulses or ripples—good and bad—in our minds. Then how can we attribute that bad impulses too come from the Lord? If we conclude that good ripples come from the Lord and bad ones from our individual minds, the difficulty arises, whether there are two creators of the world, if at all we hypothetically think there is creation. The right solution of this problem is: Being architects of our own destinies, it is we, who cause both good or bad impulses in our minds and not any deity. What we lack is conviction on our parts that "unselfishness is more paying, only people have not the patience to practice it" (page 32 Vol. 1 *Swamiji's Works*). Of course, "that is the ideal of Karmayoga" in the words of Swamiji (on page 34 Vol. 1). A Karmayogi believes in being unselfish to the utmost.

Now it is clear if you kill the motive, you are sure to get yourself killed in action. Motive is like a spar. Can we ever imagine to remove the spar even? No, never. What we need the most is to remove our selfish or sinister motive in life to have a peaceful life. The solutions of all human problems can be sought only in human minds and thus only the human minds are to be overhauled by the humans themselves. It is they who are to dismantle all the evil camps in their minds themselves.

Selfishness is the offspring of our excessive attachment here or there. All our attachments or motives are not bad in themselves. Even attachmernt with god must mean attachment with good only. We can live without God in this world, but not without good. Hence, Swami Vivekanandji too rightly says, ". . . we must not be extremely attached to anything excepting God . . . As soon as extreme attachment comes, a man loses himself, he is no more master of himself, he is a slave. If a woman is tremendously attached to a man, she becomes a slave to that man . . . There are higher things in the world than becoming a slave to a human being. Love and do good to everybody, but do not become a slave. In the first place attachment, degenerates us individually and in the second place, makes us extremely selfish . . . A good many of the wicked deeds done in the world are really done through attachment to certain persons, So, all attachment, excepting that for good works should be avoided." (on page 6 Vol. 4 *Swamiji's Works*). It is only the excessive attachment, which is the mother of wickedness in this world. Even Krishna Himself advised Arjuna in the Gita: "Arjuna, be attached to me."

Our experience especially of present day life clearly shows that our extreme attachment with God even makes us extremists or terrorists or fanatics or 'Jehadi'. Our medieval history has been a witness, of how extreme attachment caused us great upheavals in the world. Today the so-called terrorists like Osama bin Laden and others are killing innocent people even, because they are extremely attached to their own God. Of course, for me God is only a projection or conjecture of human minds. These fanatics are at war with the civilised world in the name of their own God. Although the religion of all fanatics is alike i.e., to create unnecessary disturbances or terror in the world and to kill the innocent masses to have some sinister motives. They do so, because they are all extremely attached to their God or religion or to themselves. Hence, I do not agree with Swamiji that 'we must not be extremely attached to anything excepting God.' I hold that both our extreme attachment or extreme detachment cause all wicked deeds done either in a family or in a country or in the entire world. Both these extremes are evils only, because both make us slaves, and inhumans and degenerate us. If all attach themselves with good, there will be no problem then, because it will mean an automatic detachments—of ours with our evils.

There are muddleheaded persons in the world. They have nothing to do whether there is sunrise or sunset here; whether here a river stops flowing, whether one takes birth or dies, whether one is happy or unhappy. They behave like eccentric or whimsical or lunatics. They too live in their own world, created by their own selves. Most of them are found being most selfish, mean, wretched and unattached with anyone, except themselves. This world does not need such selfish and unattached persons at all. Our attachment, our motive is a problem or evil only when, we are extremely attached somewhere—either to our exclusive bread, or to our exclusive children or ourselves or exclusive country and do not care for others too at the same time. So, what we are supposed to do is to remove not all our attachments or motives or detachments, but only excessive attachments and excessive detachments. Our mind is like a battery which needs to be charged and re-charged with '*gyan*' in our meditation again and again at every moment of life. In order to be masters and no more slaves let us keep all excessive attachments and excessive detachments quite at bay from ourselves. But can we ever be ready for it, unless we have immense faith in our own navigation?

Excessive desires are the siblings of excessive attachment in life. Had there been no excessive attachment, there would not have been excessive desires. So, what we need primarily is to avoid extreme desires of any kind. Swami Vivekanandji says in this respect: "The next is called . . . freedom from desires. He who wants to love God must get rid of extreme desires, desire nothing except God. This world is good, so far as it helps one to go to the higher world. The object of the senses are good so far as they help us to attain higher objects. We always forget that this world is a means to an end and not an end itself . . . So, wife, husband, children, money and learning are good so long as they help us forward, but as soon as they cease to do that, they are nothing, but evil. If the wife helps us to attain God, she is a good wife, so it is with a husband or a child. If money helps a man to do good to others, it is of some value, but if not, it is simply a mass of evil, and the sooner it is got rid of, the better . . . Instead of hearing foolish things, we must hear about God . . . Instead of reading foolish books we must read good ones which tell of God . . ." (on page 7-9 Vol. 4 *Swamiji's Works*)

What a good explanation regarding desire Swamiji has given here! It all means that desire in itself is not bad. This world, the wife, the husband, the children, the parents, the parents-in-law and all alike are only our necessary means to attain our end of life. And our end of life is to attain a peaceful life not only for our ownselves, but for others too around at the same time. Being escapists by nature, some suggest us to be ready to leave the world and our family members to reach Vaikunth, the hypothetical heaven. We never realise when we have made our world dirtier or filthier by our evil thinking, feelings and doings, how can we maintain that heaven purer? So, first of all let us make our world and family a purer place simply by our thinking, feeling and doing good, what we can, wherever we are to be good only.

So, let us live in the world alongwith our family members, but let the world of evils not try to make their oasis in our minds any more. We are no more to live in the world or in the family like slaves, but masters of our own destinies—good or bad. Masters of our destinies does not mean we start posing our authority before others. We're no more to be slaves of our evils.

Those who suggest us: 'desire nothing', do not understand the very implications of their stand. Even to live to eat, we need some food, we desire some water to quench our thirst, we desire some air to breathe. Let our motive be not only 'to live, but let live also' at the same time. If this world is good so far it helps us to attain higher mission in life, how can then it be dubbed as 'mithya' or illusion or dream? In fact, this world is neither good, nor evil in itself, but it is what we make it either good or bad. We see people going to temples, or mosques, or churches, or gurudwaras and, asking their God to do this or that for them, or to bless them with this or that. Thus, often we do shopping with God there, requesting Him to do this or that in our favour in return of our worship. We nave always been postponing our programme of thinking, feeling and doing good for tomorrow in the hope that God is to descend on earth with His divine-crane for our upliftment. But tomorrow never comes and when we see no chance for the Lord to come down on earth, we become totally disgusted. We never realise God is only our age old 'Projection', or 'conjecture', or 'conception' of human mind in its' ignorance of the universe. Even then our shopping or bargain goes on and on with Him daily. Hence, Swami Vivekanandji chided such people: "It is better to be an atheist than to have such an idea of religion". (on page 20-21 Vol. 4 *Swamiji's Works*) This shopping with Him can be stopped only when we know ourselves clearly, what we are and what we can be, and if we revive faith in our own making of our own lives by our ownselves, either good or bad.

Unless we know about God, we cannot desire Him. Let us desire then good, instead of God. So, we cannot remove all our desires. Only we are supposed to extinguish our extreme desires. Because we must know that civilisation does not consist in multiplication of wants, but in their voluntary reduction. Unless we reduce our wants to the minimum, we cannot live like masters, but only slaves. The slaves can never imagine of higher mission in life even. Instead of hearing, reading, writing, learning, thinking, feeling and doing foolish things, let us hear, read, write, learn, think, feel and do good only, what we can, wherever we are to have a calmer life.

But it is certain that denial of God does not mean we can afford to be inhumans or we can deny nature too. Nature has ever been in existence at all stages of the evolution in the universe. Swamiji too accepted the fact. ". . . there never was a time, when nature did not exist" (on page 422 Vol. 7 *Swamiji's Works*). Nature, being a self-regulating force, has been helping all beings to come to their lives, it has also been protecting their health and lives too. Of course, nature causes devastation to us too from time to time, if we go against it and its laws. It causes floods, earthquakes, storms, tides, volcanic rupture and the like in this or that part of the world, due to some natural or geographical reasons.

As we cannot deny nature, we cannot deny Karma theory as a general rule in our life. But if we apply it to every happening in our life—good or bad, we err. Had Karma Theory been a reality, all the beings must have been extinct long-long ago like dinosaurs, as every human kills hundreds of microbes even when one breathes. We must not forget that there is no consideration of right or wrong in the world of wilds. There is only one law applicable, i.e., Might is right or "survival of the fittest." Of course, being humans we cannot ape them in this respect. But if a lion, being a carnivorous animal, kills another animal in the jungle, it is but natural for it to satisfy its own appetite. In the same way, a butcher deals in meat to earn his living the world over, and a meat eater prepares different dishes of meat to satisfy his appetite. To apply the Karma Theory in these affairs will all be meaningless.

People remind us that the message of 'Nishkam Karmayoga' sermonised by Krishna in the Gita aimed at elimination of the general spirit i.e., 'I am the doer of this or that' from human minds. O.K. It is a good aim. I humbly hold how can this feeling of 'I am doing this or that' wither away from the actual doer's minds, when the truth has come before all of us by itself that the hypothetical Lord does nothing? He is only a product of human minds. And in case the doers do not keep this thing in their minds that, being the true architects of their own destinies, it is they actually do this or that, no matter it is good or bad, as no Lord can ever commit any bad by Himself, they won't be able to weave a better web of their lives with their own knitpins as human spiders. It is no use to keep a veil on a bride's face, when it has ben exposed already. Let no one think that I am trying to create a new situation merely out of my poor pocket. I am simply a seeker of truth. I want that whatever our destination is it must be clearly visible to all. Let there be now a flood light after crossing over a long long dark tunnel. Of course, we should not have any feeling of ego in our minds that if we do any good thing in life anywhere we oblige somebody. If we do any good, or if we fulfill our duties like a good person—why don't we feel we do good to make our own life calmer, and consequently we must feel obliged to the person concerned that he/she has given us a golden opportunity to be more peaceful? But why to presume that every 'I' is a bad 'I'. We are not to remove this 'I' at all, but only I's bad mindset, which makes the whole ocean of humanity dirtier. Let us remember in case we remove this 'I', I's whole work of life too will come to a grinding halt by itself. So, let us no more make this 'I' the very target of removal, but I's filth only. Let every 'I' work with a pure mind only to make life good.

I am of the firm view the feeling of ego, if there is, cannot be withered away merely by being non-attached with one's due or merely by being motiveless. The truth of all truths is that we can never be motiveless. Of course, if we want to weave a better web of life, being the true spiders, we must weave or re-weave with a good motive i.e., 'live and let live' only. Merely by being Lord's 'nimits or His Masters' pet dogs on a long leash, have we become less egoists or more humble in our lives? Are we now less conscious of our exclusive self? If we have become less egoists, why are our sufferings and miseries, wherever we are, either in a family or country or in the entire world, multiplying day by day? My humble request is: No doubt, if one who has come here, one must go one day. But why to die in a quack's hands? The main problem is: Unless one knows that it is he or she who weaves the fabric of life, whether good or bad, one shall never mind to re-weave it, if it needs.

Hence, I do not think it is at all right on the part of Mr. Parthasarthy in his good book '*Vedanta Treatise*' to suggest us to banish the thought of "I am doing this" on its' page 75. I know Mr. Parthasarthy, being a well-read person, is unlike me. I know one thing only that I know nothing, but I humbly hold from my own experience of life that the use of 'I', or 'me', or 'my', or mine are not bad in themselves necessarily. They are bad only, when they carry the germs of 'exclusive self' with their wings, wherever they flutter. If these 'I', 'me', my, mine dissolve the myopic view attached with their wings into the wider ocean of humanity, they become good instruments or mediums of our mutual expression. It is only in this context, we must take it that nothing is good or bad in this world, but our thinking makes it so. Why, instead of thinking at a lower level, I do not think, feel, do, desire at a higher level? Let us think good for all. Why evil at all? I humbly hold that in the heat of Gods' 'bhakti', the removal of this poor guy 'I' will be akin to touching a wrong wire only. This is all due to crisis of faith in our ownselves.

What we need is to break our artificial and unnatural shackles, which have made us slaves and not masters. It is in this context Rousseau once remarked: 'Man was born free, but he is in chains'. I agree to disagree with Mr. Parthasarthy, who says, in his book on page 75. "People are of mistaken impression that work suffers when there are no desires or motives attached to it. They are afraid that work will come to a halt if they lose their desires, But this is not true." I believe it is only his misfire in the air. May I humbly know whether Mr. Parthasarthy has no good desire or no good motive in writing this good book on Vedanta? If he feels that he has not written this book, but God, let me know, how can we question God, if we find there is something not worth accepting in it?

If the characteristic feature of the life is motion, activity and energy, we must remember then that motion, activity, energy and motive cannot be kept in water tight compartments. Actually, motive is like a fuel of the engine. If there is fuel, the engine moves. Of course, if the fuel is good, the engine works more effectively, more economically and it helps the driver to reach his destined place smoothly with certainty. Otherwise, not. Renouncement is a very good thing. It is very captivating. But why to renounce, all our motives. Why not only our bad motives? If we renounce all our motives, it will be akin to renouncement of all our activities from life. It is apt to lead us to the state of being lifeless ultimately. We have no choice between motive or no motive in fact, but between our good or evil motive only. Let us not commit foolishness that in the excitement of removing the bad motive, lest we should err to remove the motive itself altogether. Let us no more take such action in any haste. It was, in fact, only Krishna's misfire in the air, when He pleaded with Arjuna: "Thy business is with action only, never with reward . . ." (on page 66 *Vedanta Treatise*) Perhaps, He conveniently forgot that He Himself too worked, what He did, with a good motive indeed. Had there not been any motive, the life itself would have been withered away. Of course, sane work with a good motive, while insane with evil. This is the only difference between them. Mr. Parthasarthy too conveniently questions: "Why should you have any motive for work? Work itself is most rewarding . . ." (on page 66 in the same book. Frankly speaking, Mr. Parthasarthy must have penned this book *Vedanta Treatise* with a good motive to clarify so many points, regarding Vedanta philosophy. Did he write it for writing's sake only? Moreover, all our desires are not evils. Mr. Parthasarthy himself says on page 70 in the same book: "When your *vasanas* are good, you are pleasant. When your *vasanas* are bad, you are foul." What actually this poor I needs is to raise the level of his/her working higher and higher day by day. Why to commit folly to remove the poor 'I'? But can any 'I' raise oneself, unless I has immense faith in oneself?

Let us remember something very important regarding reward and punishment. Everybody knows that when a cat puts a mouse on her tongue and swallows it to satisfy her appetite it all does not mean that some deity is punishing the concerned mouse for its' past bad karmas through His '*nimit*'—the cat. In the same way, when a lizard puts a mosquito in its mouth and swallows, it all does not mean the mosquito in question is being punished by some remote control super power for its past bad deeds. Again, when cannibals used to eat even human flesh, it did not mean even remotely that the victim concerned human must have done some wrong in the past. As regards wild life Mr. D.H. Lawrence rightly says: "I never saw a wild thing sorry for itself. A smaller bird will drop frozen dead from a bough without ever having felt sorry for itself."

So, let us live in the present, make it worth living simply-thinking, feeling and doing good, and not live in the past, which has gone with the winds, just to make our present and future brighter ones.

Today our life is really becoming more akin to the words of Hobbes 'solitary, poor, nasty, brutish and short' and there seems to be more or less 'a war of everyone against everyone'. It might not be true in Hobbesian imaginary State of Nature, but these conditions are becoming quite common everywhere now. Do we ever realise who is responsible for this deterioration? Will we be honest to hijack Him, as Swami Vivekanandji did that it is He, who makes us rise. It is He, who makes us fall? Will we be uplifted simply by dragging Him in human affairs by itself?

If there is a supernatural power here, how did He allow evils freely moving here and there in His kingdom? In Swami Vivekanandji's words: "It is the same old, old question which you find discussed in the Brahma-sutras, which you find Draupadi discussing with Yudhishthira in the forest: "If there is a Personal God, all merciful, all powerful, why is the hell of an earth here, why did He create this?—He must be a partial God. There was no solution, and the only solution that can be found is what you read about the love of the Gopis . . . they (Gopis) did not care to know that He was the Lord of creation, they did not care to know that He was almighty, they did not care to know that He was omnipotent, and so forth. The only thing they understood was that He was infinite Love, that was all." (on page 257 Vol. 3 *Swamiji's Works*)

May I know, did Yudhishthira satisfy Draupadi's natural query? If He is the sole creator of this world, why did He create evils here? In fact, he had no answer of her age old pertinent query. To say 'God was infinite love', is not a solution in itself. After all, no matter how pious the God's love might be, it has no wings to flutter and no feet to walk on its own. The world needs not love for a single God, but love of all for all the living gods and goddesses indeed in our minds. It is only then we can find the true solution of the problems regarding miseries in life. God's 'infinite love' cannot create a good society by itself, unless we architects of our own destinies change our mindset. It is all futile to give a metaphysical flavour to our thoughts. That is why Pt. Nehru once said: "Indians are supposed to find pleasures in metaphysics, but I have deliberately kept aloof from them, as I found . . . they only confused me and brought me no solace or guidance . . . Religion in its limited sense did not appeal to me." It is better to believe in nature, being without beginning and without end, instead of such a God. Although god and nature are two entirely different conceptions. They are not synonyms at all.

Regarding God, Buddha had very reasonable view. Swami Vivekanandji described: " . . . Buddha . . . had a discussion with some Brahmins. They came discussing about the nature of Brahman, and the great sage asked, "Have you seen Brahman?" "No", said the Brahmin; "Or your father?" "No, neither has he", "Or your grandfather?" "I do not think even he saw Him." "My friend, how can you discuss about a person whom your father and grandfather never saw, and try to put each other down?" That is what the whole world is doing . . ." (on page 254 Vol. 3 *Swamiji's Works*) what a fine dealing Buddha had with those Brahmins! Have we not been fighting with each other on God without seeing or knowing or experiencing Him at all? Why? Because we have faith in Him, while no faith in our ownselves. Faith in ourselves does not mean we are allowed to do, what we like, no matter good or bad, but a hope from each architect of one's own destiny to do good to be good only. Has this faithlessness in our ownselves not been proved the costliest thing for our ownselves?

Of course, every human cannot be expected to be a sage. Perfection in this world is utopian only. To live in this world we are supposed to choose only the path of lesser evil. In this context, Swami Vivekanandji rightly says, "We cannot put a line of demarcation and say, this action is entirely good and this entirely evil. There is no action which does not bear good and evil fruits at the same time. To take the nearest example: I am talking to you, and some of you, perhaps, think I am doing good and at the same time I am perhaps, killing thousands of microbes in the atmosphere; I am doing evil to something else." (on page 82-83 Vol. 1, *Swamiji's Works*)

I humbly hold whether our world is good or evil primarily depends on the architects of human destinies. The world can be good only if we earnestly make our lives good. We may or may not rely on Him, but let us rely on our ownselves. Swami Vivekanandji rightly asserts: "Our attempts to lay the blame on Him, making Him the punisher, and the rewarder, are only foolish. He neither punishes, nor rewards any . . ." (on page 224-225 Vol. 2 *Swamiji's Works*). Swamiji rightly thinks that He does neither of these two. But the question is if He does not do either of these two, then how does the so-called Trinity act as the saviour and destroyer? In fact, what matters more not how many times we chant Ram-Ram, Allaha-Allaha, God-God or 'Wahe guru'-'Wahe-guru' or 'Om'-'Om', but how much good we do in our lives. This is the true yardstick to know how much religious one is. Moreover, when it is a fact that "He neither punishes, nor rewards any", is it not all then foolish on our parts to leave the works of rewarding or punishing us according to our respective works with Him? Have we not been living in the age old tunnels of illusions then especially in this respect? Our only good Karmas can save our sinking ship and change the world. So, let us restore faith in our ownselves.

In order to avoid all confusions, it was Buddha, who did not accept the existence of God. Swami Vivekanandji says, "when Buddha . . . was asked by one of his followers: Does God exist? He replied: God. When have I spoken to you about God? This I tell you, be good and do good." (on page 287 Vol. 7 *Swamiji's Works*)

How clear headed Buddha, the great was! Why and how? Because Buddha relied on him and the personal experiences of his own life. He talked only on the basis of his own experiences and proper analysis of the things. He relied not on the make-believe world. That is why, Buddha was original in his own vision and thinking. Reason was his great arch. He nowhere talked like a parrot. History has not yet seen such a bold person, who spoke so plainly about God, as he did. He had an extraordinary capacity of assessing things objectively. So, we cannot see Buddha as a carbon-copy of anybody. He was the first original thinker, the world has ever produced. It all does not mean I must accept him blindly, whatever he says.

Buddha was not mystic in his views. He did not want to create any mystery. Swami Vivekanandji says that all men are pure in the name of Vedanta. He argues: "All men are pure; all men are good. Some objections can be raised to them and you ask why some men are brutes? That man you call a brute is like the diamond in the dirt and dust—brush the dust off and it is a diamond, just as pure as if the dust had never been on it." (on page 418 Vol. 7, *Swamiji's Works*)

What a lofty flight Swamiji had in the air? The question is who is to brush the dust off? Everyone is supposed to do the same oneself. Can anyone brush off the dust of Osama bin Laden, Veerappan, Billa and Ranga, etc? This shows whether we are good or brutes, depends on what we make our ownselves. It is beyond my poor commonsense to see God even in brutes. How can we say all are pure or all men are good. Had it been so, there would not have been wickedness in this world at all. How can everyone be like a diamond in the dirt and dust, as Swamiji thinks? Buddha was not sceptical, but a realist only. This is all because we have faith that God is omnipotent and omnipresent, but we have lost all faith in our manhood.

Buddha said: "Worship and prayer . . . are all nonsense. You all say, "I thank God"—but where does He live? You do not know, and yet you are all going crazy about God." How realistic Buddha was to expose the truth! He rejected all meaningless religious practices. While people remain busy in seeking God here or there, Buddha was busy seeking the ways, as to how to eradicate human misery. Hence his recipe was: to remove our exclusive self. Buddha did not believe that it can ever be done merely by prostrating before Him. For all this we all need to do good to be good only. What a right diagnosis and what a right prescription Buddha had!

It is strange that on the one hand Swamiji says everybody is a diamond and his Christ, and on the other he holds: "There are others who deny that there is any evil at all and consider everything good. That also is a weakness . . . If something is evil—smelling. Why sprinkle it with rose water and call it fragrant? Yes, there are good and evil in the world. But you do not have to white wash Him . . ." (page 110 Vol. 8 *Swamiji's Works*)

How can we accept God has put evil in the world? why do not we accept the fact that men are the causes of both good and evil here? Why to drag Him in and out? Is it not strange that Swamiji on the one hand says everyone is his Christ, and on the other he says that there are people, who bite a person like a snake, who feeds them? How can a snake bite a person, if at all one is a Christ?

Misery comes through excessive attachments or detachments. Even saints cannot be completely detached here in this world. Swami Vivekanand ji said: "When my father died, it was a pang for months…" (on page 192 Vol. 8, *Swamiji's Works*) As birth pangs are natural, death pangs too are natural, but we should not be slaves to them. He further states: "I have worked for the world, Mary, all my life, and it does not give me a piece of bread without taking a pound of flesh." Is it not strange that he still believes that all men are divine? And God lives in all! Is it not strange that he still believes that everyman is a diamond? How? What is the use to flatter a brass by polishing it as a diamond? But let us hate Osama bin Laden's evil-doings only, and not Osama bin Laden at all for a peaceful mind.

We rise when we follow 'live and let live'. And we make our fall, when we shirk even a bit to act accordingly. So, the need of the hour is that we should not behave like the cockroaches of the gutter, but as architects of our own destinies. The cockroaches can neither change themselves, nor they can ever change the world. So, long we are not careful about it, I think we are not religious, but only pretending to be religious. The so-called theists try to tempt us by suggesting us to 'surrender and let God do everything. But our main headache is when we do not know anything about the whereabouts of the Lord, to whom should we surrender and thank? Should we surrender to human-sharks even in mere blind faith in Him? Practically speaking, when He is simply the Projection of human mind, whose will will work then? The question is what do they mean by surrender? Surrendering means practically surrendering from our entire responsibility of caring our ownselves, and surrendering from any sense of duty or doing anything. When He is nowhere, but is simply a concoction or conjecture of devotee's minds, who is to care for us, and who is perform all our duties? Surrender will mean then escaping from our entire net of day-to-day responsibilities as well as duties, wherever we are. Secondly, surrender will mean crime and sin thrive under the garb of God's responsibility. As a result of this surrender innocents have already been suffering, and they shall ever be so in the name of the same Lord. Thirdly, when the devotees have already poisoned our minds with the idea that the Lord is the sole-doer of all things in life, and whatever He does, does right, we are sure to take our sufferings merely as our *fate-accompli*. Thus, we are apt to be fatalists, cowards and perfect shirkers and all our wickets are apt to be down one after another in the series. This will be the net result of surrender. If we go on doing everything as before, what will then God do? That will not be the surrender. When He neither rewards, nor punishes anyone, why to surrender Him then?

Most of us behave like that stupid ostrich in this respect. How can these two things happen together? If one surrenders something to someone, one surrenders the responsibility of caring alongwith doing anything too. In fact, surrender and responsibility never go together. The priests of Somnath temple, when it was being looted, are a classical example of both surrender and responsibility. Hence, to me the very idea of surrender is a myth. Thus, it is futile to be crazy after the idea of surrendering and doership. If we go on doing good, what we can, wherever we are only to be good, keeping in view that we are all the architects of our own destinies—good or bad without undergoing any false idea of surrendering to the Lord, we are sure to save our boat from being hit from any rock of ego on the ocean. Secondly, we are sure to make our safe arrival at our destined place. Let us remember that a hand or two earnestly busy in doing good are hundred times better than two hands tied together before a hypothetical deity to ask Him or Her to care and do this or that for us, as mendicants do. What we need the most is to change the very gear of our thinking, feeling and doing only.

For this revolutionary change, we may or may not be able to know the hypothetical Lord, but to know ourselves as to what we are, and what we ought to be, as architects of our own destinies is a prior must for all of us. The most foolish people in this world are those, who pretend to be wiser or to know each and everything, and even make fun of others that unlike themselves, they know nothing. They never realise that if we do not know anything about God, it would not make much difference to us. But in case we fail to know about our ownselves, we shall never be able to change ourselves to change our world. So knowing ourselves is more important priority-wise today, than knowing the same Lord. Earlier we realise all our potentialities inherent for good in all of us, the better. But that is possible only when we have faith in our own making by our ownselves.

Those who claim to know God or themselves, let them listen to the great Socratese beforehand in this respect. Socratese said, "When I was not aware, when I was ignorant, I used to think that I know. Now that I know, I know only one thing—that I know not." How humble Socratese was! Let us understand him, sitting at the feet of this great 'guru'.

Swami Vivekanandji too has quoted Prof. Maxmuller from one of his books as to how a brahmin visited Socratese once in Athens. The brahmin in his usual stereotyped thinking and reasoning asked Socratese: "What is the highest knowledge? Socratese replied: "To know man is the end and aim of all knowledge." (page 433 Vol. 1 *Swamiji's Works*). On getting the unusual reply from a friend, philosopher and guide like Socratese, the same Brahmin counter-questioned him: "But how can you know man without knowing God?" (page 433 Vol. 1 *Swamiji's Works*) Rare persons in the world realise that the knowledge of man is the highest knowledge. We have been suffering from miseries, because of our own exclusive self. We know nothing about it seriously.

May I humbly know whether God is an essential window to peep into men? If yes, have we known Him so far? Let us remember: Existence precedes knowledge of something. How can we know a thing, which does not exist at all? In blind faith we can presume a rope as a snake and a ghost as God only.

Does it not all look very strange and contradictory as well that on the one hand we hold in Swami Vivckanandji's words: "Brahman is . . . incapable of being grasped by word and mind. Whatever lies beyond the reign of space, time and causation cannot be conceived by the human mind." (on page 133 Vol. 2 Swamiji's Works) Swamiji adds further: "A God known is no more God . . . He cannot be known . . . He is always the unknowable one." and on the other Swamiji claims: ". . . you have to know everything in and through the Brahman." (on page 133 Vol. 2 *Swamiji's Works*) "The Knower cannot be known, because if it were known, it will not be the knower". (on page 419 Vol. 3 *Swamiji's Works*). The question is: if the knower cannot be known, then how did Sri Ram Krishna Parmahansa, Swami Vivekanand's guru claim to know and have seen God? If he did not do this through his mind, but soul, science, does not admit its existence. It was Swamiji believed: 'All knowledge that the world has ever received comes "from the mind . . ." Why to conceal Him behind the artificial bushes of the so-called 'space, time and causation' then?

The whole universe may be like a pandora's box of wonders, but one may or may not believe it, man is the greatest wonder on earth. He is the greatest book in himself. For centuries our target of main knowledge has been God, but we have failed bitterly in our aim. But let us beware of the fact that if we fail to know the man, the real architect of his own destiny—good or bad, our conclusions or derivations regarding his role in making or unmaking of his world, what it is, would always be the most confusing and distorting. Let us remember that if we allow our minds to go hungry and spiritually starved for a long time, our glittering prosperity of matter even is apt to turn us to mammon-worshippers, being reduced to the level of its slaves, and consequently, our main aim will ever remain un-attainable. As a result of it, our approach to our world around us reduces us to mere snobs. Earlier we erect fencing against these dangers ahead, the better. So, let us avoid these two extremes: 'matter, matter' or 'God-God'. Let us no more behave like slaves, but humans, who pursue good and avoid evil. If we forget the men, the whole race will be extinct. These extremes are dangerous, because both forget the men.

There is a bitter truth in what Machiavelli says in his Prince: "Men forget more easily the death of their father, than the loss of their patrimony". Do not we make the world more attractive or almost non-attractive merely by our own looks? Let us understand the truth of all truths that we shall never give priority to humans over matter, unless we know fully the men—their minds. Let us no more behave like lunatics. Can we ever produce good men and their good world mere by turning haves into have nots or vice-versa? If we believe it, will it not be like robbing Peter to pay Paul? Our exclusive physical fitness or material sufficiency, our exclusive intellectual alertness or sharpness alongwith our spiritual dwarfness, will always be a danger for the extinction of humanity even. To be humans we shall have to change our values and priorities at the earliest possible. Do not either you or me who sprout value in gold in preference to a good man? So, it is only we who can put good men in the highest esteem in preference to gold. Let us sprout faith with love in good men in preference to matter.

Those days now must go too far, when we used to link our ailments, our sufferings and miseries in life with the anger of some deity in the sky. There was a time when we thought that malaria was caused due to anger of some deity. We were quite ignorant about the female anophelese mosquito at that time. It is strange still we link our miseries of life with the simple will of the same deity. Do we ever realise the anophelese of 'exclusive self', which has its powerful well-built oasis in our minds, is the main cause of human miseries? It was Science which told us that Sun, and not the earth is the centre of Solar system and moon is not a 'devta', but only a satellite of earth. There will never be peace here unless we change our tigerish nature, no matter we live in a bullock cart age or in a rocket era. And we cannot change our nature, unless we realise or have faith that it is nobody else, but we all of us either individually or collectively are responsible, no matter we swim or sink. A 'thing' or a 'thought' which brings human welfare as a whole nearer, is true. Otherwise, it is false. Hence, truth is not static, but dynamic.

Let us see further the paralysing effects of the dismal philosophy i.e., God is the sole doer of all things in human life, and how it helps us to throw away our own responsibilities for making ourselves and our world—good or bad on the poor shoulders of God. Let us see how people in the very high authorities are not exceptions to it. Do we know why they do it? Because they lack the requisite faith in making their own world—good or bad by themselves.

For instance, Mr. Bill Clinton, the ex-president of USA as a matter of repentance over Monica Lewinsky's affairs said: "I ask that God give me a clean heart..." But Mr. Clinton, may I know first, if God deals in giving us a clean heart, then who deals in giving us an unclean one? How long will we like to behave like that stupid ostrich? How long will we go on hijacking God in human affairs, just to find an easy escaping route from our own responsibilities for our own commissions or omissions? In Aug. 2000 (as published in *Hindustan Times*) Mr. Clinton told again in the same reference quite rightly: "I am in the second year of a process of trying to totally rebuild my life from a terrible mistake, I made." He added further: "I feel more at peace than I used to". "Spiritual life is always a work in progress and you just have to hope (for) getting better every day."... Well done, Mr. Clinton, well done. Better late than never. Because now you have realised ultimately that you yourself were responsible for your spiritual fall, and now by totally rebuilding your life, you yourself will be ever responsible for your spiritual rise, as we are all the architects of our own destinies good or bad. Earlier we realise that the poor hypothetical God has His hands neither in our rise, nor in our fall, the better. Again, earlier we realise that God is only a projection or a conjecture of human minds in its ignorance, and thus He neither deals in our virtues, nor in our crimes or sins, the better. Better late than never. Earlier we realise that we have no alternative, except to do good to be good, the better.

In this world, what it is made by all of us, the age long blind *'bhakti'* and ignorance regarding God make people bewildered to see the truth. In the name of Lords' *'hukam'*, even the great saint Nanak justified all: "...All life was created by *'hukam'*. And by *'hukam'* alone distinctions come to some, ...some are abased, some must suffer, while others find joy..."

It is strange that all conventional religions talk of the same concoted Lords' *'hukam'*. Does this blind faith in Him not put a premium on our vices?

Here is another instance in the same context. The so-called religious people blessed the wife of Dr. Raj Kumar, the very well-known famous actor of South India and consoled her by telling: "God will deliver him (her husband) safely, don't worry" from the cruel clutches of Veerappan, a very hard core criminal-cum-kidnapper of South India. May I know humbly know from these self-proclaimed pundits that if God delivered Raj Kumar quite safe to his wife, then who had actually delivered him in Veerappan's hands and, who had helped Veerappan to kidnap him? (Veerappan has been a big smuggler of sandalwood-cum-kidnapper of South India) I earnestly feel great pain to see even pundits, and scholars, unlike me, talking in such a loose fashion, which, instead of guiding someone, misguides him or her. This all shows how hollow our claims are! I humbly believe that we shall go on and on relying on God and claiming such things by virtue of our ignorance again and again in this world, so long we lack faith in making ourselves by ourselves—either good or bad.

No-doubt, such assurances console the tensed minds of the people. But don't we come across such people in our lives—people, who have blind faith in their Lord, and instead of relying on the best doctor and best prescription, they start relying on their Lord exclusively for their recovery? They stop taking all medicines in the hope that their 'Shiva' is there sitting in the sky to make all arrangements for their survival. Instead of prostrating before any hypothetical deity, why don't we go for the best medicines and best prescription and doctor to save ourselves? Because we lack faith in our own captaincy of the ship of our lives.

Merely by mugging up *'shastras'* or scriptures, we can't be real pundits or *'gyanies'*, but by grasping the whole truth, wherever it is. In fact, if there is wickedness there is no question of existence of an almighty God. Both can't co-exist together. Here by dubbing me as an atheist, or merely by accusing me for the charge that I'm provoking people to revolt against these authorities, or by ex-communicating me from their religions, won't help them. Yudhishtir might have declared an atheist as a fool, but I feel that a fool is a fool, whose mind is not in a proper working order. There is no question of any faith or no faith in this or that with a fool. On the other, the so-called atheist has all faith in oneself. He only wants to seek the truth. His greatest crime, if at all it is, is that he does not believe in the God, as maker of our own destinies-good or bad. He has no blind faith in any false navigation of our ship of life by any Lord. He has only immense faith in his own streersmanship. In fact, he is not an atheist, but thiest. A good person has nothing to do with any ego-psychosis. He believes that his life is, what he makes it-good or bad. Nature evolves the universe, and humans make their world, what it is - good or bad. Let us believe what the following Nobel laureate says the truth:

Prof. Harold W. Kroto, a Nobel laureate says, "I am just a machine made out of molecules and chemicals". Mr James Watson, another Nobel laureate believes that there is no "divine element" at work in creating life, though we are still a long way from creating life on our own".

Some people laugh at me and sometime they accuse me, dubbing me as an atheist, a person who does not believe in the existence of God. But I want to tell-them, who says I don't believe in god? Yes, the difference is there. That I believe in living gods and goddesses, and not in a Voltaire's God, who according to him is dead. In case we earnestly want to stop the further decline of human civilization, our mere performance of this or that ritural or dogma won't help us at all in this respect. Merely our age old spirtual knowledge too won't help us much. It is not enough. What we need is spiritual attainment. God may or may not be irrelevant today, but human goodness can never be. It has been the main arch on which the human civilization stands.

Nature needs not our worship, but its' proper understanding. Hypothetically speaking, if today all the beings die all of a sudden or by-and-by due to this or that reason, the work of evolution, which has been going on permanently in nature will go on as usual. Ofcourse, it will take millions of years for the life to come again on earth. This will happen again without the hands of any deity at all. Nature can never get the breathing of the evil-doors stopped at its command, as people think that God does so. While nature works silently, God works only in imagination of bhakats. Believe that faith can move even mountains, the blind faith can leave us only in dark lanes.

That is why I believe religion is neither in books nor in scriptures, nor in discourses, nor in the religious places like temples or churches or mosques or gurudwaras, nor in rituals, nor in dogmas associated with a particular religion prevailing at present. The present day world needs men-making religion, instead. This religion is not to be said or talked about loudly, or prayed either with coins or flowers here or there. It doesn't hope to get anything in return, as mendicants believe to get from some hypothetical deity. It is not essentially learning or reading or writing good things, but this men making religion is to be lived by all the crores of architects of human destinies throughout the world without any bias at all. It lies in removing the peel of a banana; so that one may not be slipped on it and in removing the rolling stone from the road, and the like.

It is not a one day, or one time affair in our lives. It is not a part of human life, but it's concerned with our whole life itself. It must be in its operation twenty four hours a day in our life. In other words, it is life in itself. We can not see it through dissection of our life. The moment we do, it is apt to be killed in action. Hence, it is not worshipping or devoting, but being or becoming or realizing. It is not either a garland of the weeds of certain good words, but like a fragrance, that comes from flowers by itself. The men-making religion revolves round the humans love for humans, and not round God's love exclusively. All the people of the world without any bias are its living gods and goddesses. So, it is always expressed in the deeds concerning human love.

It doesn't live necessarily in the lives of those, who merely say or know or believe in: 'Don't kill' or 'don't harm', and the like, but it essentially lives in the lives of those, who actually never kill and never harm, and never think bad even of anybody, whatsoever one may be consciously or out of any sinister motive or for some personal gain or profit or for selfish interest. It's right oasis is life of those, who not only care for themselves to live, but do care, so that others too may live at the same time. Why? because the very cardinal principle of men-making religion is universal love or 'Basudheva Kutumbakum'.

In fact, men-making religion has nothing to do with either a Hindu is becoming a Muslim, or a Muslim becoming a Hindu or Christian and the like. It may be a conversion, but it is not essentially a change or a revolution or tremendous change. It may be merely a superfluous change only. Men-making religion is essentially a tremendous change in the very mindset or thinking or consciousness or in our very being. It has nothing to do with any of our little mindedness or negativity or negative thought of hatred, jealousy, vengeance, betrayal, etc., or any kind of impurity that trespasses our minds. When we have no little-mindedness or selfish thought or selfish feelings or selfish doings of any sort, when our minds are pure, we at once become happy and peaceful. Otherwise, our minds flutter, become restless like a bird. So, man-making religion gives us award or punishment at once. When we convert ourselves from one religion to another, our beleif in our being remains the same usually. Even then we fail to see the people of the world simply as humans, but either as Hindu or Muslim, low or high, rich or poor, touchable or non-touchable, white or black, Indian or Pakistani, American or Russian, men or women, and the like, a fragmented humanity, and not united as one. Then we change our outer masks only. On the other, man-making religion aims at revolution in the entire being, in our entire outlook and vision. It is a change from within, not necessarily a change from without.

This man-making religion doesn't need people of stone-hearts — people, who have no feeling whether one lives or dies, whether there is a sunshine or sunset, whether a river flows or not. It gives asylum to those people, who love all without any discrimination of ours or theirs even. It embraces all people, who are attached to all, have love for all, and are detached to nobody at all. It does not live in the minds of muddle headed persons. It feels pain, when an innocent being suffers uselessly, for no cause of one's own, and it feels happiness, whenever it finds any being happy. But it keeps itself quite at bay from excessive desires or excessive attachments, or excessive-detachment for a more peaceful life. Already our life has become dry. There is no greenery of love, and now putting aside all attachments from life, man-making religion does not want to convert it into a Thar or Sahara desert - a life which has no blood, but only dry-bones

"A loveless heart is like a cremation ground", said Kabir, the poet of the people. By love he didn't mean lust, but compassion, pity feeling of help for all, true sympathy to share one's miseries and happiness, mutual tolerance, sacrifice and desire to have selfless - service of humanity without any bias. This is what man-making religion wants to attain. Kabir had an allergy against any fanaticism, no matter whether it is Muslim or Hindu or Sikh or Christian fanaticism. That is why, Kabir declared: "I am neither a Hindu, nor a Muslim, but only a human being." What an irony of fate it is that we Hindus and Muslims fought together, when Kabir was no more to decide either to bury him or to cremate him. We kept him divided even when he was dead! A person may have read all the scriptures, but in case the compassion and love have no birth in his minds, he is not a true human, but only a brute.

For Kabir to be a real pundit we need to know "dhai Akshsar prem ke" only. Thus, Kabir was the most revolutionary poet. He was after changing our mindset. That is why, he chided both fanatic Muslims and Hindus rightly alike. His following '*dohas*' are well-known in this respect:

(a) *Kankar patthar jodke masjid liye banaye,*
ta chad mulla bang de kya behra hua Khudaya';
(b) *Pahan puje Hari mile, to main poojonoo pahar'...*

So earlier we realise that religion does not lie necessarily in muttering either God or Allaha, or Ram or wahe guru, the better. Otherwise, what is the difference between muttering Ram-Ram and Roti-Roti? It lies in being good or doing good only. True love changes men's mental horizon. The highest love is not the love of God, but the love of all living gods and goddesses living around. If one can't love a human on this or that pretext one can't love a hypothetical deity even. One who loves God and forgets the men around, pretends to be religious. In the words of Kabir: "*Hari se tu mat het kar, kar Harijan Se het.*" (love not God, love god's men) What a revolutionary thought he had! But, unfortunately, who cares here for changes in one's mindset? Most of us are content with ritualistic or dogmatic changes only. Hence, our miseries are becoming chronic day by day. When will we be awakened? So far we have been doing to please the God, but have failed to make our ownselves. Man-making religion is to make men by restoring the faith in themselves.

In context of attachment Mr. Parthasarthy has referred to the true happening with his two childhood friends on page 206 in his book. One of them was a business man, another was a Sanyasi (man of renunciation). Having mutual discussions both reached the bank of a river. It was late in the evening. There were so many wild animals hiding here or there. Hence, for them it was essential to cross-over to its other side for their safety, but the boatman refused to concede their demand as they were not ready to pay him his demanded money. When the business man friend offered the boatman the money, he demanded, he atonce yielded their request.

In the meanwhile, these two friends continued their usual discussion. In due course the businessman friend enquired of the sanyasi friend in these words: "Tell me of what use is renunciation? If I had not the money today both of us would have been devoured by wolves. I feel you have done wrong in choosing the life of renunciation" The Sanyasi replied: "It is true that your money helped us today" and added... "but dear friend reflect a little deeper - was it retention that really saved our lives or resignation?"

Undoubtedly, in this world, what it is, money is one of the most important factors in our lives. We can't move even an inch further without it. It all does not mean money is the whole thing, But we cannot renounce the whole world. At least, we can't renounce to say 'my wife' or 'my husband', 'my mom' or 'my child', or 'my house', or 'my country', or 'my

Lord', as desired by Mr. Parthasarthy in his book. We can't sail in two boats at the same time i.e. if we cease to say 'my child', or 'my house', we cease to possess the child or the house in question. In this context, we can't overlook the human nature and human psychology, what they are. Moreover, our solution of the problem can't be solved merely by not saying 'my child' or 'my house', because the moment this message goes to our minds, our whole connection or link with the child and the house is broken. The question is who's is to possess or who is to care of the child or the house in such a state of detachment or renunciation? Obviously, the prescripton is worse, than the disease. Then what we must do is that we must be proficient in the true art of attachment and detachment at the same time. We have no alternative between either attachment or detachment, but we have to know as to what is to be attached and what is to be detached up to what extent at the same time. We must know the art of right ordering of our attachments as well as detachments in our individual and social life to have a peaceful life. The stereotyped solutions what generally people offer are no solutions. Before any renouncement of anything, it is better, if we renounce our evils. Let us make our minds purer.

Of course, we can't buy peace with money, as peace is not a commodity, available in the market. Peace can be had from within and not without. That is, we can have peace merely by building or rebuilding ourselves from within. When we are able to make the two railway lines track, i.e., 'live and let live'earnestly as our daily routine of our lives, we will see ourselves what magic our sincere efforts to build or rebuild ourselves can play in our lives. This world, the money, the wife, the husband, the house, the country is only a necessary means to an end. The end is human welfare at large. Let us not be slaves to either of these, but their masters only. When we care exclusively for our own child or wife or husband or country and don't care at all for other people in a family or the country at the same time and think let my country live, no matter others die, we reduce ourselves to the level of their slaves and don't remain their masters. We're not supposed to identify our lives with anyone. Let us live with them, but let us not allow them to live in our minds as our masters. Can we do it without restoring faith in our own life, what it is good or bad?

For peace definitely we have to eat to live and not live to eat, as we generally do. It's our excessive attachments, excessive detachments and excessive desires are to be renounced as early as it is possible. Both our attachments and detachments are good servants, but bad masters.

Further, on page 207 in his book Mr. Parthasarthy rightly says: "Renunciatiion indicates the state of your mind. When your mind is free from desires it is calm and composed ... An agitated mind cannot concentrate. It is not fit for meditation. Redue your desires . . . ." But being wordly we can not renounce all our desires. O.K., when we have extreme desires, it is very difficult for us to control the stream of our thoughts. Meditation is the art of putting our minds in a situation, so that we may be able to focus our minds upon a chosen thought to the exclusion of all other thoughts.

It is through putting a proper embankment on our flow of thoughts & feelings i.e. through our *vivek*, or *buddhi* or power of discrimination, we check our minds slipping into undsirable channel of thoughts. Thus, meditation is like applying balm and bandage. But excussive desires create fissures and tension.

Again on page 272 Mr. Parthasarthy in his book says: "Some say that whatever happens, happens with the will of God. That God does everything. Others deny it. They say that whatever happens, happens with man's efforts.That man does everything. Vedanta says that both are right....Vedanta says God is the prime mover of all activities ... Those who hold God responsible for destiny are right in as much as God is the substratum of all activities which determine destiny. Those who argue that man is responsible for his destiny are also right".

But we know there are sane and insane people in this world. Both have good and bad impulses in their minds respectively. How can we assume that we have evil-impulses with the will of God? Why do we hijack God in human affairs unnecessarily? Why don't we accept the truth that men are the true architects of their own destinies-good or bad? Moreover, objectively speaking, how can God be the very substratum, or the foundation of the activities of both sane and insane people, who man this world, as Mr Parthasarthy says? How can God be the prime mover of our all activities—good or bad? Unless we intend to put a premium on our vices, we cannot accept it. How can we apply God's will to our both good and bad impulses? Let us remember 'Divine Origin Theory' has been proved a myth only.

On page 275 in his book Mr. Parthasarthy shows how God is the source of all our activities by giving a false simile. He says, "God is like the Sun above. Sun is the source of all activities. Sinner or saint draws his vitality from the sun. Sun provides them both the energy to act. Sinner to be vicious. Saint to be virtuous... But all of them act according to their own nature... So is God above your activities and fruits thereof..." How fictitious the simile is! Of course, it is right to say had sun not been there in the firmament, there would not have been any life of any being, whatsoever on earth. The Sun is mainly concerned with our life, as water, food and air are. It is a truth that sun is the source of our life, but it is untruth that the sun is the source of all our activities. If there is no life, there shall be no activites - good or bad whatsoever. Being the Sun, a natural object far far away from earth, has nothing is do with our activities - good or bad.Of course, it gives life to both sane and insane. But we can't hold the sun responsible for our good or bad activities. It is the sane or insane people, who are responsible for their good or filthy minds, which are the real spring boards of these respective activities. Why to make the sun a scapegoat for our good and bad activities? Ofcourse, we are thankful to the natural object, the sun, for giving life to both good and evil persons without any bias, whatsoever. If a sane grows, and an insane arrests his growth under the same sun, the credit or discredit respectively must not go to the sun, but to the sane and insane persons concerned. If our food gives energy to us to work, no matter we are sane or insane, should we hold our respective food responsible for our activities?

Sun gives us mainly life. It is not mainly concerned with whatever activities - good or bad, we have. Good or bad activities are mainly concerned with our good or bad mindset, what we make it. It is not the sun, but our minds which are the prime sources of all our activities - good or bad. Can we ever put the sun in the dock for our bad activities? Under the same sun, consuming the same food, the same water and breathing the same air, do we not the architects of our own destinies commit good or bad activites here in this world? The sun, the food, the water, the air are, no-doubt, the sources of our lives. Both sane and insane maintain their lives due to the sun and the food they take, the water and air they consume. But how can they hold them as the sources of their good or bad activities respectively? The sources of our good or bad activities are our minds.

So, let us no more try to be escapists by assuming as Mr. Parthasarthy did, that the sun or the water or the food or the air are the sources of our good or bad activites. They are the sources of our lives only. Of course, if there is no life, their will be no activity.

Hence, I humbly hold that God is like the sun above and it is the source of all our activites, is nothing but religious obscuranitism or religious fanaticism, which is very dangerous indeed. It is glorification of God only. But it is not factual. If at all God, is here or there, He needs no glorification by His stooges.

Of course, the task of mind's management for the architects of their own destinies, is more tough than the business management. It is also undeniable that our minds can not work this way or that without the sun -

the main source of our life. If steersmen can not steer the ships of their lives without the engine and fuel, it does not mean engine or fuel is the determining source of their activities. It shows while logic conceives in faith, illogic conceives in blind-faith. Can the fuel ever determine our very ways? The fuel is mainly concerned with the working of the carriage, and not with the working of human mind.

Again on page 279 in his book Mr. Parthasarthy raises controversy unncessarily. He says' "Vedanta says your desires are innumerable... Unfulfilled desires are the cause of rebirth..." Ofcourse, the main cause of our trouble is our excessive desires. But upto the last moments of our lives we have this or that -good or bad desires in our minds. Most of them remain unfulfilled. Do not we need some food, some water and some air to be alive even? What to talk of other desires, even the so-called good people have their unfulfilled desire to have 'darshan' of their hypothetical Lord. Let us suppose hypothetically that a time may come when the whole world consists of such people only, who have no desire unfulfilled, will it not then mean the process of rebirth, if at all it is there, is completetly stopped altogether? Evolution means that birth and death are eternal natural phenomenon. So, it is all meaningless to link our desires with the course of our rebirth, as Mr. Parthasarthy did. Nobody knows about it so far authentically. Even Swami Vivekanand on page 7 Vol. 4 in his works says, "desires nothing except God"... It means desire in itself is not bad. Only extreme desires are to be avoided.

Let us no more try to distort karma theory just to prove our false sense of religiousity or blind bhakti towards the Lord. Let us no more use it like a bed-sheet, which can be spread over the bed as well as is used to wrap our bodies. The moment we do it, it becomes a myth. In fact, when we have no faith in our ownselves we try to hinge our lives in sheer being disgusted with this or that, no matter it is meaningful or not.

Moreover, regarding desires Swami Vivekanandji removes our age old confusion persisting in our minds very rightly on page 148 Vol. 2 in his works: "We all understand that desires are wrong, but what is meant by giving up desires? How could life go on? It would be the same suicidal advice, killing the desire and man too. The solution is this. Not that you should not have property, not that you should not have things which are necessary and things which are even luxuries. Have all that you want . . . only know the truth and realise it. Have no idea of proprietorship . . . All belongs to the Lord. He is in the desire that rises in your mind. If you put God in your every moment, in your conversation . . . in everthing, the whole scene changes and the world instead of appearing as one of the

relatives; we are attached to our intellectual and spiritual works . . . We have to detach ourselves to earn joy. If only we had power to detach ourselves at will, there would not be any misery" (Vol. 2, *Swamiji's Works*) Let us develop the power of attachment as well as detachment at will, when it is so desired with all the Krishna's and Gopis of the world. Can we ever forget the perfect historical example of enlightened self-attachment and self-detachment at the same time and self-identification and a deep knowledge of right ordering of loyalities of Panna, the nurse?

Had all attachments been evil, Swami Vivekanandji would never have asked us to "attach yourself to the Lord and nothing else, because everything else in unreal..." So, let us attach ourselves with good, try to detach with evil, wherever it is. As regards God we know nothing about Him. For a small person like me, my family, my neighbour, my village, my city, my country and ultimately all the people of the whole world are real. It is in this context, Swamiji suggests: "... Serve the living God!... The moment you think you are "helping", you undo the whole thing and degrade yourself". Right.

According to Edmund Burke: "Superstition is the religion of feeble mind". Those who have a feeble mind, they have their look towards either God or the Stars in the sky to know the 'why'. Is it not our sheer foolishness and climax of superstition when the very assassin of Israli P.M. said on 5-11-95: " I have instructions from God to kill the P.M.?" So, the most advisable course is: let us live in the world, but let us no more allow the evils to live in our minds anymore. Hence, Swami Vivekanandji said: "The ordinary sanyasin gives up the world, goes out and thinks of the God. The real Sanyasin lives in the world but is not of it... Live in the the midst of the battle of life. Anyone can keep calm in a cave or when asleep". (On page 84 Vol..6 *Swamiji's Works*) Rome might have been built in a day or years, but building the huge edifice of good human life takes, at least, the whole life of a person.

To give a practical shape to the idea of 'live and let live' is a difficult task. Hence, H.J. Laski rightly believed that rights of one person are duties of others. In fact, a real Sanyasin never adopts the Laissezfaire attitued towards the living gods and goddesses. If we all adopt complete detachment with the world, it is apt to be turned into a desert without a desert. Today if there is an accident on the road, the good Samaritan people, atleast, go ahead to help the victim, but in case everyone is detached with everyone, who would come forward for help? None.

Even Swami Vivekanandji felt sorry and pain on learning about the death of some of his friend. He felt "So sorry to learn the passing away of

Mrs. Sturdy! She has been a very good wife and good mother". (on page 153 Vol. 5 *Swamiji's Works)*, Swamiji felt sorry on her pasing away because, every good human including a saint, who is not muddle-headed, must feel pain naturally to see when someone is no more. Can one do it without being attached? Even Swamiji felt the passing away of his beloved father very bitterly. He expressed, "When my father died it was a pang for months". (on page 492 Vol. 8) Unless, one is attached towards one, one cann't feel pangs in his/her absence. So, to some extent they are natural.

Swami Vivekanandji might have held this view: "As soon as we identify ourselves with the work we do, we feel miserable but if we do not identify ourselves with it, we do not feel that misery". But the moot point to ponder over here is: whether it is not but natural to identify ourselves with our own work to some extent? We cannot help without being so. Didn't Swamiji himself feel very upset, when some persons tried to obstruct his high mission in U.S. by having his character - assassination merely out of his jealousy? It was Newton, who felt it very much, when his own pet got his most precious work burnt by chance with a lighted lamp. Of course, we must avoid our excessive identification with anything and any person, if we want to maintain our mental peace. Swamiji adds further: "If a beautiful picture belonging to another is burnt, a man does not generally become miserable, but when his own picture is burnt how miserable he feels! Why? It is because in one case he identifies himself with the picture, and not in the other". Well, it is but natural to feel more pain, more miserable, when one's own finger or picture or one's own beloved is burnt or butchered or raped or exploited or when one's own country is in danger, or when one's own family is in any trouble. Can we ever behave like robots even at such moments of pains in our lives? Robots are machines. They have no personal sentiments or emotions. Humans have their own minds as well as hearts. Should we too behave like idiots or muddle headed, who remain unattached, no matter whether there is sunrise, or sunset, whether there is moonshine over a flowing river or not. At least, we must not behave like those unfortunate pundits of Somnath Temple, when it was being looted. What they lacked miserably was that they didn't know the right ordering of their loyalities or the art of attachment and detachment at the same time. Well, Mira and Gopies too could not remain without getting themselves identified with their beloved Krishna.

Of course, our undue or excessive attachment or excessive detachment sometimes becomes our major cause of trouble and mental tension. So, whosoever one may be, one must avoid both these extremes in life. I always prefer people behaving like living beings, than people with stone hearts and consequently, having no emotions and no sentiments on good or bad occasions in life. Of course, those people who have excessive attachments or excessive detachments here or there in their lives, behave like idots only. They are senseless persons. In fact, we can't help without being sensitive. It is always good to be sensitive, but the moment we become over-sensitive or sentimental we cross the danger mark ahead. To be sentimental is a psyche-problem, and must be treated by a competent pychiatrist indeed.

In the name of yoga people in general, and Swami Vivekanandji in particular suggest us to do our works with no consciourness of 'I' am doing this and that'. If we lose the sense of doer of anything, we perform all our works masterly. Swamiji says, "Gita teaches Karmayoga. We should work through yoga... The consciousness that I am doing this and that is neither present, when one works through yoga. The western people do not understand this. They say that if there is no consciousness of ego, if the ego is gone how then can a man work?... If the painter losing the consciousness of his ego, becomes completely immersed in his painting, he will be able to produce masterpieces... He who is one with the lord through yoga performs all his works... and does not seek any personal benefit." (on page 247-248 Vol. 5 *Swamiji's works*)

May I humbly know when Hanuman, the well-known epitome of egolessness declares with a great pride before Rama, "I am simply your '*daas*' (Sweak), and you're my Lord," do we ever object to his using these words? If not, why not? Because, He uses this 'I' and 'my' with a good motive. Hence, let us be sensible by dropping simply the filth of the minds of these 'I' and 'my and not 'I' or 'my' at all for 'yoga'.

It is good that Gita teaches us Karmayoga and asks us to work through yoga, which means a union or a harmony among our three good aspects - thoughts, feelings and willing. When we do a work through yoga, the results wil be good. But it is beyond my comprehension as to what is wrong, if there is the consciousness of 'I am doing this or that'? The trouble is that we Eastern people want to flog every 'I' with the same ego. It's our mistaken belief that every 'I' works with the consciousness of ego. So long 'I's' mind works with a higher mission or with a good thinking, good feeling and with the spirit of good doing, whatever one can, wherever one is, and so long this 'I' does not carry any filth or ego with 'its' wings, it can not leave virus of evils, no matter where it flutters and where it sits. If there is no conscisousness of doing this and that, how can one carry the sense of 'dos' or don't with oneself? I feel when a painter works on the higher altitude of one's mission i.e., the production of masterpiece sample of one's art, when he/she dissolves all his/her little-mindedness into the vast ocean of humanity i.e. when one works for the benefit of all the people, one is found more responsible and thus one produces master pieces of one's works. Let us accept the difference between these two things i.e. first, doing good consciously by oneself, secondly, the sense of unnecessary ego attached with work, no matter whether it is good or bad. The sense of ourself doing consciously this or that good is a yoga in itself. It has no concern with any ego. Man is not a robot or a machine, which has no consciouness of doing this or that - good or bad. In case a soldier or a painter has the sense by chance in one's mind that it's not he but God is fighting or God is painting and he is only His 'nimit', the person will no more remain a soldier or a painter, but a first class His master's pet dog on a long leash only. But this stage comes only when, one lacks the desirable faith in oneself.

Of course, if I am a soldier or a painter, I must lose the consciousness of any ego that I'm the only soldier of this or that merit, or I am the only painter, who has no match in terms of quality of work in the world. Let every soldier or a painter be a good man first, and good worker next. No good worker suffers from the fit of any ego. It is because our good soldiers were good humans too in the recent Kargil war between India and Pakistan, they treated Pakistani dead soldiers on our sides quite humanly. We should be aware of the fact that if the consciousness of doing this or that withers away from the scene, then all the works themselves too are apt to wither away . This consciousness of doing this or that in itself is not bad. It must be there. What we are to renounce is the desire of thinking, feeling and doing evil only.

Let us remember we are apt to behave like pundits of Somnath temple, when it was looted, if we lose all sense of doings. Then we are apt to be escapists.

So, what we need is not to remove 'I', but the filth of I's mind. If our motive is good, it brings bliss, happiness and peace. In a nutshell, let the soldier or a painter or any worker fight and work with the sense of one's duty of excellence. If one does one's work with this sense, one is found immersed in one's work too to have the best results. Let us remember the moment a driver loses the sense that he is driving or he is on the steering wheel, he's apt to cause a fatal accident. Because one loses the sense of responsibility with the loss of the sense of doing by oneself. So, let us no more make our 'poor' 'I' a scapegoat for our own vices. Let us no more distrust every 'I' unnecessarily.

minds. Let us remember both heaven and hell are not God's creations, but our own. Let us no more waste our precious time in useless age old controversies regarding the so-called *Atma-Pramatma,* heaven-hell, and *lok-parlok.* In fact, human minds are the true epicentres of both good and evil. We may or may not have faith in Him, but we are apt to be sunk if we have no faith in our own steering of the ship of our lives.

Do planets rule over our lives? 'No', they dont, writes Amalendu Bandyopadhyay. I firmly believe had God been the creator of the world, He himself too would have been stunned to see His own creation! Swami Vivekanandji holds: "By reading books we become parrots; no one becomes learned by reading books. If a man reads, but one word of love, he indeed becomes learned". (on page 20 Vol. 4 *Swamiji's Works*) It all does not mean we should not read books. Instead, we must. But we must think over and talk less and no more behave like parrots. Parrots have no faith in themselves.

Only we are not supposed to be hypnotised by the glamour of the world, as the world is only a necessary means to an end. And the end is the welfare of the people. There has been a tendency that those who worship God, they look down upon the people, who live in the world and work for the good of the people. This is not good. Swami Vivekanandji too said: "If a man returns from the world to worship God, he must not think that those who live in the world and work for the good of the world are not worshipping God... Each is great in his own place". While the former has faith in God, the latter in men.

We wordly people are to mend our Sanskars; so that we may be able to think, feel and do good to improve the fabric of our lives. We must be very careful for what thoughts and feelings even conceive in our minds. Because they have an everlasting impact on our minds, no matter whether they're allowed to survive for a very short time or live for a longer one. Once they have entered our minds, they try to come again and again, no matter they are subsided by us. Hence, we must resist their re-conception, if the impulses are bad. Swami Vivekanandji tells us how sanskars are formed, which are responsible for a good or bad fabric of our lives. He says, "Using the simile of a lake for the mind, every wave that rises in the mind, when it subsides, does not die out entirely, but leaves a mark and a future possibility of that wave coming out again. The mark with the possibility of the wave reappearing, is what is called sanskars". We architects of our own destinies are supposed to do is to minimise the possibility of the appearance of these ripples or waves, which are not in the good of the individual and the society as a whole. If we go on resisting such bad ripples or waves coming in our minds as a daily routine earnestly we are sure to form our good sanskars by and by. But this may take days or years or the whole life time of ours. If the ripples or waves are good, they too need our protection, atleast, initially in order to be everlasting. Here too faith in one's own self is more important.

Swami Vivekanandji warns us: " If a man continously hears bad words, thinks bad thoughts, does bad actions, his mind will be full of bad impressions, and they will influence his thought and work without his being conscious of that fact — and their resultant must be evil— Similarly, if a man thinks good thought and does good works ... and even if he wishes to do evil, his mind, ... will not allow him to do so — you may place him in any company, there will be no danger for him -- By work alone man may get to where Buddha got largely by meditation and Christ by prayer". This all shows how we can make our rise or fall possible ourselves. But is it all possible without having a faith in oneself? Faith in oneself does not mean sprouting and protecting the feeling of ego in oneself.

Swami Vivekanandji tells from his own experience of life. He says, "I may meet hundreds of persons-meet also one whom I love when I retire at night—only that face comes before the mind -- I met perhaps only for one moment and which I loved; all the others have vanished. Therefore, be "unattached". -- The whole gist of the teaching is that you should work like a master and not as a slave -- ninety nine percent of mankind work like slaves and the result is misery. Work through feedom! work through love!"

In this world we can't be completely unattached with everybody and everything. We've to attach ourselves with good people and good thoughts and things. Of course, our excessive attachments and detachments both cause us miseries. Because both extremes make us slaves, instead of masters. Even our excessive attachment with a hypothetical God becomes a problem and we become ready even to finish the living gods and goddesses sometime.

Swamiji adds further: "Although a man has not studied a single system of philosophy, although he does not believe in any God, and never believed, although he has not prayed even once in his whole life, if the simple power of good actions has brought him to that state where he is ready to give up his life and else for others, he has arrived at the same point to which the religious man will come through his prayers and the philosopher through knowledge, and so you may find that the philosopher, the worker, and the devotee, all meet one point, that point being self abnegation..." (Swami Vivekanandji) Everyone is to remove one's exclusive self only. Let us try to achieve this goal of life with self-confidence. The goal is: 'live and let live.

So let us realise that our world is good or bad, because we either most of us are good or bad respectively. We can't claim to be good and say that our world is bad in itself. It is not made either by any deity, but by ourselves individually or collectively. Swami Vivekanandji too acepted this fact: "It is a lie when we say, the world is bad and we are good..." (on page 8 Vol. 8 *Swamiji's Works*) When I say nature made the universe and men made their world, it means our life or world is, what we make it. We have been negative in our approach. Always we have been insisting on not to have any attachment with the world, except the God, without knowing anything what He is, without experiencing His presence anywhere at all. Do we ever realise that whatever the world is, it is not made by itself? We can't help without both attachment as well as detachment in life. Only we are supposed to know the priorities of our attachments as well as detachments at the same time. Even Swami Vivekananadji too accepted the truth: "Both attachment and detachment perfectly developed make a man great and happy". (on page 430 Vol. 6 *Swamiji's Works*) Merely our negative outlook in life won't help us. So, let's be happy to see a bud blooming. Why to keep our faces hanging in the air to remind ourselves that the same bud is apt to be dry and fall one day? Why don't we keep it into our minds that nothing is eternal in the world. If the bud is apt to be dry and fallen one day, why don't we accept the tuth in positive light? Swami Vivekanandji asserted again: "I am learning now how to be detached as well as attached, and mentally becoming my own master" (on page 517 Vol. 8 Swamiji). He adds further: "That man alone will be able to get the best of nature, who having the power of attaching himself to a thing with all this energy, has also the power to detach himself when he should do so. The difficulty is that there must be as much power of attachment as that of detachment - But the wall never feels misery, the wall never loves, is never hurt... Surely it is better to be attached and caught than to be a wall." (on page 3 Vol. 2 *Swamiji*)

The greatest tragedy is that all of us have become more of less like stones or walls, which are neither happy, nor unhappy to see others happy or unhappy respectively. A faithless person, who may have faith in some hypothetical deity, but has no faith in oneself, behaves like a log of wood, becasue he is not attached with anybody, but detached with everyone and everything, except a hypothetical deity.

How faith in oneself has been decisive or the keystone of humans' edifice, Swami Vivekanandji gives histrocial facts to prove it. ". . . Believe in yourselves first and then believe in anything else. In the history of the world, you will find that only those nations that have believed in themselves have become great and strong. Here, to India, came an Englishman, who was only a clerk, ... he believed in himself, he believed that he was born to do great things, and that man became Lord Clive; the founder of the empire. If he had believed ... "O Lord, I am weak, and I am low" where would he have been? In a lunatic asylum. You also are made lunatics by their evil - teachings." (on page 426-427 Vol. 3 *Swamiji*)

How truthful and factual it is! What a contrast we have in our approaches here in India! While Lord Clive believed that he was born to do great things, because he believed in himself, we are taught here with one's baby's milk that the sole doer of all things is the Lord. We are simply His *nimits* or instruments, and whatever he does, does right and good. And whatever he gives and does for us, we must accept that quite happily as our *fate-accompli*, pre-determined by Him on the basis of our Karmas of our last or present birth. Another potensive dose, what's given to us is that all of us are only 'His Masters' pet dogs on a long leash'. And we can do nothing, except worshipping the Lord—the cheapest escaping route from our own respective responsibilities has been taught to us since our birth. Every child has been indoctrinated since his/her birth with: 'O Lord, I am weak and I am low'. It has made us indolent and inert. Why have we reduced us to this dismal level? Because we have no faith and no belief in ourselves. At the most we have ideals before us that we've to build a house for us to live in, that we have to get our wards married, that we have confined ourselves for attaining these aims in our lives. Ofcourse, to some extent we have made so dismal a set-up of our society that we men of ordinary clay can't think of anything else, except these aims of our lives. But do we ever sincerely think that these are only the necessary means in our lives? They are not our ends. The end of human life is peace. And the peace can be had not merely by getting a glorious and cosy house built and merely by earning a good source of living, but by building ourselves from within or by followng earnestly the principle 'live and let live'. Unless we build ourselves from within, we are sure to behave like lunatics and we are sure to find ourselves in a lunatic asylum. In this respect, merely by getting a glorious abode of God built and installing a beautiful idol or statue in it won't help us at all. It is all our illusion. To change ourselves and our world, we have no alternative, except to build ourselves from within. It all does not mean we do not need a good house to live in, or we do not need good food to eat, or we should not marry or we should not earn a good living. We must do all these things but honestly and whole heartedly. But we can't overlook our ultimate aim i.e. peace. We should not be the slaves to them, but only their masters, because they are only our necessary means to live and not at all the end of life. We must remember that we are born to do greater things in life than these.

The question is: has not the age old indoctrinatiion of this philosophy of 'weak and low' paralysed us both physically and mentally? Has it not made us perfect cowards, fatalists, shirkers, escapists and parasites? What a downfall we have caused to our ownselves! Let's no more mug up each and everything that's written by some sage in an age for this or that reason in a scripture. That sage now is gone and that age and time too have gone. Let us no more repeat those things like parrots. I don't mean we should have a boycott of reading those things. If they help us in understanding ourselves and the nature well, they are good. otherwise not.

Today we see people happy, holding this view that they're simply the puppets in Lord's hands and thus they're simply to dance and be happy, as He pulls their strings, sitting behind the curtain. It appears that the view in question has sucked all faith from our lives.

If we accept that we're all the architects of our own destinies, so we can steer the ship of our lives without any clutch or brake etc., this is the wrong meaning of human free-will. Moreover, that is never possible in a civilized polity.The hands of Rule Of Law must be powerful to deal with such unlawful persons. Again, faith in our ownselves doesn't mean at all that we are free to snatch other's bread at our own will, or we can also capture other's territory, as British Government did in India and elsewhere, or we can snatch other's freedom to keep them as our slaves.

Rather faith in oneself means faith in thinking, feeling, and doing excellent for the entire humanity. Let no one think that he/she is the only person here to live, but rather one must cultivate this attitude of one's mind that there are others too like oneself, who are also to live in this world.

'Live and let live' are the crude forms of simultaneous philosophies of both 'materialism' and 'spiritualism', which are to co-exist together. They are not primarily two activities, but they are the names of two visions, or two outlooks or two mindset or two ways of life. While materialism gives priority in life 'to live' and that too at the cost of others sometime. The spiritualism gives priority to the idea of 'let live' The goal of materialism is 'live', the goal of spiritualism is: 'let live'. Hence, our salvation from miseries lies in the co-existence of both these attitudes in life. Spiritualism has nothing to do with the performance of any kind of rituals or dogmas or '*asans*'. It has nothing to do with wearing any mask of religiousity. It is not at all running away from the world, which is our self-creation, but on the other hand it is living in the world with a deep desire or sense of fulfulling high missions in life, one after another. Actually spiritual person's high vision reflects his whole thoughts, his all feelings and doings. A real spiritual person prefers higher values to valuables in life. He can surrender these valuables, because he gives priority to attaining higher mission in life i.e. peace and happiness, not as a coward, but as brave person. Certainly, he will fight for the honour of the country but he can never lick the boots of his superior to keep oneself in the office or position or service by hook or by crook. Man down the ages, has been thirsting for peace and happiness. A spiritual person can have them from within and not with out. Peace is neither essentially attached with the bullock cart age, nor essentially detached with the present rocket or atomic era. Because peace is essentially a state of mind, which can be had merely by following earnestly 'live and let live' at the same time. The cause of strife, quarrel, battle and war has always been the same i.e, the human little - mindedness in different forms. Peace can be had not necessarily if somone chants Ram, Allaha, God or 'guru' several times a day, but when we have an earnest urge in our minds to follow the 'mission of swim and sink' together with all the living gods and goddesses as far as it is possible. Otherwise, chanting of Ram and Roti makes no difference.

Every good or bad happening in our lives leaves a lesson behind it to teach the people. Only men of contemplation imbibe the lesson and forget the event. On the other hand, the thoughtless forget the lesson and go on brooding the tragic event.

Here in India, if we want to open a petty grocery shop, leaving apart all other smaller or bigger works, what we do in our lives we usually link our success in our endeavour with the mercy or blessings of an Unknown. It's all our illusion if we think that we do so, because we want to be humble or we want to keep ourselves at bay from any ego in life. Don't we see usually those, who prostrate before the Lord to worship Him most of them are found misbehaving with the living goods and goddessess—their own sisters and brothers around? Of course, exceptions are there. Due to lack of desired faith in our ownselves we work, but work half-heartedly, with the result, if by coincidence we succeed in our aim somewhere, we at once tie up the crown of success on the forehead of God, and if by chance we fail to achieve our aim we start cursing our own fate, as if it was all pre-determined by some Lord on the basis of our past Karmas. Most of us never realise that if we rise in our lives, it is because we raise ourselves by doing good, and if we fall somewhere, it is because we make us down either individually or collectively. Only a jaundiced can see a ray of ego in this truth. So, earlier we raise ourselves, the better.

Do we ever realise that a good swimmer too is apt to be drowned in the swift current, if he has no faith in his own skill, no matter then how much faith he has got in his Lord. So, it is no use to live like morally degraded people. It is no use to have a 'psyche of low and weak'. It is in this context, it is relevant to quote Swami Vivekanandji, who says: "It is the coward and the fool who says, "This is fate" -- But it is the strongman, who stands up and says, "I will make my fate" -- You will find that astrology and all these mystical things are generally signs of a weak mind --" (on page 184 Vol. 8 *Swamiji's Works*)

That is why Swami Vivakanandji gave a clarion call to all the children of the world to boost their morale high:

"Therefore, children — do not sit idle" (on page 428 Vol. 3 *Swamiji's Works*)

"Arise, awake, and stop not till the goal is reached. Arise, awake! Awake from the hypnotism of weakness. -- stand up assert yourself" (on page 193 Vol. 3 *Swamiji's Works*) I have a firm view that if we rise and wake-up spiritually, we are sure to move the mountains from our ways, make our own destinies, and draw our own fate lines.

Let us not forget this even for a moment that the removal of these artificial divine crutches from our armpits does not mean at all the replacement of the crutches of any of our ego there to move on. Let everyone of us realise one's own duty in this respect. This is why, it is rightly said :

'*Shama her range mey jalti hai Sahar hone tak'*.

(I shall do, whatever is within my capacity) Now enough is enough. There is no question to see towards our back. No-doubt. hurdles here or there are apt to come, but the architects of their own destinies are to remove them.

In the respect, we are supposed to remember the warning signals and the immortal lines of Robert Frost too just to boost our morale:

"The woods are lovely, dark and deep,
But I have promises to keep,
And miles to go before I sleep.
And miles to go before I sleep."
—(Robert Frost)

In the ocean of life there are rocks, the most dangerous sharks, crocodiles, and the like, but we should not be afraid to face them. If we are cowards, we cannot remove them from our ways. It is only our bravery and firm will which are to go ahead like more powerful rocks. Being the true architects of our own destinies we are to complete our high mission in life one after another to change our lives or the world.

In fact, I have no allergy of any sort against the so-called God or soul. Whether they exist or not, I know nothing about them. But I have the humble conviction whether there is God or no God, soul or no soul, we human beings have no alternative, except to do good to be good, what we can, wherever we are to be good only.

Those who have staunch faith in their God, when they find they have no argument left in their armoury, their usual plea has been to believe that there must be some power, or energy or unusual force to run this whole universe. I too humbly hold that if one of the forms of God is energy (of course, I know some hold that God is formless), and especially atomic energy, which can cause us both the greatest construction as well as destruction in the world, when it is produced not through the destruction of matter, but through the process of fission or fusion of 'atom', should we then accept an atomic bomb, consisting of atomic energy, as God? Let us remember that all the living and non-living materials here in the world are made up of certain basic units, known as atoms, which are made up of three fundamental particles i.e. 'protons', 'neutrons' and 'electrons'. Even you and me, and so all of us and my poor pen with which I'm humbly writing this '*Architect of human destiny*?' and the book, copy, the table I have with me — all are made up of the same atoms. In our own country too 'Prithvi' (earth), 'Jal' (water), 'Agni' (fire), 'Yayu' (air) and 'Akash' (space) are known as five fundamental particles consisting in an atom. It is these fanatics, who keep their Lord in these atoms even. How can an atom by itself consisting of energy, maintain and control the whole world, no matter how powerful it may be? Hence, I feel this is nothing, but simply a jaundiced approach to the matter in question. Matter or energy can neither create, nor sustain, nor destroy by itself. Both the use or misuse of an atom or energy mainly depends on humans. As the time passes new discoveries are apt to come into being, but their use or misuse will always depend on humans.

It is told that about 5000 years ago rishi 'Sri' Ved Vyasji questioned the people of his time, as to why they didn't observe the limitations or restraints regarding 'dharma', 'artha' and 'Kam' in their lives? It is told the rishi resented very much to see nobody paid him any heed regarding these matters mentioned above. Let us understand that our salvation lies in following our own 'dharam' only, which is the science and art of right actions. Our salvation i.e., freedom from miseries lies in earning our own livings honestly or by remembering' the principle i.e., 'means justify the end'. Thirdly, we can get salvation only when we follow only legitimate and desired '*kam*' in the world. If we do not listen to the voice of reasoning of the saint, let us remember we won't get 'moxa' from our miseries then.

'Here is then the warning for us:

'Na Samjhoge to mit jaoge, duniya walon,
tumhari daastan bhi na hogi daastanon mein'.

(If you don't pay any head even now you people of the whole world will be destroyed and your species will be extinct and tale will not be in the stories narrated).

In Swami Vivekanandji's own words: "It (the Vedanta) does not show that the world is vain and does not exist, but it says, "understand, what this world is, so that it may not hurt you". (on page 312 Vol. 2 *Swamiji's Works*)

In this context let's remember:

'Bazaar may rehta hoona, magar kharidar nahi hoon,
duniya may rehta hoona, mager talebdar nehi hoon'.

So, it's a warning for these, who without understanding the world, want to run away from the world simply dubbing it mithya',

'Sansar se bhage firte hoo,
Bhagwan ko tum Kya paoge—

The nucleus of fanaticism is self-centerdness and self-aggrandizement even at the cost of others, and hence, it is demon like. So, it must be condemned by all.

If really everyone of us understands as to what must be done and what not, we are sure to change our hell into heaven. Then if today in the words of Swamiji: "... in this world (there is) ninety percent misery and ten percent happiness. Perhaps, after a while it will appear as ninety percent happiness, and we shall call it heaven...". This all needs prior faith in our ownselves. Otherwise, we won't be able to turn our hell into heaven. (on page 303 Vol. 2 *Swamiji's Works*)

We all usually talk of change. But what does it mean actually? It means we are to change ourselves from within. In other words our mindset or our whole process of thought is to be changed by ourselves first. In this context, Mr. Clinton, the ex-President of U.S rightly said: "Prosperity and power are important and we must maintain them. But the greatest progress we have made is in the human heart. In the end, all the world's wealth and a thousand armies are no match for the strength and decency of the human spirit." Let us remember arms are meant to create wounds, while only our spiritual development can heal them. What men do depend on their power of discrimination, Vivek and '*buddhi*'.

We should keep it into our minds what is pleasent to our senses may not be good, and what is good, may not be pleasant. Neither our wealth, nor our Lord, if at all He exists, is an end in itself. The end is human welfare at large. So, let us no more behave like slaves, but perfect masters only.

I am well aware that the believers in God may floor me in a debate, because what I humbly hold in this book: '*Architect of human destiny*?' is based not on our sacred books or scriptures but on the basis of experiences of the lives of common men of the world. I hold these views only as a seeker of truth. I am not against anybody or anything. Hence, I hardly need to assure my patrons that if I'm proved wrong in my humble views, I won't treat it as my personal defeat, but the victory of truth only. That too would be the happiest occasion in my life to see the truth shining in the world.

What I humbly believe is that the world needs new humans — humans, who have no moth-eaten minds and having new eyes with new eye-glasses on to see the truth themselves with an angle of vision, which is far away from any bias, and pre-commitment regarding an ideology. So far we have learnt to make an Unknown the very architect of our own destinies. Hence this human world, what it is—good or bad—has been His mindsport or the '*leela*' only. So, it has zeroed our own accountability for both the good or bad fabric of our lives, what we have. So far as our understanding goes, we have been believing that God is the Master-weaver of the web of our lives, and consequently, we have accepted the easy route that it's not we, but the Master Himself who is to mend the web, if at all it requires anywhere. So far we have been treating ourselves as passive spectators of the whole melodrama, staged by all of us. The whole output of the philosophy is before all of us. Let us examine and weigh the very dividends of this philosophy as such without any bias or prejudice.

How hypocrite we have been that on the one hand we have been believing that it is He, who makes us rise, and it is He, who makes us fall, and on the other, we have been declaring from our tops that men are the masters of their own fate, as they have the complete free-will to determine it! When we have made God as the sole maker of our lives, the absurdity of human-free-will to determine their own fate is quite obvious. How can we make-fool all the people all the time? Let us remember that if faith in our ownselves is lost, everything is lost.

In my humble opinion our salvation from miseries lies in accepting our own parentage of the baby-world, no matter the baby is beautiful or ugly. Can we ever bring up our own baby well by escaping from our own responsibilities? So let us no more accept anything by closing our eyes, no matter from where it comes. A seeker of truth can never do that.

In this context, it is relevant to quote immortal words of Buddha, who advised us: "Examine my teachings like a goldsmith investigates the purity of gold - If there are any impurities reject them. Don't accept them merely because Buddha is saying so".

In this world, what it is, the age long views regarding the causes of one's physical, mental, social, economic and political inequalities have ever been a bone of contention. This question has been troubling people's minds even before the advent of Buddha on the world stage. What was viewed was that it was the God, who caused all these inequalities on the basis of our past karmas. The questions like why one is brought up with silver spoon in one's mouth, and another is born in the womb of poverty; why one is born to a millionaire and another to a pauper; why one is born as a mental prodigy and another as an idiot; why one is born with saintly characteristics and another with criminal tendencies; why one is born with the qualities of a linguist, and another with the characteristics of an artist or a mathematician, or a musician or a writer etc. from one's cradle—all were knocking Buddha's mind too for their satisfactory answers.

Before examining in details as a goldsmith, as to what Buddha, the great human giant, says about the causes of these inequalities, let us not overlook the fact that there have been even great scientists like Einstein and others, who were not genious at their initial stage of life, but later on became the greatest Scientists in their own fields. We can not overlook either heredity or envirornment, what major role they play in making one's life, what it is. Moreover, we can not ignore the social, political, economic conditions and individual factors, which are responsible for the existence of such inequalities in human beings the world over. Let us remember that Ratnaker was neither a born dacoit, nor a born saint. In ancient Greece, the so-called slaves were treated even as inanimate objects by the so-called freemen, and they were even sold and bought there like commodities. These slaves, who were in majority, had no rights and no privileges at all. The moot question is: was the real cause of their inequality in their status lay in the past Karmas of all the slaves alike, or actually in the peculiar social, political and economic conditions made by the people in ancient Greek city-states?

Let us remember what treatment — good or bad - one gets from another in this world depends more upon one's mental - set up. There are now people in India - people who no more look down upon Sudras-their own brethern, but still there are people, who use their missiles of hatred against these people. It is a historical fact that when Alexander came to India, he was taught by Aristotle to treat all non-Greeks as inferiors, as barbarians and as slaves. But on meeting these people in question, Alexander was helpless to act according to the advice of his 'guru'. Dr. Radhakrishnan refers this case to show that if we apply our *vivek* or power of discrimination, as what to do, and what not, we can change the very course of human history, as nothing is inevitable and nothing is pre-determined. Dr. Sahib says, "There was a time when Alexander came here (in India). He was taught by Aristotle to treat all non-Greeks as inferiors, as barbarians, as slaves. "You must not deal with them," was the advice, he gave to Alexander—But what did Alexander do? He came out looked at the Persians, looked at the Afghans, looked at the Indians... and said "How can I treat them as inferiors? How can I treat them as barbarians? These are people with great intellectual powers with great spiritual insight-How can such people be treated as inferiors?"

Thus, Alexander did not give a wrong direction to the course of human history, at least, in this respect. Here I am not discussing what unfortunate other things he did. Now we know what Aristotle proposed, and how Alexander disposed it.

So, let us then seek the right casues of all events or incidents or happenings in history. I think to link the very cause of inequalities with one's past karmas, is nothing, but the revival of the same age old view of pre-determinism in different garb.

The view of one's past karmas says: 'The definite invisible cause or causes of visible effect may not necessarily be confined to present life, but could be traced to a proximate or remote past birth'.

Those who believe that one's past karmas are very potential ask: why should identical twins, who are physically alike, inheriting the same genes, enjoying the same privileges of upbringing, be temperamentally, intellectually and morally totally different? They believe that the theory of heredity can not satisfactorily account for the birth of a cirminal in a long line of honourable ancestors, for the birth of a saint in a family of evil repute, for the arising of infant prodigies and great spiritual teachers. They say that they come across identical twins, which were born from the same germs, under the same conditions of time and environment — one of whom is an angel and other a demon. Thus they believe that both heredity and environment fail to answer all these queries. Let us not forget that we are all the architects of our own destinies, not only from the time of our birth, but from the time of our conception.

Let us know now the views of Buddha, regarding the causes of inequalities that exist in the world among humans, and which ultimately determine the lives of the people and their world, what it is.

Perplexed to see the apparent inequality or disparity in humans, a young truth-seeker named Subha approached the Buddha one day and questioned him: "What is the reason, what is the cause, O Lord, that we find amongst mankind the short-lived and long lived, the diseased and the healthy, the ugly and the beautiful, and powerless and powerful, the poor and the rich, the low born and the high born, the ignorant and the wise"?

The Buddha's reply was:—

{as mentioned in the book—'*The Buddha and His Teachings*' by Narada. Buddhist Missionary Society, Malaysia (page 338 onwards)

"All living beings have actions (Kamma) as their own, their inheritance, their congenital cause, their kinsman, their refuge. It is Kamma that differentiates beings into low and high states." Buddha then explained the causes of such differences in accordance with the law of Cause and Effect.

If a person destroys life, is a hunter, besmears his hand with blood, is engaged in killing and wounding, and is not merciful towards living beings, he, as a result of his killing, when born amongst mankind, will be short-lived."

Buddha further states: "If a person avoids killing ... is merciful,... he, as a result of his non killing when born amongst mankind, will be long-lived".

To know and to investigate Buddha's views as a goldsmith regarding the subject cited before, an obvious question arises had it been a fact, what Buddha holds about short lived and long lived here, what would have happened with all the butchers; who earn their livelihood through their work, with the meat-eaters, who fill in their bellies with their dishes of meat, with the soldiers, whose dharma is to kill their enemies; and especially with the doctors, who bring the real solace to the very doors of suffering and dying humanity as a result of their own researches on animals in the labs? Of course, these doctors are not hunters, but their hands too are besmeared with blood in their labs. The question is: should they give shelter to the fear in their minds that they will be short-lived, when born again, if at all it is a fact, what Buddha holds?

Moreover, it is also a fact that I myself too might be killing hundreds of microbes through the course of my writing this book. Should I then stop seeking the truth through the project? In the same way, when a mosquito bites me, I try to kill it mercilessly. Sometime I also get my hand too besmeared with it's blood. I must remember that if a mosquito has it's birthright to seek human blood for taking protein from it, I also have the birth right to kill the said mosquito to survive and to use even the disinfectants for the same. We are well aware that these mosquitoes (she) cannot stop biting us. But being humans should we stop killing them, in view of the ideas of Buddha that when born again, we shall be short-lived due to that?

Buddha again answers the query of his disciple and says, "If a person is in the habit of harming others... he, as a result of his harmfulness, when born amongst mankind, will suffer from various diseases...

...If a person is not in the habit of harming others he will enjoy good health."

Again, to keep ourselves embraced with facts side by side , what Buddha holds, let us ask ourselves: had it been a fact, what Buddha says about diseased and healthy persons in the world, what would have happened with all of us the world over, as we are not in the habit of harming others, but actually have been killing crores of microbes, at least, unconsciously, as they are bound to be killed, while we are busy in this or that activity in our life throughout? Sometime we do harm to others too. Should we all grant an asylum to the fear in our minds that as a result of harming or killing the beings (even unconsciously) all of us will suffer from various diseases in the next birth?

The moot point is: Can we even live or do any activities in our lives without harming or killing the beings around unconsciously, at least?

How fantastic the belief seems to be that Buddha's foot was slightly injured, when Devadatta (Buddha's own cousin-cum-disciple) made a futile attempt to kill him out of his jeolousy, because Buddha too killed a step-brother of himself in the previous birth with the object of appropriating his property. (Referred on page 369 — *The Buddha and His Teachings* by Narada)! I wonder, not because I am against the principle i.e., as you sow, so shall you reap, but because how could it be linked particularly with an episode like this so authentically, unless we have a fool-proof record of our past birth? From this angle of vision, becausue everyone must be committing this or that wrong in one's own life, may be unconsciously, hence, no one of us can ever be happier in one's life.

We may try to save our own skin by presuming that there is nothing good or evil in the world, but thinking makes it so. When Buddha's foot was injured, because he too did some wrong in his previous birth, as supposed wrongly or rightly, does it not clearly mean that even God, the doer of all things (as supposed by so many) differentiates between good and evil activities of ours?

If here in the world everyone of us reaps, what one sows sooner or later necessarily, then why to feel sorry or mourn the crucifixion of Christ and the people like him in the world then? Why to establish courts, enact this or that law to govern, when everyone is to reap only what one sows? Does it not all look like a wishful thinking of our minds? From this fatalistic viewpoint, one who sips the cow's milk even, eats curd, takes vegetables and fruits or cereals and the like must be ready to listen to the music of his own doings sooner or later.

If we go on with our minds, laden with this dismal view, our life will then become then more cumbersome, and as a result of it we are apt to find ourselves more or less in a lunatic asylum. Let us remember: health and disease have more or less always been the integral parts of each sane's or insane's life. Both are natural to some extent.

Buddha answers the query of his disciple further and says, "If a person is . . . irritated by a trivial word, gives vent to anger, ill-will and resentment . . . will become ugly . . .

"If a person is . . . not irritated even by a torrent of abuse, does not give vent to anger . . . will become beautiful."

Again, to keep ourselves well-equipped with latest facts in view of what Buddha says, let us accept the glaring facts that by our negative thinking i.e., like having unnecessary anger, jealousy, cunningness, hate, ill-will, feeling of vengeance, and the like our whole chemistry of our bodies and minds is disturbed, which affects both our physical and mental health ultimately with harmful consequences. Moreover, our positive and peaceful attitude in life becomes the cause of our good health, undoubtedly. In this respect, Buddha's views are definitely praiseworthy.

But the point is how many persons are there in the world, who are not irritated, don't give vent to their anger easily due to right or wrong reason, and don't find themselves in a fit or cyclone of ill-will and resentment even on trivial matters from time to time? If they are more in numbers and obviously they must be, then there must be more ugly persons in the world. But the main cause of ugliness or beauty is either our heredity or environment according to Bio-technology. No more speculation, please.

Buddha states further: "If a person is jealous—of the gains of others . . . he as a result of his jealousy, when born . . . will be powerless.

"If a person is not jealous, ... he, as a result of his absence of jealousy, when born—will be powerful."

In this respect in short, we must be aware that there might be very few persons in the world, who are not jealous of the gains of others. Hardly there may be the few, who never act as dogs in the manger. From this angle of vision then more or less all must be powerless. But here we find that the hard core criminals are more powerful. They are the laws in themselves. What is Veerappan? What is Osama bin Laden? Have they not been the most powerful law breakers in India today? In fact, one's power of body and mind lies mainly in one's heredity and environment. With the passage of time it is reduced naturally. Of course, I don't deny that we lose the power of the body and mind of ours in jealousy, anger, hate, feeling of vengeance, etc.

Buddha states and replies further: "If a person does not give anything for charity, he, as a result of his greediness, when born ...will be poor".

"If a person is bent on charitabe giving, he as a result of his generosity, when "born ... will be rich."

Well, it is an undeniable fact that most of the people in the world are poor. They remain hand-to-mouth in their lives. They in fact, have nothing left with them in spare to give for charity. The question of charity comes only when most of them are in a postion to have even their basic needs fulfilled. In fact, the main cause of one's poverty or one's affluence lies in the economic and political structure of the place indeed, where one lives. If one does not act according to one's capacity, one won't be able to produce enough and, consequently, one must be poor. In addition to it if one doesn't get one's due according to one's work or need, one is apt to be poor. The question of charity comes only when on gets one's own due in the world. Moreover, is it not a fact, that here lakhs of people, who earn their wealth by wrong means, they become philanthropists in their turns? They donate easily for the construction of a religious place, or a hospital, or to a charitable trust to please their Lord. Ofcourse, all affluent people don't sail in the same boat. They are in execptions. But it is not correct to say that all persons have become rich through their charity. It is a wrong diagnosis of a case indeed. Most of the time the truth is found on the other side of the fencing. Because conventional religions have been teaching the anatomy of the poverty to the poors. Marx has rightly said that religion is the opium of the masses. It is what teaches them to tolerate it. These doses act as sedatives, calmpose and tranquilizers for the time being.

Buddha further analyses the cause of low birth and says: "If a person is stubborn, haughty, honours not those, who are worthy of honour, he as a result of his arrogance, when born . . . will be of low birth . . ."

"If a person is not stubborn, not haughty honours those, who are worthy of honour, he, as a result of his humility when born . . . will be of high birth".

We are all familiar with the fact that in this world, what it is, people who really deserve respect of people, who are worthy of people's honour are seldom put in high esteem. First of all, all such people , whose greatest weakness is that they are ahead of their age or time and thus such people are either hit by brickbats or shot at by the people out of mere misunderstanding. The great Christ, the great Socratese, the great Galelio, the great Gandhi and the like come into this category. Secondly, when they are no more in the world, they are buried under big stones by the people simply as a ritual. This is the irony of fate of most of the so-called big people in the world.

From the point of view of Buddha, most of us must be of low birth, because most of us are haughty, seldom honour those, who actually deserve our high esteem. But the facts are quite deep. It is our social-set-up, which categorises as to who is of low, and who's of high birth.

Further, Buddha says, " If a person does not approach the learned and the virtuous and inquire what is good and what is evil, what is right and what is wrong, what should be practised, and what not should be practised, what should be done, and what not should be done, what conduces to one's welfare, and what to one's ruin, he as a result of his non-inquiring spirit, when born . . . will be ignorant . . ."

"If a person does approach the learned and the virtuous . . . he, as a result of his inquiring spirit when born . . . will be intelligent".

But the fact is that in this world, where money and muscle-power are everything for most of the people, there are natually only the remaining few people, who approach the learned and virtuous and enquire what is good and what is evil, what is right and what is wrong, and the like. Most of the people even pose themselves, as if they know each and everything in the world, and hence, they never feel the need to approach the learned people for the knowledge. Most of the people live in their own world, created by their own. They have no such mindset, or bent of mind or taste to enquire about such things mentioned above. They remain self-centered in their own lives. In short, most of us have non-inquiring spirit. They want that their 'end' must be good for them, no matter whether their 'means' may or may not be good to achieve the end. Most of us are either mammon-worshippers or God - worshippers. Most of us have nothing to do with the the questions related to higher life. Let us remember our spiritual knowledge is one thing, spiritual attainment is another.

From this angle of vision of Buddha most of the people of the world must be ignorant or idiots. But the facts are bitter to taste. No matter one knocks the learned's or virtuous doors or not, but it is a scientific fact that one's intelligence or idiocy depends here on one's heredity and environment. It all does not mean the denial of the importance of inquiring or non-inquiring spirit much. There are persons here who have a deep desire to know, but their environment does not come to their rescue in this respect. It becomes the greatest hurdle for them.

Thus, with the utmost apology before the great Buddha, I humbly say that these above said inferences regarding one's past karmas, what Buddha has derived, seem to be based more on speculation than on facts.

Let us accept the facts that all humans - both human giants like Buddha, and a Lilliputian like me alike are subject to err. Evolution has ever been going on in the arena of thoughts too. It is through this evolution only, truth comes to light. Let us be then ready to rejoice the victory of truth ultimately, no matter who possesses it, and who doesn't. The great thing in this world is not so much , as to where we are today, but in what direction we have been navigating our ships of life. Perhaps, to complete our voyage of truth will take the whole human life. The most important thing in this respect is whether we are sailing in the right direction or not.

Of course, I do accept Buddha's plea: "we are heirs of our own actions." (on page 342 - *The Buddha and His Teachings*) But I know nothing abut our past karmas. There is no doubt even the least in it that we are the heirs of our own actions, done by individually or collectively. That is why, I humbly say that our life or the world is not what the hypothetical remote control supernatural Power makes it, but what we humans make, what it is—good or bad.

The Buddhist hold it's due to one's difference in Karma appears the difference in one's gain and loss, fame and disgrace, blame and praise, happiness and misery. I do agree that the difference is primarily concerned with one's own life's present Karmas. But we can't ignore the fact that the world is not divine, and it is not a one man's show. Is it not a fact, that so many times besides an individual concerned, others around too have a major or minor hand in one's gain or loss, in one's fame or defame, in one's happiness or misery?

Can we ever forget how Buddha himself had to undergo his own character-assassination by a lady, who accused him once that she was pregnant from Buddha himself? Fortunately, it was all proved a fabricated lie later on. Should we take it for granted that Buddha had to undergo such accusation, because of some of his past action? Again, can we ever forget how Swami Vivekananadji too had to bear the burnt of his own character assassination in US. out of some people's personal jealousy? If we go on connecting our fortunes or misfortunes with our past or present this way, we shall be nowhere.

To conclude, we can say it humbly that the whole edifice of past karmas, what Buddha, the great had erected, was dangerously founded more on speculations, than on facts. Moreover, who knows in reality about one's past activities here in this world? At least, for commoners like me, it is beyond our capacity even to dream of it. I don't know whether Buddha had ever given any authentic talk regarding his past karmas. Let us no more try to scratch our past unnecessarily. Let us live in the present, make it a better one to change ourselves and our future world too.

Let us remember here in the world there are neither born angels, nor born demons, as good or evil has no genes. Buddha too was not a born Buddha, but he became a great human 'guru' and got 'nirvana' ultimately through his meditations only. According to advaned bio-technology, heredity and environment are the two master-keys to know one's present. We have got no such keys with us to know one's past, if at all it is there. Being architects of our own destinies we can change our present to a great extent, if at all we have a rocky will-cum-understaning, as Ratnakar did.

Certainly, both heredity and environment play an important role in making the brain or the mindset of a child, that functions in a particular way, because of the brain-chemistry. Perhaps, this is the domain of a doctor to change it to have the desired results. Now great hope lies with the science, which now, can change the genes too. Of course, we are to give a suitable environemnt to every babe since his/her conception even. There is a good news that now there is a lot we can do about the problems of our children's behaviour through men-making education and through men-making religion. To add in this respect, it is now evidently clear that even the hard core criminals especially in Tihar Jail in Delhi are finding a revolutionary change in their mindset and entire net of behaviour, because they are under going the courses of 'Yoga', 'pranayama' and meditation etc.

Now it is most essential to know what the modern scientists say about the causes of this inequality in mankind. They seek it's cause either in our heredity or one's environment.

Julian Huxley, one of the most distinguished Biologists and evolutionists writes on the basis of his own studies and experiments.

"Some genes control colour, others height or weight, others fertility or length of life, others vigour and the reverse, others shape or proportions.

Possibly all, certainly the vast majority, of hereditary characteristics are gene-controlled. For mental characters, there is every evidence that they are inheritable . . . That which is inherited in our personality and bodily peculiarities depends somehow upon the interaction of this assorted battery of genes with which we are equipped at fertilization." (on page 335 *The Buddha and His Teachings*, by Narada)

These are all scientific facts, and not even scientific fictions or speculations.

At the Chicago Darwinian contennial in 1959 by prominent evolutionists Sri. Julian Huxley said: "Evolution had no room for the supernatural. The earth and its inhabitants were not created, they evolved".

At the same conference Huxley told the 2500 assembled delegates: "We all accept the fact of evolution... The evolution of life is no longer a theory. It is a fact. It is the basis of all our thinking". He asserts: "The first point to make about Darwin's Theory is that it is no longer a theory, but a fact", In 1963 the book '*Biology for you*' confirms: "All reputable biologists have agreed that the evolution of life on the earth is an established fact".

The evolutionists assert that the first speck of life on earth arose by itself from inanimate matter. All matter on earth is composed of basic chemical elements. It is said that the first speck of life was seen in water.

Thus, the "questioning of The Theory of Evoution is like attacking the Theory of Gravity", says Isaac Asimov, an American scientist. He states further: "It is a fact, not speculation". In fact, unless we know what evolution is, we shall go on highlighting the Theory of Creation. The evolutionists believe that men evolved out of an ape like creature sometime between two million and ten million years ago. This ape like creature probably evolved from a type of monkey millions of years earlier. The monkey was evolved from a primitive primate resembling a modern tree shrew. "Like all other mammals the shrew evolved from an amphibian, and the amphibian evolved from a fish. — The first sign of life — simple one called organism (amoeba) developed in the ocean". (*Science World*). (Fosil-records) Scientists hold that for evolution to have happend, lifeless chemicals had to come together to form a living cell accidently. Let us remember that faith in science and faith in our ownselves in making our lives-good or bad is our precious asset.

On 15th Dec, 1967 in California, when Biochemists said that they had produced in Test tube for the first time a fully active DNA. virus (jerms smaller than bacteria), they were confirming that accident must have taken place in nature millions of years ago, which led to some lifeless inanimate chemicals changing into one called organisms as a result of evolution. Thus, men had succeeded in producing "a simple or primitive form of life".

Our irony of fate would ever be that one day scientists are definitely supposed to be able to produce artificial life in a lab soon, but that life may or may not necessarily be of desired personality, what this human world needs the most. Because nature produces life on earth in a raw form, but it's men-making education and men-making religion turn it into a fine and finished product.

Evolutionists in recent years have generally agreed on a line of ascent from ape to men. A vital link in their chain is the creature called Australopithecus, fossils of which were found in Africa. It was a small brain case, having jaw bone, and was pictured as stooped over and fish looking.

In 1971 The *New York Times* declared: "It was Australopithecus... that eventually evolved.. into Homosapiens, or modern man". *Los Angeles Times* noted in 1972: "Current evolutionary theory holds that Homosapiens—modern man—evolved within the past million years from Australopithecus, a fossil with physical characteristics of both ape and men". Late in 1972 Richard Leaky and his team found in Africa skull and a leg bone of a creature that is said to have lived at the same time as Australopithecus. But it is claimed to have human characteristics.

Keeping in view all these facts, it does not seem to be a fact that 'God made the country and men made the town'. What seems to be more correct now is. That nature evolved the universe and men made their own world and even their gods and goddesses according to their sheer own images and vision. It is due to this there are as many gods and goddesses here in the world as there are people.

It is also a fact that we may be nearer to the church today, but far thest from godly qualities. That is why Nietzsche had to declare: "God is dead." It is now the time of science, and not of theology, because science believes in facts and not in speculations or superstitions.

At this stage it is difficult to believe, what Krishna says, "I am the source of all creation: everything in the world moves because of Me." Well, we move towards good and evil both. How can we accept His creativity in all these movements? When there is no creation, how can He be the source of all creation?

Now, whether we are created or our life is predetermined by an Almighty, who controls our destinies, or we are the products of our own past or present karmas are practically the samething. The main difference lies in these two words, i.e. the God or the Karmas. I don't accept both of them, as both are determinists in character. In fact, this Theory of Karma is an intelligent replacement of the old Theory of Remote control super natural Power as determining force in disguise. After all, who knows about them authentically?

It looks strange to me that Buddhists aimed at the final destruction of all their karmas, so that it may bring a complete halt of their so-called cycle of birth and rebirth to them. I humbly feel that it is only the negative view of life. So long there is life, we can't stop our Karmas. Even our sleeping, eating, drinking water and breathing air - all are our Karmas. How can we stop them? Moreover, if there are miseries or sufferings in the world, there is happiness too. Both are products of human minds. They are like sunrise and sunset. Does it not give the stink of the same age old hate-campaign to our nostrils, which has been going on against the world? How can then we fulfill our aim, i.e, to do good to be good by removing our exclusive self?

It is a matter of great pity that Buddhism too administers the opium of 'Karmic doctrine', especially to the poor people of the world; so that they may remain bogged down forever in the marshy land of superstition and fatalism.

Does it not imply that "You are born poor in this life on account of your past evil Karma. He is born rich on account of his past good karma. So be satisfied with your humble lot, but do good to be rich in your next life?" Does it not imply again: "You are being oppressed now, because of your past evil Karma. That is your destiny. Be humble and bear your sufferings patiently. Do good now. You can be certain of a better and happier life after death"?

The Buddhists might deny and say that the Buddhists' doctrine of Karma does not expound such fatalistic views. They may argue that Buddha did not teach this law of Karma to protect the rich and comfort the poor by promising illusing happiness in an after life. They may place that Karma is neither fate, nor predestination imposed upon us by some mysterious unknown power. It is one's own doing reacting on oneself and so one has the power to direct the course of Karma to some extent. How far one diverts it, depends on oneself

But I don't think practically Buddhist's doctrine of Karma won't be fatalistic ultimately. I don't think then the thing like free-human-will has any scope to change one's destiny. Formerly, a human being became practically the prisoner of Gods' long leash, now he/she will find himself or herself more or less behind the bars of his own past Karmas. There is only the change of prison. I find Buddhism too ultimately was bogged down quite deep in the marshy land of karmas only. From here I don't think any one can have such a powerful crane to get it uplifted from such a depth. What these believers in God used to do with the help of a Remote Contol supernatural Power, these Buddhists are apt to do the same with their new deity of Karma. Their tracks are more or less the same. Hence, it too is not acceptable to me. It is strange that our past Karmas become so active in our present life by themselves, as Buddha did not believe in any God! I don't expect such a philosophy of Karma from Buddha - a truly enlightened man indeed. I know from Karma, Buddha did not necessarily mean past actions only. It means both. But Buddha stressed too much on our past activities. By introducing past karmas, Buddha made his thought speculative. Practically speaking, keeping in view of the impact of our past karmas, it is very difficult for us to think that a criminal today may be a saint tomorrow, and a good person of yesterday may be a vicious one today. According to Buddhism it is Karma that conditions rebirth. Past Karmas condition the present birth, and present Karmas in combination with past Karmas, condition the future. It means Rousseau was not correct to say 'man was born free, but he's in chains' in Buddha's perceptions. But he is right, because it is we who shackle ourselves with evils in present life. When we know nothing about our past, Rousseau was right to hold 'man was born free'.

Moreover, Buddhists believe that their theory of rebirth is different from the theory of transmigration of soul, because they don't believe in a soul. If body changes it's form at the time of one's death, how do one's past actions become so potential in present, is beyond our comprehension.

On page 344 (in his book - *The Buddha and His Teachings*) Mr. Narada supports Buddha by asserting: "Such a fatalistic doctrine is not the Buddhist Law of Karma". This may or may not be theoretically correct estimate of this good writer, but practically speaking, it is not correct. Nobody realises that the world is not divine and it is not a one man's show. One's poverty, one's helplessness, one's miseries and the like, which are actually man-made, are apt to be then justified behind this dark bush of Karma as before. If at all we accept that past karmas affect our present life even hyothetically, we commoners are not like Buddha, who was a great enlightened person, to tell us which action of our past or present is linked with what. It will ever remain beyond our comprehension. Being stet so, we shall ever be helpless to mend ourselves, because we are ignorant: whether our past was wrong or present is wrong. A true seeker of truth must be aware of the implications of each and everything. It is my firm conviction that had Buddha, who was a great human giant, properly weighed his Theory of 'Karma' - it's both pros-and-cons - he himself would have rejected it to see it as a painful riddle of human mind. So my humble advice is, let us live only in the present, let us no more try to scratch our past, if at all it can be known by us, and make our present better by following the principle, 'Live and let live' earnestly; so that our future too may become better and better. I know nothing whether I had my past life. I am not sure whether I would have a future life of my own as well. I still feel that Buddha was the Ist human great guru, who got all of us freed from the divine shackle and man-made miseries, and his entire thought was aimed at bringing great revolution to each human's door. But I humbly suspect Buddha's 'Theory of Karma' and rebirth, which I feel are very speculative in character. They must be examined by experts before taking any final decision about them. In addition to it, I humbly hold that Buddha's view that 'life is full of sufferings' and there is no substance in it is also to be objectively examined further.

So, it is all a humble advice to all: let us no more talk of our past Karmas and rebirth, so long we have no authentic proof to prove their existence as we don't believe in making God, the Chief-navigator of our lives.

Swami Vivekanandji, in spite of being a staunch believer in God, had to accept the truth: "I do not believe in a God, who cannot give me bread here, giving me eternal bliss in heaven". (on page 368 Vol. 4 *Swamiji's Works*) He adds: "I do not believe in a God or religion, which cannot wipe the widow's tears or bring a piece of bread to the orphan's mouth... I do not call it religion so long as it is confined to books and dogmas". (on page 50 Vol. 5 *Swamiji's Works*).

So, it is no use to conjure up ghosts and say whatever our present is, it is (fate) determined by our past activities essentially. Swamiji rightly warned us: "Do you see how much abused the Karma Theory of your Hinduism has been?..." (page 45 Vol. 6 *Swamiji's Works*) I feel we have committed a blunder by handing over the accelerator, the steering, the clutch and brakes of our fate in His hands, when we were quite ignorant about the universe.

Buddha didn't believe in soul. If one gets one's present in inheritance of one's past activities essentially, and if it is not the death of soul, when one dies, then we don't know how is one's past transformed into the present?

We all know that birth and death are two stages in our lives. Everybody's life is made of atoms. When human machinery stops working, the same atoms, which are the constituent parts of everybody's life,mingle with the earth again.

Science, says that everthing is in a state of change according to the Law of Motion, and nothing is immortal here. Then what is immortal? What goes from one's past to present? And how it so happens? What is in-herited by a person newly born? Why are one's accounts of one's commissions or omissions not cleared in one's past life?

In fact, if we go on brooding about all these issues, we're sure to find ourselves more or less in a lunatic asylum. So, let us live in this world, but let us not to leave the world a worse place for others to live in, when we're no more here; so that, at least, others may live in a better world and may not dream even to renouce it at all.

Buddha rightly didn't believe in a God, because in the views of Einstein: "If this being (God) is omnipotent, then every occurance including every human action, every human thought and every human feeling and aspiration is also His work, how is it possible to think of holding men responsible for their deeds and thoughts before such an Almighty Being?."

The undeniable scientific fact is that we are not created by God, but we are the products of the sperm and ovum cells, provided by our parents. A fact is a fact. Let no one take it as ego-centric. With regard to the origin of life, it's the domain of Science to explain it.

Buddha believed: "The very craving is that which leads to rebirth". First of all, the very sentence stinks of negativity. This human world is neither good, nor bad in itself. It's what, we make it. Then, why to be afraid of re-birth? If there's one's rebirth, then why don't we make it our mission to make the world a better place to live in after getting re-birth? As regards craving is concerned, the moot point to ponder over here is: Can we ever cease to crave (or to have a strong desire) competely in this world, what it is so long we live? Won't we ever desire some food to live even, some water to quench our thirst, necessary air to breathe? Man does not live by bread alone. He has a very high mission in his life. That mission can be fulfilled by attaining peace of mind. For peace of mind, one craves to see God eye to eye, no matter He exists or not. Another craves to follow 'live and let live.' Can a believer in God ever cease to crave for Lord's darshan? No. Can a person, who expects to embrace peace by following 'live and let live' ever cease to crave? No, never. Of course, we should not crave, what makes us its slave.

If hypothetically speaking, we all cease to crave for anything in life, it will mean, as per Buddha's version, their will be no more re-birth then. Will it not then mean the extinction of the entire human race one day like dinosaurs? Would Buddha ever be ready to see the light of that day too, had he been alive today? Of course, I do believe civilisation does not consist in multiplication of wants, but in their voluntary reduction. Again, I do agree our excessive desires make us slave, instead of their masters. So, we must avoid our excessive desires. Of course, we can not eliminate all our desires, so long we live. Hence, I humbly feel that it is not in a good taste to know that Buddha concluded his discourse by declaring: "This is my last birth. Now there is no more rebirth." It is said that on the very night of Buddha's Enlightenment he developed retro cognitive knowledge, which enabled him to read his past lives too. Hence Buddha declared: "I recalled my varied lot in former existences as follows: First one life, then two lives... Twenty upto fifty lives, then a hundred, a thousand, a hundred thousand and so forth." (on page 408 '*The Buddha and His Teachings*).

But this is all beyond the comprehension of common people like me. Hence, it is no use to have any craving to know about our previous lives. Buddha being Enlightened might be knowing, as to what bridges the gap between one's death and again one's birth. If it is rebirth consciousness, which tells us about our past lives, then the question is how does it walk down to the new born baby's mind on its own? If according to Buddha nothing is permanent here, then is this birth consciousness inmortal? If it is so, where does it live in the time gap period between one's death and one's rebirth again? Is there any difference between the so-called soul and this birth consciousness?

Of course, there is no question for the acceptance of 'Charvaks' view (Rishi-Brashpati), i.e., 'eat drink and be merry'. But when our dead bodies are mingled in atoms again, it is very important to examine Charvak's plea: from what will come our rebirth? To know the truth, it needs proper scientific investigation.

Buddhism became the fan of past Karma. And in it's fanaticism it believes that 'Sex is determined by past Karma at the very conception of the being". (on page 424 *The Buddha and His Teachings*). It is strange that instead of 'X' and 'Y' chromosomes, the Buddhists believe one's sex is determined by one's past Karmas. It is a serious challenge to modern Bio-Technology. They hold that it is due to one's past Karmas men are even changed into animals and vice-versa in their next birth.

Dissent is the essence of democracy. Let everyone have the freedom to have one's own view, so long as they don't become a hindrance in anybody's proper growth. Buddha too believed: "Hatred does not cease through hatred but through love alone they cease". Insults of great men in the world have been a common feature. Buddha himself too was insulted and abused here. Jesus Christ too was insulted, humilated and utlimately crucified by us. Socratese was insulted even by his wife. Lincoln and Gandhi too were shot dead, because of our introlerance.

If we take these insults, humilations, ill-treatments as the natural effects of one's past Karmas, we are to sow the seeds of poisonous saplings, which will produce the fruits of fatalism, cowardice, escapism, etc-etc.

The question is why don't we tag them with our little mindedness only? Why to enter the dark room of one's past Karmas unnecessarily?

Peace can neither be had by humilating or ill-treating others, nor by snatching other's due, but by sharing our own with others. Alexander went to conquer the whole world, so did Hitler. Both were terribly disappointed in their aims. Had by chance they conquered the whole world, even then they would have bitterly failed to attain peace of their respective minds. Why? Because peace can be had only from within and not without.We can embrace peace only by conquering over our little-mindedness or exclusive self, which have been the greatest causes of our miseries.

It's good that Buddha didn't treat himself as the last word in the dictionary of wisdom. He nowhere crowned his views with any divinity Hence, he invited all to examine his views as a goldsmith does. In fact, freedom of thought, doctrine of equality, faith in human dignity and utmost faith in each human to right the wrong, or to turn hell into heaven as an architect of one's destiny, were the few cardinal principles of Buddha.

But the psyche of 'low and weak' has kept our minds on an age old long holiday. The scientists of the world warn us that brains atrophy without use, and the less we use our brain, the more likely we are to suffer from senility, mental confusion, mental depression, mental unrest, loss of memory and even the dreaded Alzheimer's disease. In short, if we don't use our mind, we lose it. The recent findings show that the continuous use of the brain protects us against ravages of dementia and Alzheimer's disease. Dr. Robert Katzman of the University of California at San Diego claims that learning activities can protect the brain from being moronic, and education helps in keeping brain cells alive upto a longer time. So, let all the believers in God no more allow their minds to have such feelings of low and weak. Even those who do not believe in Him, if they keep their minds inert or dorment for a long time, they too have the danger that their brains too may atrophy without use. We can't claim to have our brains in use merely by going through T.V. serials or by skipping over news columns and the like. So, let us then talk less, think more before doing anything. If we follow this course earnestly, we've less chances of such danger in life.

But if we go on looking at the world with negative glasses, the world will look to us, as if it is a big bundle of problems. Here Buddha too looked at the world with a negative vision. Hence, he found even birth, decay disease, death and everything in life lying in the gear of suffering. Buddha proclaimed that life was nothing but sorrow. There is no substance in it. Delivering his first sermon after attaining Buddhatava, Buddha said:

'Birth is suffering, decay is suffering, disease is suffering, death is suffering, to be united with the unpleasent is suffering, to be separated from the pleasant is suffering, not to get what one desires is suffering. In brief, the five aggregates of attachment are suffering'. (page 89-90 *The Buddha And His Teachings* by Narada)

Undoubtedly there are sufferings in life, but I humbly think Buddha highlighted them too much. In fact, the fabric of our life is made of two yarns—happiness and sorrow. Both are interwoven and interlocked by us. Both are obverse and reverse sides of the same coin. Moreover, both of them are more a state of our minds. They are more concerned with the attitude of one's mind. In this context, there is an interesting story of two children. Once, their mother sent one of them to the market to buy cooking oil in a bottle. While coming back home, by chance that child fell down alongwith the bottle full of oil. Consequently, half of the oil of the bottle flowed out. On seeing it the child started crying out of fear. Then the mother sent her other child to the market for the same purpose. By chance, another child too fell down and half of the bottle too flowed out. Only half of he bottle of oil remained. On seeing it that other child, instead of crying and weeping, became happy and told his mother: 'mummy, I am happy unlike my brother, because I have saved half of the bottle of oil.' This shows our happiness or sorrow in life depends on our vision or outlook of life to a great extent. In the story, half of the bottle of oil flowed out both the times, but in one case it's loss caused one's crying and weeping, while in another the same loss caused another brother even happiness. Is it not due to the magic of our vision?

Let us now coolly analyse, what our life is? Whether it is full of sufferings? Whether really there is no substance in it, as Buddha thought about it? In fact, the birth pangs, old age, disease and death — all are natural phases more or less in everybody's life. Everyone is seen undergoing them here sooner or later. They have like gifts of nature for all of us, no matter whether they are sweet or sour. Of course, by removing the exclusive self from our lives, and by living a natural life, or by coming nearer to nature, we can definitely minimise our sufferings or miseries in life to a great extent.

Why to forget: if sorrow comes in life, can happiness lag behind? If autumn comes, can spring lag behind? If those good days have gone far, will not these sad days too go one day soon? By having a positive view in life we can turn our bed of thorns into bed of roses.

Undoubtedly, at the ti me of delivery a mom undergoes birth pangs. It is wrong to say they are sufferings. By dubbing them as sufferings, I feel, as if we hurt the sweet or the pious hopes of a would be mother, because it is a fact that every would be mother invites those birth-pangs herself consciously or unconsciously, thinking they are the ultimate carriers of pleasure or happiness of a new born babe to her and to the entire family. In reality, these birth-pangs are inherent in the whole natural process of everyone's birth. Those would be mothers, who realise this reality before hand, they minimise their pinch. Moreover, they are momentary phases of one's birth. They are not at all permanently associated with one's birth. In fact, these birth-pangs are a sort of necessary labour or efforts, one must undergo them to gain something in return in life. Can a farmer ever get his yield in his field without undergoing some pains? Again, can a labourer in a factory ever produce any finished product without undergoing some pains or without doing same labour? Again, can a student ever pass in one's examinatin without undergoing pains day and night?

So, pain and gain co-exist together in life. If there is no pain, there is no gain in life usually. Hence, there is an imminent need to change our whole mindset first. If we do it, even the pain is apt to become good and desirable. By highlighting sufferings in life unnecessarily, we only strengthen the hate-campaign aganist this human world, which has been going on for ages and, consequently, makes people cowards and escapists only. Only by removing the exclusive self from our lives, what Buddha prescribed, we are sure to see substance and charm in the world. Let us no more try to shirk from coming here in the world again and again, if there is a rebirth just to follow Vivekanand, Tagore and Bhagat Singh in this respect particulary. Let us know how to live and how to die.

As regards decay, disease and death—they too have been seen by Buddha with negative glasses. According to the Law of Motion matter has ever been in a state of change or flux. So, decay, disease and ultimate death are natual milestones or stages more or less in everybody's life. They are associated with this change in matter. Our body is made of matter. Matter can't be kept intact. Our body, what it was at the time of one's birth, doesn't remain so even after a moment. It is changed. So, decay, disease and death all are inherent in this natural process of change.

When there is change, decay must be there, and disease is naturally associated with the natural decay. Decay brings disease ultimately. Why do we lose our eye-sight, when we become old especially? Because of the same decay. Of course, we lose our natural eye-sight due to some deficiency as well. If this decay takes place speedily in the body, diseases and old age too trespass our bodies speedily. Why to make a fuss of it? Of course, we must have a necessary cure to arrest this decay so rapidly. Let us remember the scientific fact: That everything and every being are made of the same matter or atom and everyone is dissolved in the same matter or atom ultimately.

So decay, disease and ultimate death - all are parts of our lives. Our life can never be immuned of them. If birth is a one shore, death is another shore of life. In old age, we are unable to do, what we could easily do, when we were quite young. If we take this change as natural and in a positive way, our pain doesn't pinch us much. Thus, we can minimise our pains in life, simply by changing our eye-glasses.

Only the natural inability to enjoy life as before or feeling of natural pinch with the passage of time is another name of a disease. What does a doctor do? He tries to remove these inabilities either completely or to some tolerable extent by prescribing his medicines or cure of the disease.

In fact, if we understand that birth and death are not sufferings, but are two inevitable natural stages in everybody's life, the natural separation even of the most beloved person from us won't become so unbearable, as it usually becomes. Time is a great healer. With proper understanding, even our deep wounds are easily healed automatically by and by. Of course, scars remain.

People's stereotyped style of thinking suggests us liberation through our renunciation. The question is: renunciation of what? For liberation from our '*dukhas*' (miseries), if we renounce our 'exclusive self' from our lives, this renunciation then is acceptable and praise-worthy. But if we think of renouncing our own world, just to attain liberation from the so-called cycle of births and deaths, as Buddha too thought about it, as if the world is nothing, but an embodiment of evils and sufferings and there is no good in it, we are then badly mistaken. In fact the view in question is the greatest hurdle to see change first in our ownselves and then in the world too. Brave only know how to live and die. Mr. Nathan Hale was hanged in 1776, aged 21 only. Being captured as a spy during the American war for Independence he died at the hands of the British army without any trial. Before dying he said, "I regret that I have but one life to give for my country." Who can dare to put his 'I' and 'my' in the dock of little mindedness or ego? Who can dare to ask such I's to renounce themselves?

At the last stage of life, known as sanyas, people have been supposed to think exclusively of God, and not of the world for the remaining period of one's life; so that they may be relieved from the cyle of birth and death ultimately. Just to attain this goal of life, people used to go to the caves in the mountains formerly to worship God there in a perfect isolated environment. Let us remember that people used to worship there only one God, who is still unknown and, invisible to them, while by living in the world, and by making it a better place to live in just to follow our old principle i.e.; live and let live, we can really worship crores of our living gods and goddesses. Let us prefer public salvation (moksha) to private salvation. Let us beware of the dangerous negativity, which unfortunately developed in Buddha's mind regarding human life particularly.

Hence, the old conception of *sanyas* must now be over for all times to come. That should no more be our goal of life. In fact, we have been suffering from the age old negativity about the world of ours and instead of rebuilding our own world, by building ourselves from within particularly, we have been having a poisonous hate-campaign against our own world, which is made-good or bad either by you or me only. When we dub the world as '*mithya*' or illusion or dream, it is all the product of the same age old hate-campaign.

Why to seek a 'Vaikunth', a heaven in the other world? Why don't we make our own world a paradise on earth simply by our own good thinking, feelings and doings? To whom we have been befooling to leave our own world like escapists, or cowards or shirkers? Can we turn the 'Vaikunth' into a better place to live in , when it is we and we have spoiled this present world? Why don't we behave like brave persons by restructuring our whole mindset, which has become an easy oasis of our own little-mindedness and ego? But can we ever even dream to do it, unless we have faith in turning our hell into heaven ourselves? Hence, I treat this faith like an anchor.

Can Sanyas, what we talk about very easily, make us better human beings necessarily? Can it make our world a better place to live in than before necessarily? Can we live a more purposeful, more meanigful and really a creative life through sanyas or it is apt to make our life quite dull, non-creative and purposeless? One used to seek personal salvation through Sanyas or through renunciation of the world. But can we have salvation of the people through it?

Thus, the days of the uncreative sanyas to achieve liberation from the so-called cycle of birth and death must be ended for all times to come. This is not the age to run away from the world, but an age to make it a better place to live in, as we are all the architects of our own destinies-good and bad. When we think, feel and do something to make ourselves better human beings and better world, our whole net of thinking, feeling and doings becomes the best prayer to attain peace and happiness in life. That is the best meditation, we can have. When a good change takes place in our own being by our ownselves, we become the Karmayogi in the rightest sense of the term. So, let us not to renounce the world, but renouce our exclusive self only to give a new meaning to our religion. Let us know then the men-making religion. All other religions are false. They create fissures here or there. So, its no use to fear birth or decay or disease or ultimate death, as by behaving well with the living gods and goddesses, we are to live even after our death. Let us understand them, what they are actually. Salvation lies only in their proper understanding. We can't help without attachment and detachment both at the same time. We are only to know the right ordering of both attachments and detachments in our lives at the same time. If sometimes we are united with the unpleasant or separated from the pleasant, let us no more try to behave like slaves, but only masters of the situations. A time may come when we do not get, what we desire, in spite of our best efforts in life, we should not be the slaves of our desires, but their masters only. After all it is a human world and moreover it is not a one man's show. Ultimate master-key of peace lies with the change of our 'mindset'. The more we are able to do it, the more peaceful we become. Of course, unnatural pangs, or man-made decay or disease or death shall ever remain more painful and even unbearable. Our attachment and detachment generate heat and not light, when they are assoiciated with our little-mindedness only. When we shrink ourselves, instead of working as balm, both create fissures in a family, in a community and in a country and in the world. Only our exteme desires, extreme attachment and extreme detachment are to be avoided. By knowing well the art of attachment and detachment at the same time we can learn how to live more peacefully even among our pleasures and sorrow both. Otherwise, we are apt to be the slaves of them.

Let us remember that the charm or no charm in the world lies in the beholder. It is we, who give due or undue weightage to a thing, or thought or person in our life. When it is due, we become happy, when it is undue, we suffer. So, our happiness or unhappiness depends on our understanding. We suffer, because we have a feeling that we can satisfy all our desires, no matter how. And we suffer also, because we feel we can eliminate all our desires. Both extremes are undesirable, unnatural and avoidable. Let us remember our extreme desires and wickedness are like siblings.

Undoubtedly, problems are apt to arise, when we live together either in a family or the world, but if we are honest in solving our problems, we won't face much difficulties. But in reality most of us are not honest in our dealings. Naturally, then problems are apt to create tension beyond an individual control. Robinson Cruso was happier in an island, because he was alone there.

But it is not our attachment, which is causing us trouble. Let us realise that every member of the family is apt to go uncared for, if they are not properly attached here with each other. Can a mother bring her babe up properly, if she is not attached with that? Can a soldier defend the border's of ones own country, unless one is poroperly attached with it? In fact, our attachment becomes a source of tension here or there, when we attach ourlselves with the things or thoughts or person not worth-attachment. In the same way, our detachment too becomes a problem for us when we detach our selves with the things, thoughts and person not worth-detachment.

How both our right attachment and right detachment in life are necessary at the same time, can be known from a real dialogue between Narendra, a college student, who became Vivekanand, the great saint later on and Swami Ram Krishna, his great 'guru'. Narendra put the question before him: "Have you seen God?" His 'guru' replied: "Yes, I see Him just as I see you here..." "God can be realised", he went on, "One can see and talk to Him as I am seeing and talking to you. But who cares? People shed torrents of tears for their wife and children, for wealth, for property, but who does it so for the sake of God? If one weeps sincerely for Him, he surely mainfests himself". This shows attachment in itself is not an evil. We can not help without attachment and detachment here or there. They are must to some extent. That is why, here the great saint wants the detached to be attached and attached to be detached. Of course, whether God exists or not that is a different question. To be happy, let our choice be right at a time.

In the context, of both attachment and detachment let us see how Buddha, the great managed them both in his own life. Buddha said: "I am the happiest of mortals. There is no one happier than I am." To know how Buddha had felt to be the happiest of all mortals, let us first know that Buddha was born as a prince with a silver-spoon in his mouth, but the miseries of the people in general struck him very deeply. Being a man of quite different nature, having a peculiar mind of his own, working on different channel, he could not find comforts or answer to his query, as to why there are miseries in human lives, in his personal pleasures of his family life. Hence being quite disturbed, he definitely renounced his family, and even left his new born son and wife behind one night. On the following day when his wife came to know about his renouncement, she felt it very much.

It is said that 'on getting the news of the birth of a son to him, Buddha was not overjoyed. Prince Siddhartha exclaimed : "An impediment (Rahu) has been born; a fetter has arisen", Buddha thought him as an impediment, because, perhaps, he had a mind to play a more important role than a dutiful husband and father, or even as a would be king on his inheritance. Buddha had a sweeping, but unpassionate glance at his wife and son before his departure.

Undoubtedly, great was Buddha's compassion and love for his beloved wife and son, but greater was Buddha's compassion and love for the suffering humanity. As Buddha's spirit to get the humanity relieved from miseries, was very high in his mind, I don't mind much his words either 'impediment' or 'fetter' for his child. I take them as the natural corollary of it.

Of course, he knew that everything was in abundance for the left out in kingdom. He stole away with a light heart from the palace at midnight for fulfilling this higher mission. Alone and penniless he set out in search of truth and peace. Everyone can very well imagine that it was not the renunciation of an old man, who had already a good taste of his whole life from every point of view. Nor it was the renunicatiion of a poor man, who was forced by necessity to renounce one's family and the world. It was the renunciation (at the age of 29) of a prince, who was in the full bloom of his youth at that time and who rolled in wealth. Really speaking, Prince Siddhartha's renunciation too was unparalleled in the whole human history.

Buddha adopted the path of voluntary poverty. Barefooted and bare-headed he was with no possession with him, except a bowl to collect his food and robes just sufficient for his body. Although Buddha came back to Kapilavastu, when Rahul, his own son, was only seven years old only for sometime. He got enlightenment then.

Thus, Buddha was one of the greatest human 'gurus' ever born not only in his life, but in his renunciation and death too. If 'gu' means darkness and 'ru' means a dispeller, Buddha was definitely the greatest 'guru', who created real hopes even in the minds of hopless. It is these hopes, which are the real wombs of change in the world.

As the issue of people's miseries were uppermost and weighing very heavily on his mind, his step of the renunciation of his family must not be felt much by us. Let us remember Buddha, no doubt, detached himself from his family as a result of his renunciation, he would not have perfectly attached himself with the people's cause, had he not taken this extreme step for the betterment of the entire ocean of humanity. Buddha thus got his personal self dissolved in the wider ocean of humanity. Buddha's greatness lies in the knowledge of his art of right ordering of both his attachments and detachments at the same time. Buddha preferred loyalty for the people's cause to the loyality of his personal pleasures.

To seek the answer of people's miseries, Buddha wandered searching for truth from one teacher to another. At last, he attained Enlightenment i.e. '*gyan*' or 'moksha' or emancipation. Thus, unlike so many '*Sadhaks*' in the world, Buddha preferred people's salvation i.e. '*nirvana*' or freedom from all '*dukh*' to his personal salvation.

Keeping all these facts in view, I don't think that any person of judicious mind will ever even dare to dub Buddha as an escapist, because he renounced his family. Why? Because, definitely he renounced his family, but at the same time he made himself an integral part of a bigger family of the people of the whole world. Buddha's whole life clearly shows how we are all the architects of our own destinies—good or bad.

When Buddha got enlightenment and when he realised that the main cure of people's problem lies only in removing their personal or 'exclusive self', it was but natural for that geat man of destiny to feel, as if he was the 'happiest of all mortals' to get his immediate very high mission fulfilled. The pleasures of personal life could never enslave the would be great human giant like Buddha. The joy or happiness what Buddha preferred to personal pleasures was really like a jewel that was beyond any price.

The most important thing what happened evidently in this whole episode was that by simply detaching himself from the personal pleasures. Buddha kept himslf intact the most attached person constantly with-the uppermost people's problem i.e., the emancipation of the people from their miseries. What a proficient knower of the art of attachment and detachment Buddha was!

Though Buddha remained alive upto the age of eighty he was busy working as one of the greatest missionaries. He was severely criticised, roundly abused, insulted, charged with baseless allegations and ruthelessly attacked as no other human *'guru'* had ever been. His chief atonement and inspiration were ordinary persons and followers of heretical schools, whose traditional teachings and superstitious rites and ceremonies Buddha justly criticised in his novel way.

Buddha was not a superstitious person. His opposition was but natural by conservative people, whose life was based on superstitions. Sri. V.D. Gupta, an ex Vice-Chancellor of Gorakhpur University wrote: "The Buddha said staring at the planets and stars and practising good and bad luck through astrology should be discarded. Vivekanand said, that belief in astrology... indicated a weak mind... Swami Dayanand espoused Science and not superstition"... (printed in *Hindustan Times* on 26-1-2001 in an article published by Sri Khushwant Singh)

Centuries ago the Romans raised a slogan — "Carthage must be destroyed". And it was reduced to ashes. It's said it was a barbarous age. But in reality no age or time or place is barbarous or otherwise. It is, what we make it either by our own commissions or omissions. The history of barbarism has been repeating in the world, because brutes have not changed their nature. Let us remember Ram-Ravana, Krishan-Duryodhana, Gandhi-Hitler have always been there in every age and time so far. The real oasis of good or evil is our mind.

Like Buddha, the persons, who make their lives purposeful or meaningful they can only have the sense of some fulfillment in their lives. But to make life meaningful, we shall have to satisfy our sense of creativity, which is in reality the fountain head of our joy and happiness in life. The sense of creativity is satisfied only when one has a high mission in life. One who has a high mission in one's life, is free from tension more or less. When one is having almost tension free life, one feels naturally, as if one is on a vacation, free from any bondage, even while doing everything for a higher cause.

If Mahatma Gandhiji worked 15 hours a day for 50 years in his life and still was having a peaceful life, there was reason for it. Once, when he was asked, "Don't you want vacation, Mr. Gandhi?" Gandhiji quietly replied: "I am always on vacation". It implied that by detaching himself with a lesser cause and attaching himself with a higher cause or mission in his life i.e his peoples' service, Gandhiji always remained quite happy. Attachment with a high mission in life does not mean Gandhiji could ever even dream to conquer other's territories. At the advent of partition of India, Gandhiji even requested Govt. of India to pay almost Rs. 55,000 crores to Pakistan, which were due to Pakistan in his eyes. So Gandhiji kept himself quite away or detached with any temptations, whatsoever. It them, as both are determinists in character. In fact, this Theory of Karma is an intelligent replacement of the old Theory of Remote control super natural Power as determining force in disguise. After all, who knows about them authentically?

It looks strange to me that Buddhists aimed at the final destruction of all their karmas, so that it may bring a complete halt of their so-called cycle of birth and rebirth to them. I humbly feel that it is only the negative view of life. So long there is life, we can't stop our Karmas. Even our sleeping, eating, drinking water and breathing air - all are our Karmas. How can we stop them? Moreover, if there are miseries or sufferings in the world, there is happiness too. Both are products of human minds. They are like sunrise and sunset. Does it not give the stink of the same age old hate-campaign to our nostrils, which has been going on against the world? How can then we fulfill our aim, i.e, to do good to be good by removing our exclusive self?

It is a matter of great pity that Buddhism too administers the opium of 'Karmic doctrine', especially to the poor people of the world; so that they may remain bogged down forever in the marshy land of superstition and fatalism.

Does it not imply that "You are born poor in this life on account of your past evil Karma. He is born rich on account of his past good karma. So be satisfied with your humble lot, but do good to be rich in your next life?" Does it not imply again: "You are being oppressed now, because of your past evil Karma. That is your destiny. Be humble and bear your sufferings patiently. Do good now. You can be certain of a better and happier life after death"?

The Buddhists might deny and say that the Buddhists' doctrine of Karma does not expound such fatalistic views. They may argue that Buddha did not teach this law of Karma to protect the rich and comfort the poor by promising illusing happiness in an after life. They may place that Karma is neither fate, nor predestination imposed upon us by some mysterious unknown power. It is one's own doing reacting on oneself and so one has the power to direct the course of Karma to some extent. How far one diverts it, depends on oneself

But I don't think practically Buddhist's doctrine of Karma won't be fatalistic ultimately. I don't think then the thing like free-human-will has any scope to change one's destiny. Formerly, a human being became practically the prisoner of Gods' long leash, now he/she will find himself or herself more or less behind the bars of his own past Karmas. There is only the change of prison. I find Buddhism too ultimately was bogged result of evolution. Thus, men had succeeded in producing "a simple or primitive form of life".

Our irony of fate would ever be that one day scientists are definitely supposed to be able to produce artificial life in a lab soon, but that life may or may not necessarily be of desired personality, what this human world needs the most. Because nature produces life on earth in a raw form, but it's men-making education and men-making religion turn it into a fine and finished product.

Evolutionists in recent years have generally agreed on a line of ascent from ape to men. A vital link in their chain is the creature called Australopithecus, fossils of which were found in Africa. It was a small brain case, having jaw bone, and was pictured as stooped over and fish looking.

In 1971 The *New York Times* declared: "It was Australopithecus... that eventually evolved.. into Homosapiens, or modern man". *Los Angeles Times* noted in 1972: "Current evolutionary theory holds that Homosapiens—modern man—evolved within the past million years from Australopithecus, a fossil with physical characteristics of both ape and men". Late in 1972 Richard Leaky and his team found in Africa skull and a leg bone of a creature that is said to have lived at the same time as Australopithecus. But it is claimed to have human characteristics.

Keeping in view all these facts, it does not seem to be a fact that 'God made the country and men made the town'. What seems to be more correct now is: That nature evolved the universe and men made their own world and even their gods and goddesses according to their sheer own images and vision. It is due to this there are as many gods and goddesses here in the world as there are people.

It is also a fact that we may be nearer to the church today, but far thest from godly qualities. That is why Nietzsche had to declare: "God is dead." It is now the time of science, and not of theology, because science believes in facts and not in speculations or superstitions.

At this stage it is difficult to believe, what Krishna says, "I am the source of all creation: everything in the world moves because of Me." Well, we move towards good and evil both. How can we accept His creativity in all these movements? When there is no creation, how can He be the source of all creation?

Now, whether we are created or our life is predetermined by an Almighty, who controls our destinies, or we are the products of our own past or present karmas are practically the samething. The main difference lies in these two words, i.e. the God or the Karmas. I don't accept both of is his proficiency in this art that delivered him inner peace of mind. In fact people's-service became a life-play for him. We too can be on a 365 days vacation in a year even, while performing our works worth-doing, worth attaching and worth detaching at the sametime in our lives.

This art is the real master-key to our happiness and joy in life. This is the very secret of success of all the great human teachers. when we get real happiness in life, our life too becomes full of substance. Even Gandhiji wanted to be reborn only as an untouchable, if at all it was a must; so that by experiencing oneself the ill-treatment what they were getting, he might be able to eradicate untouchability from its roots even. This shows Gandhi ji wanted to live with a high mission in his life.

If we cannot see substance in a purposeful life here, we can't see it anywherelse. India is not a country of youths. In fact, it has been a country, where old people have been taking birth for centuries. Of course, some exceptions are there. It is because in India people of the 'pyche of old, weak and low' are born here. If youth is only the name of a physical state of our bodies, then definitely there are crorers of youths in India, but if youth is essentially the name of the state of our minds, then youths in India are very few in numbers. Had there been really youths in India, at least, they would not have been bogged down in the marshy land of age old deadly superstitions and delusions. What I humbly feel is that the burning flame to attain high mission in life has been lacking very badly in the so-called youths' minds particularly in India and generally in the world. The psyche of 'low and weak' has been eating all of us like white-ants for centuries. People with this 'mindset' are apt to wait for the so-called Lord even for their petty works in their lives. Why? Because they have got artificial divine crutches under their armpits. So long as they live in the world of superstitions, they can't think even of changing them-selves to change their world. From high mission, I don't mean only 'simple living and high thinking', but also doing something in one's own field of work, which aims at the welfare of the whole humanity. In short, we all need faith in making of our lives ourselves, which has been sucked by the philosophy of 'weak and low',

In Chicago Swami Vivekanandji, one of the greatest human 'gurus' gave us a clarion call: "Come up, O lion, and shake off the delusion that you are the sheep..." Perhaps, it was a call particularly to the persons of the mindset of the same 'old and weak'. But who pays any heed to the call of a saint now in this world, what it is made by all of us?

Undoubtedly, Swamiji has tried to boost our morale by calling us 'O'lion', but does it not put us in a natural, but strange dilemma: what to do and what not? Because, it is Swami Vivekanandji preaches us: 'He is the cause of our both rise or fall, and 'without His mercy even a blade of grass cannot grow, and without His blessings we can not breathe even and so on and so forth. Like Swamiji there are thousands of people here, who believe that we're only 'His Master's- pet dogs on a long leash', and now in Chicago Swamiji calls us: 'O lion, . . . shake off the delusion that you are the sheep . . . !" Are these delusions too God-ordained? Let us remember pets cannot unchain themselves from their delusions, and become lions automatcally. Only masters can unchain their pets and behave like lions. So the earlier we change our mindset, the better.

Do we still really think that this deadly age old poison, which we have been sucking for centuries, is to be flushed away by some deity? If not, then whom are we waiting for this job too? How long would we like to behave like that stupid ostrich?

Netaji Subhash Chandra Bose, one of our greatest freedom fighters too once asked us before independence: "You give me your blood, I shall give you freedom". Surely, we got freedom in 1947, but did we get this freedom to slit each other's throat or to change our brutal nature', and, consequently, our world? Let us remember Netaji did not have his call for the people of 'low' and weak' psyche. Obviously, our beloved Netaji could deliver us freedom through good people only.

When Swami Vivekanandji founded Ram Krishna Mission, he too roared in the same tone and spirit again: "Give me a few men and women, who are really pure and selfless, I shall shake the world." At that time he must have forgotten, what he himself said earlier that it is He, who makes us rise and it is He who makes us down!

Undoubtedly, this great call of the great saint clearly implies that only new men and women, who are really pure and selfless, or only good humans, who not only care for themselves to live' but equally care for all the people of the world 'to let live' at the same time, are needed either to shake or to change the world, what the great Marx had dreamt. Because, it is only good people that can establish genuine peace, wherever they are. Again, because it is only they who can weave or re-weave entirely a different web of their lives as human spiders with their own knitpins without having any blemish of their moral decay anymore anywhere.

Our salvation lies really in becoming humans and not brutes. Even the Vedas ask us to be only "Manurbhava" i.e., '*He manava tu manava ban*'. But how can we be so, unless we all earnestly follow real 'manava-dharam' i.e., "*Atamnah Pratikulani Paresham na samacharet". (Jo baat tumeh apna liya aachi nahin lagti, oose dusron ke liya mat karo)* "? This we have already seen, no matter how important the economic changes are, they themselves can not change the brute in men. For this we are to follow Buddha, who advised us:

(1) 'Do no evil'

(2) 'Do good to be good'

(3) 'Purify your mind'

Buddha's great message for all of us was not to be the 'fan' of anybody or anything, whatsoever, and not even of his in this world, because fanaticism, instead of changing any human or his world for good, has ever been forming the dark clouds of miseries everywhere. Buddha was not allergic to enlightened self, but to exclusive or personal self', which is attained by us at the cost of others even, and which is the very nucleous of fanaticism. Buddha was against any exreme i.e., to gain or attain something either by completely losing oneself or by completely getting others lost around. He believed in a via-media or golden-mean. That is why, he believed not in personal salvation, but in people's salvation through mitigating their exclusive self for the elimination of their miseries.

Earlier we realise these issues earnesly, the better. Better late than never.

We can forget God, but not men. Today, unfortunately, we remember the God, but forget the men. Do we ever realise that by forgetting the men what remains here? In this context, let us remember Swami Vivekanandji: "May I be born again and again, and suffer thousand miseries, so that I may worship the only God I know that exists, the only God I believe in, the sum total of all souls, and above all, my God the wicked, my God the miserable, my god the power of all races, of all species". Here Swamiji's mission was not the liberation from the cycle of the births and deaths at all. What a high mission of life he had! Swami Vivekanandji was really a holy man, not because he used to wear saffron robes, but he felt one with the whole (the whole ocean of humanity). He was holy, because his pious heart throbbed with the happiness and sorrow of all the people of the world. So, let no one think Swamiji was holy, because he was well-versed in our esteemed scriptures, but because, being one of the greatest architects of one's own destiny he made his being truly holy.

In this context, I feel it is most relevant to quote Bhagat Singh, one of the greatest patriots ever born in the world and how he thought about the so-called God. He said: "By the end of 1928 I had been convinced as to the baselessness of the theory of existence of an Almighty supreme being, who created, guided and controlled the universe," He asked if God created the world in six days, as mentioned in the Bible and proclaimed at the end of that "all was well", let Him read the bloody pages of human history and then explain only what He meant by all being well. When asked: "if no God existed, how did the people come to believe in Him". Bhagat Singh promptly replied: "As they come to believe in ghosts and evil spirits ... God was brought into imaginary existence to encourage men to face boldly all trying circumstances... the idea of God is helpful to men in distress".

One may call Bhagat Singh an atheist, but I think he was one of the greatest theists, as he had tremendous faith in his manhood to serve his beloved motherland. We can know Bhagat Singh as to what stuff he was made of by his following statement. Just one day before the hanging of Bhagat Singh, the Sikh chief warden Chattar Singh approached Bhagat Singh and said: 'I have only one request to make. The end is very near. Now you take the name 'Wahe Guru' and read Gurubani (The Sikh Gita). Here I have brought the 'Gutka' (the little book) for you.'

In fact, it is told Bhagat Singh asked himself as to what did this so-called God do to him, except his execution? Where was He at that moment? What was his fault? Bhagat Singh's goal of life was not the liberation from the cycle of deaths and births. He knew remarkably how to live and die for his country.

The brave and the most rational Bhagat Singh was asked before hanging: "Have you any last wish?" He answered: 'May I be born and serve the motherland again?" What Swami Vivekanandji said before, Bhagat Singh said the same at the time of his last breath. It is said that Bhagat Singh sang the following famous couplet before going to his gallows:

"Dil Se no niklegi markar bhi watan ki ulfat,
Merri Mitti Se bhi khusbhoo-e-watan aegi".

—Bhagat Singh

Can we ever dub him as an atheist by any judicious angle of vision? The world needs such youths and such architects of their own destinies.

I have got no answer at all in my poor mind, when following questions crop up there: Where was He, when the very head of Guru Teg Bahadur, one of our the bravest 'gurus' was being cut? Where was He living, when the great Guru Gobind Singh got his two beloved sons set alive among bricks voluntarily for his motherland? Is He almighty or powerless? Does He exist everywhere or exist nowhere?

I recollect an Urdu couplet here to add:

'Insan woh nahi, Jo hawa ke sath badle,
Insan woh hai, jo hawa ka rukh badle.

I want to assure Marx, the great that only such '*Insans*' (humans) can change themselves and only such persons can change the world as well and fulfill his great dream. Let Marx no more rely on any good 'matter', but only on good men.

The real foundation of our world is the goodness of men or the human virtues or human - excellence. The more there are devils in this world, the more it shakes. Our world or our life is neither good, nor evil in itself, but it is what we make it either individually or collectively. It is the true mirror of what we are. It is a gross lie to say that we are good, and our world is bad. Our hypocrisy won't pay to us anymore. Let's no more give a distorting image of our world by hijacking God in and out of human affairs, simply according to our own convenience. We may or may not have faith in Him, but faith in humans as the true steersmen of the ship of our lives, is like an anchor. Without it, we had neither good past, nor we shall have our present good, nor future.

If we are really earnest to change ourselves first and then our world, we have the patent solution, prescribed by Buddha, the great:

'Do good to be good only' — Buddha.

It is only then we can make the foundation of our world almost unshakable, no matter how many tremors come.

Swami Vivekanandji too viewed: "This is the age of the worship of 'Virat', the visible God" 21st Century is an age of men, and not of God. Rather, it is better to say that it is an age of living gods and goddesses—the real architects of their own destinies—good or bad, and not of a hypothetical divine entity, who has never been known, or seen, or felt, or experienced actually by any one of us. They need not our worship at all, but our earnest love for all without any discrimination, if we really want to change ourselves first, and then our world too.

Of course, the age of the worship of 'Virat', the visible God' does not mean, we can afford to be brutes anymore. Let us throw away now this or that mask, we wear. Let us 'be men' first and men last in the true sense of the term. So far this world has been considered only 'His'. Now being its true spiders let us weave or reweave to make fine the web of our life or world, as that may be almost free from all the red or black patches of our own evils. Earlier we realise it, the better: Better late than never. If we really want to change the world to establish peace everywhere, no matter we are in a family, or in a '*mohalla*', or in a village, or city, or in a country, we have no alternative, but almost all of us will have to leave first the age long path of our ego at our earliest possible. Because ego is nothing, but our excessive attachment with our ownselves even at the cost of others around. So long as human spiders, we don't leave weaving a web out or our ownselves exclusively to catch others in our nets, and don't think and care earnestly for others too at the same time, peace will ever remain a mirage, no matter there is God or no God, soul or no soul. Of course, perfection in this world is only utopian. So, let us put an end to our ego. Otherwise, ego will put an end to our ownselves. This ego is the mother of all our vices. Let us realise it.

We are all like potters, wherever and in whatever position we are. So, let us no more commit any 'Zulum' against any of our brothers and sisters around in this world. Let us rather help them if possible in their lives. So, being potters let us remember the following immortal '*dohas*' of Kabir as our 24 hours guide in our lives:

(i) *'Mati' kahe kumhar se, tu kyon ronde moya,*
ik din aisa aayega, main roondoo gi toye'.

(ii) *'Jab hamm aayen jagat mey, sab hansen hamm roye,*
Aisi karni kar chalen ham hasen jug roye'

—Kabir

If we do it earnestly, thinking well in advance before doing anything in life that we are all the architects of our own destinies—good as well as bad, I have no-doubt at all that we are sure to change ourselves and our world too simultaneously, and consequently, all of us can live in real peace.

This way we can pay our real tribute to Marx and fulfill his great dream too.

Index